A. L. Karras is presently Secretary Treasurer of Cumberland Community College in Saskatchewan. His years of experience as a woodsman prompted him to write *North to Cree Lake*. He lives in Nipawin, Saskatchewan, where he continues to write other non-fiction books.

NORTH TO CREE LAKE

BY

A. L. KARRAS

ILLUSTRATED BY LASZLO KUBINYI

PaperJacks

Markham, Ontario, Canada

A CANADIAN

PaperJacks LTD.

One of a series of Canadian books
by PaperJacks Ltd.

NORTH TO CREE LAKE

Paper Jacks edition published 1975
3rd Printing October 1980

ISBN 0-7701-0175-5

Printed and bound in Canada

This PaperJacks edition is published by arrangement
with Simon & Schuster Inc.

Introduction

ONE NIGHT last autumn I watched the moon rise heavy and full. As it climbed higher it cast its light upon a stand of native poplars where the leaves hung in colourful array of bright green and vivid yellow. The scene set me to remembering many a similar view during the years that I had spent in Saskatchewan's northern wilderness. Recalled with remarkable clarity were many moonlit scenes of woods and water and hills far to the north of my present home. The moon had lighted similar views for the first white men ever to enter this land. Here, I thought, was something that had not changed. Thoughts of the present were crowded out by memories of yesteryear. I lowered my gaze and for a time I studied the autumn colours of the poplars where the leaves shook a little in the night breeze.

Sometime later I looked again at the moon. The vapour trail of a jet aircraft cut directly across the moon's face.

This book was written from memory of events that happened before Man was literally reaching for the moon.

The locale of the story is an area where no tin cans, or bottles, or paper, or other man-made litter was to be found at the places where the few human residents made their campfires. Here charred wood, wood chips, stumps, and axe-blazed trees and a bit of discarded buckskin would likely be the only evidence of human visitation, for this land had not yet received an influx of tourists, or developers, or promoters, or sportsmen, or despoilers.

This book deals with that part of Saskatchewan's north central area which begins at the commercial forest belt near the city of Prince Albert and extends over three hundred miles of wooded wilderness to the north to end in the jack pine forests to the north of Cree Lake.

The story begins in the autumn of 1932 and ends in the spring of 1939.

For centuries the old established routes of the fur trade had existed on the Churchill River, the Athabasca to the west, and Reindeer Lake to the east, yet the area concerned in this book had seen comparatively little travel. Ancient canoe routes made access to this region possible in summer, but few men ventured there, for the way was long and treacherous to the uninitiated, the work hard and punishing. It was upstream travelling much of the way, through swift-flowing rivers with much portaging and tracking to pass the many rapids. Above all, the thought of spending a winter in isolation, loneliness, and the awesome cold of this land kept out all white men except a very select few.

The geographical centre of Saskatchewan is in the vicinity of Montreal Lake but at that time there were no all-weather roads north of a line drawn east and west across the province at that point. The modes of access to the area northward were by canoe or dog team in season or by aircraft. No bulldozers were in use to crush down the bush and grade the ground for vehicular traffic. All portages at the rapids were marked by footpaths, well worn through the moss down to the sand and rock beneath, made by the feet of laden packers: Indian, Métis, and white men who had toiled here through the centuries. There were no wheel marks or rails anywhere within hundreds of miles to alter the appearance of the ground from what it had been before any white men had passed this way.

When the prairies to the south were being settled, largely by white European immigrants, the search for farmland drove the late comers north to the parklands and into the fringes of the commercial forest. Here I saw evidence that the wave had sucked back a little, foiled by thick stands of big trees, extra tough roots, rocks, swamps, and muskeg. Mosquitoes, blackflies, bulldog flies, and sandflies tormented the homesteaders and their livestock beyond belief in summer.

The farmers left this land to the Indians and the Métis of mixed Indian and white blood, the commercial fishermen, the loggers, and the white trappers. Some of these people, although they ranged extensively as far as the Churchill River, did not venture in appreciable numbers any great distance beyond. A few travelled into the coniferous forest that extends all the way to Lake Athabasca and beyond the northwest corner of Saskatchewan. Fewer still were those who journeyed into the thin taiga forest to the northeast past Wollaston and Reindeer lakes, the taiga that dwindles and is replaced farther to the northeast by Arctic tundra.

This country was still the old North, land of mystery and deep silences. The silences of summer were occasionally shattered by aircraft, or on the navigable waterways by the outboard motor of some permanent resident who, with muffler removed for extra power, ripped his big freighter canoe through the rivers and lakes en route out to civilization or returning from it before freeze-up in the fall. The occasional crack of his big game rifle, the sound of axe or saw in wood, and the yelping and howling of his dogs sometimes broke the stillness. In summer, too, the roaring of rapids and cataracts could be heard over long distances when the wind was just right in the evening stillness. The resounding crashes of great peals of thunder in the rockbound country above the Churchill River, the lonely call of loons all summer long, the gay chorus of frogs and migrating waterfowl in spring, the whine of millions of mosquitoes in early summer—all were silenced by the congealing cold of winter when all of nature's sounds were replaced by the soughing of the cold wind through the frozen trees, the running, booming crack as the frost split the thickening lake ice from shore to shore, and the occasional howling of big timber wolves from the hills in the distance.

The barren ground caribou or reindeer migrated in the hundreds of thousands to this region in the dead of winter far from their summer range on the tundras to the north. This fact was at that time unknown to most of Saskatchewan's southern residents.

Already there were few places in this land that did not show evidence of visitation by humans, for a few white men had wandered through the country long before the southern wheatlands had been settled. Trading posts at Green Lake and Ile-à-la-Crosse were in business well before the homestead era, for the fur trade was established long before wheat was exported. There had been some prospecting activity. In 1935 a trapper told me he had seen the neat round holes of a diamond drill in the big rock outcroppings near Porter Lake, some distance north of the Churchill River. A producing gold mine existed on the north shore of Lake Athabasca. To the north also stood the trading posts of Fort Chipewyan and Stony Rapids, yet these were more easily accessible by water than the area about which this book is written.

The Indians had been there long before the whites first came. At certain places where the rocks rose sheer along the lakeshores, hieroglyphic legends were scratched in the lichens that covered the rocks. Indian campsites were to be found on every major waterway, some so old as to be almost obliterated by time. Old Indian cemeteries were located on lakeshores or other places that had been picked as appropriate gravesites.

Down along the edges of the settlements the homesteaders were clearing land by felling trees with axes and grubbing roots by hand. The chain saw and bulldozer did not yet exist there.

This story tells of white men who vanished quietly into the

bush in late summer and were seen and heard of no more in the frontier villages until the new leaves had opened in the following spring. It tells of their experiences that range through success and failure, heat and bitter cold, triumph and black despair, of work and sweat, of such leisure and peace as cannot be found Outside, as trappers term civilization. Everything told in this book has happened to someone, somewhere in the Northland. In our rapidly changing world and by its reshuffling of values, it is possible that the story of this kind of man may become distorted or lost and if this book will in any way assist to keep the record of a way of life that has now almost ceased to exist, then this is part of the book's purpose. The identity of some of the white trappers has been deliberately camouflaged for reasons that will become apparent.

Today, great earth-moving machines are gouging into the vast tar sands near Fort McMurray in Alberta just west of the area concerned. In Saskatchewan, highways are steadily creeping northward. Although it is economically sobering to build a mile of highway through Precambrian rock, it is but a matter of time until roads will be built through the region and the old North of the white trapper will be dead. Then will follow the big game hunters, the sports fishermen, tourists, filling stations, motels, and littered campsites.

This story happened long before the news was circulated via the American sports magazines of the tremendous sports fishing that is to be found all the way from the parklands to the Arctic coast.

As a boy still in my teens, I entered the precincts of this land. I came as a greenhorn and through seven years travelled its then unmapped lakes and rivers over its muskegs and through its woods and by actual experience gained a firsthand knowledge of the ways of the North, its moods, its bounty, its unproductiveness, its pitfalls and terrors, and some of its secrets.

Just old enough to read, I became fascinated by the fur price lists that came by mail from the big fur companies. Listed were the furbearing animals native to that part of the prairies where I lived. I knew of coyote, badger, skunk, weasel, muskrat, and jack-rabbit but what of the silver, cross, and red foxes? What about mink, otter, beaver, marten, fisher, lynx, timber wolf, wolverine, and bear? These were not found on the bald prairie in those days. I learned that they were native to the wooded country far to the north.

I had developed a healthy interest in hunting and trapping by the time I could legally carry a rifle. In company with my older brother, Ab, I stalked the big prairie hares or jackrabbits by tracking them in the snow until we located them sometimes sitting in the open with their backs to the winter wind. Ab often awed me with the way he could pick them off with a .22 rifle at long range and with open sights, a talent that was to be a great asset to us in later years. Thoughts of stalking a bull moose or trapping wolves excited us to the point where we vowed some-day to see the northern part of our province for ourselves.

The fact that most of the world was in a state of economic stagnation that some called the Great Depression, gave us a logi-cal reason to go north. There were no jobs in our small town. We had grown to young manhood and since civilization apparently had nothing to offer we decided to escape its tentacles.

It was demonstrated quite clearly to me that in the deepest wilderness one could expect, at any time, a visit from the devil. The Chipewyan Indians, I learned later, were acutely aware of his presence, spoke of him often and called him *Dishlini*.

1

BIG RIVER

ALMOST EVERY city, town, and village in the northern section of Saskatchewan's settled area has at one time or another made the claim that it is "The Gateway to the North." In the early 1930s there was only one community that could rightfully claim such a title although it did not do so at that time. Due to its geographical position and its situation on a navigable waterway from which travel by water was possible to the most remote hinterland of northern Canada all the way to the Arctic and from which a traveller could board a train south into civilization or travel by car to the same destination on a passable road, its claim could not be disputed. From this point, no railroad northward existed nor did any all-weather roads. This community was the little village of Big River.

I first went to Big River in mid-October of 1932. With my brother Ab, and our friend Bob, I boarded the Canadian National Railways' "mixed" train at Prince Albert for the ninety-odd-mile run to Big River to the northwest. The old steam locomotive dragged the dozen or so red-painted boxcars and one passenger coach leisurely through partly cleared farmland, discharged freight at each stop along the way and in the early afternoon rattled into Shellbrook, the last divisional point.

Here we encountered the dividing line between the settlements and the wilderness. The bush closed in and the only clearing was on the railroad right-of-way. Solid stands of trees crowded in from both sides with no clearings to either side. Much swamp and wooded muskeg existed along the way and as the weather was yet quite mild, water could be seen oozing into the ditches along the tracks. The train puffed its way slowly through the endless bush and I thought of the speed with which the trains travelled on the straight, level, and well-ballasted tracks of the Soo Line on which my hometown of Yellow Grass was located. Outside the creaking passenger coach I could see leafless poplars, and spruce, jack pine and dreary-looking tamarack. The sky was heavily overcast and I experienced a new sensation which I later diagnosed as homesickness, for I was eighteen, on my first long trip away from home.

The passengers seemed to change also as soon as we left Shellbrook. The old passenger coach with green plush seats contained about twenty passengers. At one end was a men's clubroom. At the other stood a pot-bellied stove. As we left Shellbrook someone produced a deck of playing cards and a lively poker game erupted at the stove end of the coach in which some passengers and some of the train crew joined. I walked down to the men's room. Four men, all dressed in outdoor clothing, were drinking beer openly, despite the Saskatchewan liquor laws of the day which stated that alcoholic beverages must be consumed in a private dwelling. A heated discussion was in progress and the flushed participants were all talking at the same time. They invited me to join them but I declined the invitation with thanks and rejoined my companions.

All the passengers were men. I overheard snatches of conversations about good times in Prince Albert, boasts of liquor binges and of female companions. There was talk I had not heard before of commercial fishing, Indians, dogs, and fur. Apparently most of these travellers knew each other and the people along the way, for at each stop they filed out of the coach onto the station platform and visited with the local citizens who came to the station. At one village stop an attractive young woman came up to my side of the coach. The man sitting in the seat ahead of me raised the window and said, "The verdict was guilty."

The woman moved away and the window was lowered.

The train departed and we sat and watched the landscape which varied only as to variety of trees. Ab, always the hunter,

once pointed out a running white-tailed buck in a thin poplar stand and later a weasel in the grass, its coat already changing to winter white.

A middle-aged man with liquor-reddened face lurched down the aisle and stopped where we sat.

"Where you fellas going?" he asked.

Ab answered, "Big River."

The man was silent for a moment, rubbed his unshaven chin and observed, "I thought I knew all the fish in Big River."

Bob, a bit nettled, told him, "I have been in Big River before."

The man weaved on to rejoin his friends in the clubroom.

Bob had indeed been to Big River. Two years earlier he and Ab had arrived in Prince Albert in November looking for a spot to locate where they might establish a trapline that winter.

"If you want to go trapping the place to go is Big River," said a stranger whom they met on the station platform. "Take my word for it, boys, that is the best place."

They took his advice, and found that the stranger had been right. So they went to Big River and through the offices of Morgan who operated a boarding house there, they purchased two trapping cabins together with various articles of equipment including traps. The cabins were situated one near the north end of Crooked Lake (a local name; the map name is Cowan Lake), about thirty miles from town, the second about nine miles to the east of cabin number one on a small waterway known as Rat Creek (Taggart Creek).

The venture was dogged by misfortune from the very beginning. The boys hired one Albert Fortin to haul their supplies by horse team to the north end of Crooked Lake. Halfway to their destination they encountered a pressure ridge on the lake ice where the horses broke through, struggled briefly, put their heads down into the water and were drowned. Fortunately the rack caught on the ice and the supplies and equipment were saved. It meant, however, that from there everything had to be hauled by hand sleigh to their destination. Winter was well established by the time they were settled in the Crooked Lake cabin. They did not realize it at the time, but the most productive time for trapping had passed by.

Bill Mahoney, the dam keeper at Crooked Lake Dam lived nearby. A retired schoolteacher, he had elected to live his last years as close to the wilds as possible. Almost seventy years old, he was an authority on the outdoors and a crack rifle shot. He gave Ab and Bob a good deal of advice on how to live in the woods and directed them to the Rat Creek cabin.

On their first trip over, Ab shot a fat cow moose which they discovered not far from the snug little cabin. It was midwinter before they were well settled here and they stayed until April. With little practical experience they caught few mink and weasel so that the venture was a failure financially.

So fascinated were they by the life that they agreed to return at some future time. Attracted by some force that could not be described in words they confessed to being haunted by the memory of the Rat Creek country. They would go back.

Here they were two years later, with myself as a third partner, on the train to Big River. It was dark now, the kerosene lamps had been lit and hung in their brackets on the ceiling of the coach.

It was black night when we detrained. We collected our baggage and stumbled across the unlit, deeply rutted street to Morgan's Boarding House. Our host, big and friendly, soon made us welcome and expressed surprise on seeing Ab and Bob once again. We sat down to an evening meal around a large rectangular table in company with the train crew and several strangers. Bowls of boiled potatoes, stewed meat, gravy, and beans, with platters of homemade bread were passed around from one guest to another. Morgan toted a big enamelled coffee pot about and kept refilling our cups. The supper was terminated with a quarter of an apple pie each.

The stew had been delicious. Later, in our room, I remarked about it. The boys said that it was probably moose meat, for they had heard it rumoured that Morgan put moose meat on the table and was able to camouflage his stew so well that he had been known to feed it to the local and visiting game wardens on more than one occasion.

At Morgan's I saw my first wood stove that had been converted from a 45-imperial-gallon gasoline drum. At that time these stoves were to be found in most business establishments throughout the North. A simple, yet most practical stove, the drum was placed sideways on a stand or sandbox. A door and controllable draft hole were fashioned in one end and the smoke pipe led upward from the top of the opposite end. The stove cancelled out much unnecessary wood cutting for it would take logs in excess of three-foot lengths. I was to see many more versions of this stove.

This was my introduction to Big River. I visited the village several times over the next seven years and knew many of the residents well enough to call them by their first names. The morals of many of the village folk could be termed lusty and loose. There were husband-and-wife exchanges with the consent of all concerned and there were exchanges that were not so docile. In reality, however, their morals differed from their counterparts in the south only in that their sins were committed without regard for what people said or thought and were done openly. These same people would rally to the aid of anyone in serious difficulty and proved it on many an occasion. They lacked hypocrisy.

For a time there was in Big River a young man whom the people called The Pilgrim. He represented well the young men of his day for he was handsome, friendly, broke, and unemployed. The village rejoiced one day when it was learned that he had been accepted for permanent employment at the newly opened gold mine on far away Lake Athabasca. Most of the villagers shook his hand and wished him well before he boarded the bush plane. This event helped to keep alive the hope for the future which the generation of The Pilgrim somehow never lost through the years of the Great Depression.

I noted a zest for living that existed nowhere else as it did here. Most of these people were rugged individualists who stood on their own two feet—come what may. They poked jibes at and joked with one another and a turn around the town was always good for a laugh or two.

Big River is named for a stream that flows into the south end of Crooked Lake just above the village site. The stream is neither big nor is it a river. It does, however, feed the lake which stretches some thirty-five miles in a narrow ribbon generally northward of the village. The level of the lake has long been kept constant by a dam near the north end where the Crooked River (Cowan River) begins. Originally built by The Company as the old logging company was known, the dam was used to keep the lake water high enough so that the log booms could be towed to the sawmill. The sawmill in the 1930s was not operative. The story was that it had closed down more than a decade before after much of the merchantable timber had been destroyed by a monstrous forest fire. Sometime later the mill itself had burned somewhat mysteriously and now consisted of rubble, rusting shafts, saws, and various other sawmill machinery. Stretching northward along the lakeshore were the derelicts of another era. Rusting and rotting hulks of big towboats lay there in melancholy disarray. The "Alligator," a steam-driven contraption that could travel on land or in the water, was now a pile of junk that could only be identified by those who knew what had been its purpose.

The sawdust burner stood solid, firm, and straight, for it was made of black-sheeted steel, the sections bolted together. This awesome structure, a steel cylinder with screened dome, stood one hundred feet high. It was so situated that it could be seen rising above the bush from both the south and north approaches to the village.

The old mill pond when I first saw it was a treacherous reach of water, clogged with "deadheads" or waterlogged logs that had one end slanted down and stuck in the mud of the lake bottom, the other end at the surface ready to impale the canoe or boat of an unwary traveller.

The village consisted of perhaps 200 people who could be classed as permanent residents. There were four general stores, the boarding house, a hotel, post office, outpost hospital, a few dozen houses, a church, and a school, the usual railway-owned buildings, a small sawmill, and several fish warehouses, and fish-company buildings. The busiest place in the village was Godin's store over the front door of which hung a homemade sign that read "O. P. Godin—Marchand Général." Godin, a shrewd, sharp-nosed French Canadian, made his business decisions while listening to his customers and biting on his pipe. He sold any article of food, clothing, or equipment that made life tolerable in the bush. He sold merchandise as varied as ladies' hats and bear traps and bought from his customers grain, hay, fur, lumber, railroad ties, fish, and seneca roots, a medicinal herb that grows wild in the region. Godin spoke but a few words in one day and these he preferred to utter in French.

From any of the general stores a man could buy a year's grubstake and supplies, tote it down to the government-built dock on the nearby lake shore, load it into his canoe and embark almost unnoticed for such remote places as Hatchet Lake, Cree Lake, or Buffalo Lake. He could go across the Methy Portage to the Clearwater River and from there all the way to Aklavik on the Arctic coast. He could follow the Churchill River to Hudson Bay —it was the traveller's choice.

Big River was the crossroads from which people entered or left the North. Strangers appearing in the village might be salesmen from far to the south or some trapper from away north. I heard Dick Hall, the federal member of Parliament for a vast northern constituency, in heated discussion with some of his constituents from Reindeer Lake. This discussion took place in front of the Lakeview Hotel. I saw Jules Marion, the provincial member of the Saskatchewan legislature, conversing softly in the Cree language with a group of Indians in Godin's store. I saw bronzed, lean, and silent men who went about their business with a purpose, and when their affairs were completed they shoved off from the dock in their big freighter canoes, cranked up their outboard motors and headed north; and no one knew their destination and in some cases the travellers themselves did not know exactly where they were going.

Big River had a diversified economy that was foreign to any Saskatchewan community that depends on agriculture for its livelihood. It had long been a fish distributing centre. Big River Fisheries the original big fish distributor was an American firm that shipped the choice catch by rail to Chicago. Waite Fisheries was established sometime later and was beginning to expand even during the Depression. Homesteaders had already hacked out a large acreage to the south and east, an area that was suited to the production of oats. Horses were used in the hauling industry, so the oats found a local market. In winter some farmers took to freighting fish from the far northern lakes such as Buffalo, Doré, Snake (Pinehouse), and La Ronge. They could turn to logging for the small sawmill or they could cut railroad ties in the big jack pine country. Big River residents might take a hand at trapping in winter or they could stay at home and keep the larder full of moose and deer meat, for these animals could be found anywhere back in the bush. Incongruously, the whole northern area of nearly half a province was governed for the most part by prairie dwellers who had nothing in common with this land and even less concern for its welfare. The fact was that the southern half of this province was largely ignorant of the north as to its physical features, its resources, and particularly its potential and future value, a fact that exists in lesser degree to this day.

An active place both in volume and political activity was the government-operated beer and wine store. Each time the government changed—so did the vendor, so that this person was always a supporter of the government of the day. The village residents and the northerners who visited town were hard drinkers with few exceptions, for it seems the farther north one travels the greater the thirst of the people. A couple of dollars bought a gallon of "Concord" or "Catawba"—potent fortified wines on which a robust man could turn green if he indulged with abandon.

In spring and early summer, on a grassy bank down near the government dock could be found the canoes of the professional white trappers. They were turned bottom up against the weather and roped and pegged down against the wind. The canoes were of excellent quality and make, Peterborough and Chestnut

2

MEMORABLE MEALS

THE WEATHER was unseasonably mild for late October, the wind was calm, and we made a good run of some ten miles down Crooked Lake. Just before dusk closed in we found a tiny beach on the west side and came in for a landing. Irvine and George whom we had hired to freight our outfit as far as Crooked Lake Dam were both experienced woodsmen and fine fellows as we found out around the campfire that night. They provided the big inboard-engined boat which, although a slow-moving craft, looked seaworthy and made steady progress when cruising. The fact that everything was stowed aboard by late in the afternoon was the signal to pull out so that darkness found us camped for the night at this spot.

We spent a very comfortable night where we spread our bedrolls under the stars in an open area surrounded by second-growth poplars. Previous to our retiring, George had mentioned that it might be a good idea to find a spot where the hips fit into a hollow in the ground. This was a hint which I have since used to good advantage. Later on I found that if you try to sleep with your hips on a rise in the ground you are indeed in for a rough night.

The next day started well enough. We were under way at daylight. The wind was still down but the sky was now heavily overcast and the temperature just above the freezing mark. The motorboat towed a large wooden skiff, loaded with our supplies, in which Ab sat in the stern and steered with a broad paddle.

A couple of miles out I saw my very first bull moose, looming big and dark against the spruce that grew along shore. Irvine playfully pointed his shotgun at him, but he was well out of range and we passed him by, for we were in a hurry to get down the lake while the good weather held. In every sheltered bay and backwater the surface of the calm water was black with thousands of migrating ducks which were poised here for southward flight when the weather turned colder. Every man aboard was in high spirits. We leaned back and took in the sights with a good deal of interest.

As things so often happen in the North, this condition was about to change. Irvine, who had kept his shotgun within reach as he piloted the motorboat, had shot a spoonbill and two mallards that had ventured within shotgun range of the two boats. This made it necessary to make three great circles with the boats in order to retrieve the ducks. I wondered at him wasting so much time when we all knew that we should be travelling. I was to be thankful for those ducks later that day.

After a while the wind came up from the northeast, and we were soon working against moderate waves. Irvine was having ignition trouble with the ancient, resurrected automobile engine which served as our power unit. It cut out on him a couple of times and finally he borrowed my jackknife to work on the battery terminals. He came up from these mysteries with a grin that showed strong snoose-stained teeth, assuring us our troubles were over.

Our troubles were over for only a short time. The engine laboured steadily but the wind was rising. When the wind reached near-gale proportions Irvine began to angle into the waves so that we could reach shore. The waves, now white-capped, rode right up the lake in a mighty sweep. The boats had been built for rough lake water and rode the waves well. The sky had become much darker, the eastern shore hazed over and sleet began to pelt into the lake. An errant wisp of spray found the vulnerable ignition system of the engine and our progress halted abruptly.

Rolling in the troughs of the big waves we were faced with new problems. Although the motorboat was seaworthy, the great weight of the motor would drag her to the bottom should she fill

with water. The smaller skiff was being balanced by Ab, now on his feet and balancing the craft like a ballet dancer so that she would ship as little water as possible as she rolled in the waves. This he did by timing each cresting wave and shifting his weight so that the gunwhale tilted up each time it met an oncoming roller. He demonstrated his very good sea legs acquired during his logging experience in British Columbia. We pulled the skiff to the downwind side and hung on.

Even so, the skiff took on a lot of water. The wind shifted more to the east and after a time the wild blasts flung us in to shore. We had no choice of landing places and came ashore amid snags and downed timber at the shoreline. Our supplies were awash by the time we had completed a landing in the big white spruce trees that grew right down to the water.

We built a great fire and proceeded to dry the outfit. Clothing and bedding were spread out on poles near the heat. Food was checked, dried, and repacked. We found the damage to be not too great as flour seals itself in cotton bags. Our sacks of sugar didn't fare as well and although still usable would be lumpy. We considered ourselves fortunate indeed that the entire outfit had not become lost with perhaps some drownings to boot.

It had been snowing heavily for some time, so that a few inches of snow covered the ground. The temperature was dropping steadily.

The five of us, after wrestling with heavy freight for the better part of the day, setting up camp, chopping wood, and doing the camp chores in the cold air, were developing most astonishing appetites. George, a well-experienced outdoor cook, took charge of preparing the evening meal. I appointed myself his assistant. From our equipment he selected an oversized galvanized iron water pail. He soon had it partly filled with lake water and slung over a fine cooking fire. It was hung on what he called a pothook, which is a stout pole, notched to hold the pail handle at one end, the other sharpened and pounded into the ground at an angle. Into the pail went Irvine's three ducks, plucked, singed, eviscerated, washed, and cut up—in that order. He added the giblets—hearts, livers and gizzards—all expertly prepared. Irvine picked up his ever handy shotgun, placed a chew of snoose inside his lower lip and walked up along some poplar-covered ridges nearby. Here he shot the heads off two ruffed grouse as they strutted almost underfoot. These birds received similar treatment to the ducks and joined them in the boiling pail. George now chose from our supplies an assortment of potatoes, turnips, and onions which, peeled and chopped, were later added to the stew. Still later several handfuls of rice became part of the recipe. Finally George added salt, pepper, a dash of curry powder, and dumplings that he mixed up himself of flour, water, and baking powder.

There was magic that came with the aroma of that stew. The cold breeze bore it our way to whet already keen appetites. Something changes in a man's appetite in this country and he is continually amazed at the quantities of food which he consumes. I recall that as we rolled into our beds that evening the stew pail stood empty. Five men had eaten it all. I recall too that my sleep was unbroken, devoid of dreams and discomfort, until daylight. Lying side by side in our spruce-bough shelter open to the fire we did not even feel the cold.

This had been my first memorable meal of the North. There were other meals to remember. Late that winter Ab and I walked out to Big River to get the mail—a distance of forty miles. We made about twenty-five miles the first day, slogging heavily on the snow-covered lake ice, and later on the logging roads in the bush along the west side of Crooked Lake. The days were lengthening, for it was late March. Four feet of snow covered the ground back in the woods and although seasoned by almost a full winter in the bush we were footsore and aching in the front thigh muscles when we made camp among the trees that evening.

Off again at daylight the next morning we entered a part of the Big River Forest Reserve where a fair-sized logging operation was under way. We followed the horse-drawn sleigh trails now and we found the footing firm and smooth. Where the felled timber had been trimmed we saw several feeding deer that did not bother to bound away as we passed. Rustling food was not easy for deer at this season and here they had found a bonanza where the tops of the fallen forest monarchs lay. Fine stands of the various species of trees grew here and we walked through a sort of Disneyland setting with fine tall trees, tame deer, and all the various forms of woods life all about, chipmunks, varying hares, red squirrels, woodpeckers—the entire cast had been present. Since loggers do not usually molest wild life the animals grow so tame that some can be fed by hand. I once saw a black-tailed buck standing astride a sleigh load of logs that had been left unattended overnight. There are snapshots around Big River to prove it.

After we had made about six miles that morning and hunger was niggling away at our stomachs we sighted the logging camp buildings. Jim Cowie, the camp cook was alone since the men were at work in the cutting area. He demonstrated true northern hospitality by placing on the table the best that the camp had to offer. Roast prime beef, boiled potatoes, gravy, homemade bread, butter, jam, and hot black coffee which we laced with canned milk and sugar. The meal was completed with dessert consisting of a six-inch square of molasses cake covered with a heavy sweet sauce.

Back in our trapper's cabin we had been living largely on meat –deer, moose, and woodland caribou. The meat, together with bannock and stewed dried fruit made up our diet. The fact that we were trail-hungry and privileged to sit down and partake of a meal so different from our isolation fare makes it the more memorable.

Several years later Ab and I sat with five Chipewyan Indian hunters around the camp stove at Cree Lake Outpost. It was in the dead of winter and the dead of night. It was so cold outside that no one ventured to guess what the thermometer read. The stove served two purposes. We kept it full of jack pine logs to warm us and to heat the great aluminum pot. This utensil had been filled with fist-sized pieces of caribou brisket, ribs, and back meat, hacked from frozen, skinned reindeer carcasses on the big jack pine stump just outside the door. The cutting was done with a sharp axe. The barren ground caribou or reindeer had recently migrated in great numbers to this region. The Indians rejoiced for there would be food for their families and their dogs for the balance of the winter.

We all helped ourselves to the meat. We lifted out the boiled pieces with a fork, picked off the inevitable deer hairs and chewed from the bones, eating meat only. When empty, the pot was refilled, reboiled, and the eating process repeated. Three months out on our winter traplines had created such appetites as only the winter outdoor dweller can experience. We craved fats and sugars to combat the cold. These cuts of meat were from well-conditioned animals and had alternate layers of lean and fat especially on the rib cages and back areas which were about as tasty as any meat I had ever eaten. Outside in civilization I was never one to relish fat meat, but here my tastes had undergone a marked change.

One of the Chipewyans came in with an assortment of cut-up deer shoulders and thighs and some leg bones with joints cut off.

This was dumped in the pot and boiled. The marrow was blown out of the bones by inserting the small end of the boiled bone in the mouth and forcing out the contents by blowing. The resulting sound of escaping air and fatty material is not pleasant to hear, but it was the accepted way of getting at the marrow.

Another Indian produced a string of caribou tongues from his pack which were boiled and eaten. This is considered the prime cut of the caribou and a noted northern delicacy.

The water from almost every stream, river, and lake where we travelled made an acceptable cup of tea. Only the brown waters of poorly drained swamps failed in this regard. We found early in our trapping experience that coffee is no substitute for tea on a winter trail. Tea refreshes and stimulates so that it is possible to travel for hours before the feelings of weariness and hunger return.

We had to learn to make tea properly. In winter the loose, powdery surface snow was never used, for when packed into a tin pail and slung over a fire the snow against the tin melts first and is absorbed by the unmelted snow in a blotterlike action, whereupon a disagreeable smoky taste results. The snow nearer the ground has crystallized. This snow, as it melts, runs down to the pail bottom and the scorched taste is avoided. The water is brought to a rolling boil, the proper amount of tea leaves are added, the pail is removed from the fire and the tea allowed to steep for about four minutes; the tea produced was found to be the most to our liking. I have never tasted tea to compare with this recipe anywhere else, neither restaurant tea nor the tea made at home in a teapot.

I was introduced to a special way to prepare a fish over the open fire, when I first travelled up the Deer River. This sizable river rises far to the north of the Churchill River and runs generally southward. Frank, our travelling companion, picked up a net-scarred jumbo whitefish, still alive and floating downstream; apparently it had escaped from some other traveller's net farther upstream. It was time to stop for the noonday meal. Frank set to work immediately, splitting the fish down the back so that it lay open in a great slab, the two halves joined together by the belly. The backbone, entrails, and gills were then removed with the scales and fins left intact. He inserted two small, peeled, sharpened willow branches under the skin, the entire length of each half, then added both prongs of a Y-shaped willow branch under the skin and across the fish. The resulting package was now rigid and easily propped up at the proper angle to the glowing fire by forcing the stem of the Y into the earth.

The fish began to sizzle and bake. In a few minutes the meat cooked to an appetizing brown colour. When Frank thought that it had baked enough on one side he turned the willow so that the skin side was next to the heat. Later he gave the meat side a few minutes more, took the willow and fish, placed it on a large flat rock and removed the willows that he had run through the fish.

We sat around the rock and dug the fish out of its skin dish. We used a salt shaker to good effect. The meat was still sizzling with most of the natural juices trapped beneath the crisp brown covering so that the meat had cooked in the sealed-in meat juices. I noticed that Frank had used the salt shaker during the baking process. This, I believe, adds something to the flavour of outdoor cooking. Also, the fire and angle at which the fish faces the heat is part of a success such as this.

A fish prepared thus is not to be compared with the panfried variety, for there is nearly always a greater time lag between the catching and the preparing of the fish than had been the case in Frank's whitefish.

I have never eaten more delicious fish. We ate it right down to the skin which, with a few bones, was all that remained. Frank had eaten part of the head, which he stated was more nutritious. This dish cannot be duplicated for flavour from frozen fish that you can purchase in a supermarket. I have eaten fish in expensive hotel dining rooms where the entree was soggy and bland in flavour because the original pristine taste was long lost during cold storage.

Again on the Deer River, but two years later, Big Nick Lenni taught me how to cook a moose nose. We were travelling in a brigade of seven boats and several canoes containing Chipewyan hunters and their families. Two weeks out of Meadow Lake, Ab and I, in the lead of the brigade, shot a young bull moose as he stood at the river's edge. We horsed the carcass ashore and cut up the meat, loading it all in the boat, including the head and hide.

Nick cut off the nose and stripped it through the nostrils onto a forked willow. He burned off the hair and blistered the skin over the campfire so that the outer layer could be peeled off. The nose, now about the size of a large coconut and of similar colour was cut into chocolate-bar-shaped pieces and boiled for about two and one-half hours. I sliced off a piece with my hunting knife and tasted the dubious-looking serving. I had to admit that the taste was good. It had a distinctive taste similar to smoked fat pork, with a hint of birch and willow, jack pine tips and water lilies on which this animal feeds. Thereafter we never discarded the nose of the moose.

Breakfast at our main trapping cabin at Cree Lake was usually sourdough hotcakes, small steaks and gravy, and tea. Gravy, I learned, was made to our preference when the steak was well browned, the gravy ingredients added (flour, water, salt, and pepper) and allowed to bubble with the meat for a time. Here again seasoning was added during the cooking process. Breakfast was varied by dumping large quantities of stewed dried fruit over a stack of hotcakes.

Sourdough bread and hotcakes were standard fare. Sourdough when properly handled is a joy to eat, but it must be used by an expert who has mastered his recipes by trial and error. Sourdough is an abomination when improperly prepared. The secret lies in just what quantities of soda are added to cut the acid content of the action of yeast on flour, sugar, and water.

Meat was often eaten every meal in the week. We found that any of the antlered species—Virginia deer, mule deer, woodland caribou, moose, and reindeer—made choice eating when the animal is in good condition. We were continually amazed at the quantities of meat which we tucked away at mealtime.

Many a meal was made with land birds as the main course. Ruffed grouse, spruce hen, ptarmigan, prairie chicken in winter and the various edible waterfowl in season. These were stuffed and roasted in our stovepipe oven—a welcome change from venison.

We were in the midst of open-water muskrat trapping when the ducks returned on their spring migration. Some of these, unfortunately for them, blundered into our traps so that fat mallards, teals, and canvasbacks appeared on our table. Often while eating we discovered shotgun pellets in the flesh, pellets picked up farther south, for we owned no shotgun.

The land yielded up to us its fruits. In jack pine country, blueberries grow in varying degrees of profusion from a few small berries in mature jack pine stands to fantastically abundant large juicy berries in country that has been burnt over. Beginning about the third year after a fire the condition becomes ideal. In such places on certain best-favoured hillsides, we picked blueberries by the bucketful. At the hilltop we spread a tarp on the ground and poured the berries from the pail lifted as high as possible so that the breeze carried away all the leaves. Combined with sugar and reconstituted powdered whole milk, this was a fine diet supplement from August to freeze-up and the first snows that covered the low bushes. As late as midwinter, I have found them where ridges had been bared of snow by the wind–still unwrinkled and pebble-hard in nature's own deep freeze–and eaten them by handfuls.

Fresh north-country blueberry pie is something to remember and to cherish. We had learned how to make good pie pastry. We possessed deep pie plates in which it was possible to bake a pie three or four inches thick. Such a blueberry filling made with sagacious use of sugar and spices such as cinnamon, nutmeg, or cloves, produced pies the like of which cannot be duplicated in pastry shops or the best dining houses on earth.

Throughout this land there are scattered peat bogs that yield cranberries. We picked them from their moss beds where they lay bright red joined by threadlike stems to the main plant. We used them in sauce form to garnish the meat on our table.

Once, along in the month of April when the sun first warmed the southern slopes of the muskeg hummocks, I discovered some cranberries that had been preserved by the frost. I had become aware of a craving for fresh fruits long absent and unobtainable. I crouched down and picked them, not as firm as in the autumn but still edible and flavourful. Several spruce hens had found them, too, for I flushed the birds from the frozen swamp as I crossed to the other side.

I recall several poor meals. Once, while muskrat trapping about ten miles from our Rat Creek camp we ran out of venison. Rather than spend time hunting down an animal that we could only partially use, we decided to try muskrat which is considered edible in this country. We severed the hind legs from several of the best-looking carcasses and fried them over the campfire. I did not consider the result to be a success.

On the trail to Big River, I met a homesteader on his way by horse team and sleigh to Green Lake. We boiled the tea pail together and he produced a bologna sausage which he called dog. This was a poor grade of sausage, encased in a long narrow waxed cotton bag. The meat was green half an inch inward from the sack casing. I made a pretense of eating this just to please my host.

Miller served me a bear steak at his homesteader's shack halfway down Crooked Lake. The male cinnamon bear from whose rump the steak had been cut had just come out of hibernation in April when Miller felled it with his .30 Winchester rifle. I do not recommend this as a meal to enjoy.

Recalled also is three weeks of a steady diet of rabbits when our regular meat supply ran out in the dead of winter on my first year in the bush.

At Cree Lake Christmas dinner was rotated each year; at our cabin, at Martin's cabin at Stony Narrows and at Frank's cabin at the east side. In 1936 we met at Frank's and the dinner menu follows:

Caribou Brisket Soup
Moose Steak
Boiled Moose Nose
Fresh baked bannock with canned butter and honey
Raisin pie
Doughnuts Pickles
Candy Rum
Tea

Each year we hoarded some of our choice food, brought in by canoe from Outside just for this day. We relaxed afterward, lit our pipes and compared notes, not having seen each other in some months. This was a memorable meal, indeed.

3

RAT CREEK 1932-1933

AFTER THE near loss of our outfit on Crooked Lake, we waited out the storm for two days. As the winds abated, we loaded up the boats, and Irvine and George finally landed us at Crooked Lake Dam. The weather had turned so cold that for the last hundred yards to the dock we had to smash ice that had become thick enough to stop the boats. They tarried only long enough to see the cargo unloaded and although the sun had already set they reckoned they could make it to Big River nonstop that night by the light of an increscent moon and thus avoid the danger of becoming frozen in.

Bill Mahoney, the dam keeper, put up the three of us for the night. He gave us space in his warehouse to store our supplies. At daybreak, we began the task of packing—on our backs—all our supplies and equipment to the cabin at Rat Creek.

Ab and Bob figured it at six or seven miles by a trail blazed through the trees in a circuitous route that skirted several swamps, led through alder bottoms, and finally struck out through the big white poplars and mature spruce over level ground. As we neared Rat Creek the trail led up and down hilly country until we found the cabin.

The first thing that I had to learn was to watch my footing. Gone was the easy prairie walking, for the area from whence I came was treeless and had little rock or stone. I found that tripping over a snag or root while carrying a heavy pack will give you a rude jolt. Stubbing the toe on the end of a stick or small stump can be very painful as our footwear was ankle height rubbers over moose-hide moccasins and socks.

The outfit was packed over, one round trip a day. Alternately, one man stayed at the cabin and two men packed freight. The cabin was cleaned up and we settled down for the winter. On one of the last packing trips Ab shot a large mule deer doe. We had been augmenting our food supplies with ruffed grouse, spruce hens, and at the still open creek we shot ducks. We packed in the venison and hung it in the little log lean-to at the back of the cabin.

The cabin, I learned, had a history. Tucked back in the inside bend of the creek, it had been purposely hidden in dense poplar and spruce so that a traveller on the creek could not see the log structure. It was well made of straight spruce logs with a double board roof and a plank floor, one of the better cabins I was to see in the North. This had been the base of operations for a man known around Big River as Utah. He was a maker of home brew and dealt with the loggers, Indians, and certain northern traders. He had departed a few years back, it was said, with the law in hot pursuit. Bob, one day, discovered a small paper stuck between two logs in the wall beside his bunk. Scrutiny of this paper brought to light that Utah had been issued a "permit to leave" by his home state since he had been, among other things, a syphilitic. Hung on the walls were pieces of equipment such as one would not expect to see in a trapper's cabin. In the lean-to stood a hardwood mash box with a thermometer on a nail above it. A sixteen-foot length of three-quarter-inch steel cable hung in the cabin, a thing that puzzled us, for we could not relate this to the moonshiner's activities. It had never been used, it was still complete with shipping tag from the T. Eaton Co., the famous mail-order house of western Canada.

An excellent cast-iron wood stove was in one corner of the cabin. The cabin floor was about twelve feet square and we found the stove to be quite adequate for our needs. It took wood up to eighteen inches in length and was fed through a door in one end. After we had fitted our stovepipe oven with new pipes, we found that it drew very well. Here, I was to learn, it was essential to have a good stove as life centers around it for preparing food as well as for warmth.

Although Ab and Bob had spent a winter here they had learned little of the art of taking furbearing animals. The three of us now set to work, and since we knew so little, did everything wrong. At the cabin there were a number of weasel boxes, built of boards, about a foot long and eight inches wide. They were closed in from all sides with a small hole cut in one corner. The top was removable so that the box could be baited and a trap set in it. The boxes were so designed that the larger animals such as rabbits could not get caught. We caught a dozen weasels by this method along with many flying squirrels that thudded on the cabin roof at night but were never seen by day. We set our larger numbers two, three, and four traps for foxes whose tracks were now everywhere as they ranged along the creek and out on the lake ice. Rabbits blundered into all these traps that we set in the woods. I noticed that fox tracks dotted each snow-covered muskrat house, and I set traps on them, not knowing that foxes climb on them only once and that just after the ice forms. One morning I saw something dark move beside one of the muskrat houses. My hopes for a cross fox were short-lived, for it happened that my trap held an unhappy horned owl that had lit on the muskrat house while hunting in the night. We worked hard at trapping. Downstream we made sets at the rapids, hoping to catch mink, but the cold weather froze the shallow rapids, the creek backed up and flooded our traps so that we found them only in the spring when the ice had melted away.

We learned early that we could expect no helpful hints on trapping from other trappers. Generally closemouthed and evasive as to successful methods, they might tell you certain things that would prove to be red herrings and were not to be regarded seriously. Professional secrets were carefully guarded and certainly not communicated to strangers. The mark of a successful trapper was measured by the number of furs he gathered. Those that failed were regarded as greenhorns and incompetents and became a laughing stock in Big River.

Bill Mahoney told us that we would have a neighbor at Rat Lake that winter. His name was Chris Timson and he lived about seven miles south of our cabin. Tall, blond, and raw-boned, with long hair and full blond beard, he had been in the area for some years. Formerly in partnership with a countryman named Holgar Petersen, he now operated alone from a central point on the west side of Rat Lake.

Ab and Bob set off one morning to pay him a visit. They kept in the tall timber back of the lakeshore until they found one of his trapping trails and tracked him to his neat little cabin; they found him at home. Chris, a great talker, made them welcome, assured them that the country was big enough for us all, served them a meal and, as they left for home, presented them with a gift of two jumbo whitefish just out of the net.

The weather was unseasonably mild for November as the boys arrived home at dusk. The whitefish, not yet frozen, I prepared for our evening meal by the light of our kerosene lamp. I cut the meat into steaks and rolled each piece in flour. Fried quickly in lard to a deep brown, we thoroughly enjoyed it for it was choice quality and very fresh. I found that there is a good deal of difference between these fish and those I had eaten in the south that had been frozen for some time.

The snowshoe rabbit population was at the height of its cycle. Rabbit tracks were everywhere. Where we had cut down some big poplars for stove fuel they congregated in dozens to strip the branches of bark. At dusk we watched them arrive along the rabbit runs.

As the days grew shorter and the snows deeper, I found coyote and fox tracks on the rabbit runs and it appeared that they fared well on rabbits, for many remnants of their kills were scattered about. The horned owls that hooted at night from their favourite lookouts in the tall poplars were having little trouble in finding food. The piercing scream of a taloned rabbit was often heard in the night. As winter progressed the rabbits began to die of tuleremia, the rabbit disease that all but wipes them out. I watched the demise of many of them. These looked unthrifty and while feeding would flop over on one side, moaning, struggling, and kicking until they died.

Almost as lethal as the rabbit disease was the creek itself. Kept open by the warm current of lake water, it froze over only in the coldest weather, became snow covered and, with the coming of warmer weather, many snow-bridged, unsafe areas developed. I saw many rabbit trails lead out onto the creek, only to end at a small black hole where they had been sucked under by the current after they had broken through. In the spring their carcasses could be seen floating in the eddies where they were found by the bears coming out of hibernation.

Just before Christmas, Ab and I walked out to Big River—forty miles one way. The snow was not deep out on Crooked Lake and we made it to the first settlements by nightfall, leg weary, stiff, and sore. By morning, although rested, we were so stiff that it took a few miles of walking to limber up. The welcome sight of the sawdust burner appeared in the distance, and we arrived in the village at noon. Morgan welcomed us and fed us well once again. After one night in town we headed back with the mail and just enough supplies to make comfortable loads that would not slow us down, arriving back at the cabin on the fifth day, with all traces of stiffness gone. We were already hardened to walking long distances.

January arrived and with it our first heavy snowfall. I had seen it snow heavily in southern Saskatchewan, but had never seen snow like this. We awoke one windless morning to grey skies and grey air as snow sifted down into our little circular clearing in the big trees. It snowed all day until each stump wore a white twelve-inch snowcap. Familiar logs and stumps were buried completely. At sundown the sun broke through the thick overcast for a few seconds, and the afterglow coloured the tops of the tall snow-crowned spruce in back of the cabin. Then the clouds closed in once more and it snowed more heavily than before. Standing in the clearing and looking up, one could imagine oneself under a giant confetti cutter whose handle never ceased to turn. We retired to our bunks that night under the spell of profound silence, for there were no sounds from birds or animals, all holed up in the snow.

Next morning the sky cleared and the cold sunlight shone on a white world. Our long rows of stacked stovewood were topped with eighteen inches of new snow. The rows had at first been five feet above ground level, but now showed only a foot above the level of surrounding snow. Our thermometer registered —40° F. and the trees popped with loud reports as they split with the frost.

All our traps were now useless until they could be dug out and reset. Travel without snowshoes was impractical and we set to work making snowshoes according to instructions from Bill Mahoney as to how to make frames and weave the webbing in a star-shaped pattern. Travel was still a great deal more difficult and our hunting range was curtailed.

Ab, one day, while trailing a moose in the poplar and birch stands north of the cabin, came upon a fresh track of a fox which he followed to its den. Since no track led away from the den, he plugged all den entrances with logs, knowing that he had a fox bottled up in there. He legged it back to the cabin for Bob and what digging tools we could muster. They spent two full days chipping at the frozen sand and finally extricated a big, male red fox, returning home in triumph.

At this time our supplies of meat dwindled, then disappeared altogether. Ab, the most effective hunter among us, was doing his best to provide venison, but with the deep snow he could cover only limited areas; nor did it help that now the hours of daylight were too few. I accompanied him on an afternoon, trailing eight mule deer that moved from one frozen swamp to another, pawing away the deep snow to find frozen green grass beneath. We made a careful stalk, but sighted them only as they faded into a thick stand of willows, grey shapes in the grey dusk vanishing into grey brush.

We were in no danger of starvation for we had a stock of staples, but we missed the good red meat. A herd of woodland caribou passed the cabin in the night. Ab set out to trail them next morning, but he was beaten from the start, for these animals seem to travel constantly and effortlessly.

We were becoming desperate for meat. One evening we shot

two snowshoe rabbits, prepared and roasted them in the stovepipe oven and ate them at our evening meal. Not as flavourful as venison, yet we found the meat acceptable eating. We ate rabbit each day for three weeks by which time we began to find that they were no longer acceptable as food. I have never eaten rabbit since.

During this time Ab was making new efforts to obtain meat. He broke snowshoe trails in the prime moose country north of the cabin and ranged as far as some big open muskegs to the east near Voisin Lake. He returned to the cabin in high spirits one evening, a grey snowy figure, packing a haunch of a big bull caribou. Coming on fresh sign, he had trailed the herd into muskeg country and dropped the bull with an expert shot. The meat proved to be good eating and we feasted on steaks and roasts. We had hamburgers made with our hand-operated meat grinder. The meat was packed in, taking several trips. When it was hung in our lean-to we felt more secure, knowing that we now had almost enough meat to see the winter out. All in all we consumed eight game animals that season: six deer, one moose, and the bull caribou.

The winter birds were our constant companions. Whisky jacks would steal any scrap of food that they could pilfer and would light on the table if the door was left open and the food unattended. Chickadees called from their sheltered feeding grounds beside the cabin. Several species of woodpecker flitted among the big trees. There were birds that I had not seen before, for they did not dwell in a prairie habitat.

The howling of coyotes was frequently heard. Although we tried desperately to trap them they eluded us, never going near our traps. Their chorus echoed tantalizingly from the thick woods, seeming so near that we sometimes sneaked over the next ridge to try to glimpse them but we were unsuccessful. Ab said that coyotes howl more often when a change is coming in the weather. On one of his hunting forays he had a quick look at two coyotes crossing the creek ice and promptly picked one off with his deer rifle. This was the only coyote taken by our party that winter.

January passed, yet the winter showed no signs of abating. February, I learned, was the mating month for foxes and coyotes. Their tracks led up and down the creek and crisscrossed on the lake ice. These tracks goaded us to reset the traps at likely stopping places, but the results were always the same—unsuccessful.

Intense cold spells kept us close to the cabin. We had no radio receiving set and spent a good deal of time playing cards. Our stack of magazines and papers grew rumpled and of no further interest. Arguments developed easily and fist fights were narrowly averted. I was experiencing for the first time what, in the wilderness, is called cabin fever. When the weather moderated, we hunted and plied our traplines. Differences were forgotten and normal relationships were resumed.

Oddly, we had no visitors at our cabin between November and May that year. The Indians did not show up at all. This is unusual even in the remotest areas and made our isolation the most complete of any winter I spent in the North.

Winter was now on the wane. The snow on the exposed slopes facing the south began to show signs of melting and settling. The February calendar sheet was ripped off, bringing March and the beginning of the muskrat-trapping season.

We went at the muskrat trapping with more enthusiasm than skill. There were many muskrats in the creek and out on the lake for their houses and feeding stations or push-ups were to be seen in great numbers. The weather was mild; we opened the push-ups and set our traps. While the weather was warm we took about fifty muskrats but a sudden cold snap sealed all the push-up entrances and we pulled up our traps.

At this time Bob decided that he had had enough of trapping. He would return to his home in the south and take up farming. This proved to be a sound decision, for, after two winters in the bush, he realized that he was not suited to trapping and had nothing to show for his efforts. We divided our furs; he took his clothing and personal effects, loading his big packsack in a neat load. We accompanied him through the woods to Crooked Lake, shook hands, and parted good friends as ever.

Ab and I continued with the muskrat trapping. March was

slipping by and we had days in which the snow softened and settled. Woodpeckers drummed all day upon their favourite trees, and later the ruffed grouse thundered their signals from haunts where the warm sun struck the wooded hillsides west of our cabin. Red squirrels chattered and barked and chased one another around and around the boles of the big spruce. The snow sank a little more each day. One morning I saw crows flying overhead.

During the last days of March Ab and I again made the trip to Big River. The cold temperatures had descended once more and put an end to spring's advance. Our purpose in walking to town was twofold: to sell our furs and pick up the mail. Our cash return for the furs just about finished our trapping careers. Fur prices were down, the fur dealers said. Muskrats were bought at twenty-five cents each. The red fox, dug out after two days of hard labour was worth one dollar. The buyer explained that it was badly rubbed, past prime, and since the government royalty was seventy-five cents we would have a return of twenty-five cents. The coyote shot on the creek was full-furred and worth five dollars—less than twenty dollars for the lot! We had to accept and struck out for the cabin that same day—we couldn't afford to stay in town.

Winter had passed. It had not been a severe one as I later found out, but we had experienced its cold, its sudden weather changes, deep snows, and complete isolation. We had listened to the coyote chorus by day and occasionally the howl of timber wolves in the night. As we lay in our bunks horned owls were hooting by moonlight. Once in the dead of night a small weasel entered the cabin through a hole in the moss chinking. Where the moonlight streamed into the cabin, through the window, we watched the weasel pounce on a tiny shrew. Thereafter the ever present mice and shrews ceased to exist about the cabin. We had awakened each morning from unbroken sleep to bright days and brilliant sunlight on a million snow-laden spruce trees. We had watched the sun dip low towards Capricorn, hesitate and swing back to the equator. We had spent a winter in the bush, excellent training for what was to come in the future.

Early one morning as I went down to the creek to dip a bucket of water, two mallards took flight, the first I had seen that spring. In a few days the migrants arrived in full force. Ducks, geese, mudhens, loons, snipes, terns, herons, bitterns, gulls, and sandpipers descended on the creek since the lake was still icebound. Such ducks as I had never seen before: mergansers, blackducks, redheads, goldeneyes, and those we could not name, with their various calls made such noise that can only be associated with the coming of spring in the wilderness.

Frogs added an incredible din to the spring song.

Small streams, created by the rapidly melting snows, bubbled and tinkled through the woods and into Rat Creek—a most pleasant sound. Songbirds whose songs we had never heard sang beautifully at evening and again just at dawn.

On the footpath another morning, going for water from the creek, as I followed the curve of the trail around a clump of grey willows I saw my first wild black bear. Plodding along the far creek bank he did not see me. I skipped back to the cabin.

"Get up, Ab. There's a big black bear on the other side of the creek!" I whispered.

He hit the floor, grabbed his 6.5 Mannlicher and soon a shot cracked the morning silence. Mallards leaped skyward quacking in alarm. The bear lunged into an alder thicket.

"We had better eat our breakfast before we look for him," Ab said.

This appeared to me to be sound reasoning. I had heard of wounded bears charging their pursuers. After breakfast we found the bear, quite dead, lying on his side, just beyond the alders on a poplar-studded hillside. We skinned it out right down to the toes with their claws which we left with the skin. Large for a black bear, it was a mature male with thick shiny black pelt. Stretched and dried it measured about seven feet each way and served as a floor rug as long as we lived at Rat Creek. We both noticed that a skinned bear carcass somewhat resembled a heavily muscled man.

One fine spring evening, with the nip of winter back in the air, I worked my way with the wooden boat, part of the equipment bought with the cabin, through the dead reeds and bulrushes, making the rounds of my open-water muskrat sets. Muskrats were plentiful and could be seen swimming about everywhere. Suddenly, quite close to the boat, I saw a fish leap from the water. Looking down into the crystal clear water, I saw a fine jackfish. Then several more passed under the boat. The creek was swarming with fish, for the spawning season was at hand.

During the next few days we entertained ourselves by snaring jackfish with brass rabbit wire. Fashioning a running loop, all that was required was to put it over the side of the boat and guide it over the head of a fish, then with a heave the fish was boated. We found them good eating after a steady winter meat diet.

The jackfish run was spectacular, but the pickerel run that followed was even better. They now swarmed up the creek to spawn in the eleven-mile-long lake that began about a mile upstream from the cabin. Pickerel, we found, were better to eat, the flesh being firm and flavourful. To this day it is my belief that pickerel taken from water free of industrial and sewage pollution is hard to beat for downright good eating.

We continued our muskrat trapping through April and on into May when the poplars first showed a tinge of green. On May 15 Chris Timson arrived at our camp in his sailing boat. He was on his way to Big River with his fur catch. Would we come along? We would. Rat Lake, he told us, had been cleared of ice the day before by a steady south wind and Crooked Lake would probably be ice-free also.

Travelling downstream in the warm sun was most enjoyable. The current swept us along effortlessly and our two boats made good time, for the creek was now a torrent with the spring flood. The pickerel run was in full swing and we saw thousands wriggling through the rapids, their spiked back fins often above water.

At the sluggish Crooked River we turned upstream. The river was high with all the backwaters flooded and the trees standing in water in some areas. We continued on past Crooked Lake Dam where Bill Mahoney had all gates wide open to let the high waters drain away. Out on Crooked Lake Chris instructed us on how to rig a sail with our tarpaulin. A fair wind filled it and swept us down the lake.

For us, sailing was a new experience. The land slipped steadily by as Ab steered the craft from the stern. Redwing blackbirds sang their spring song in the reeds along shore, the air was full of the wing sounds of travelling waterfowl, fish jumped from the water and the sun shone bright and warm all day long. We had short periods ashore to boil the tea pail and eat our meals and to doze in the sun.

On the second day, from ten miles out we sighted the sawdust burner. The wind held fair and we landed at the government dock at noon. The denuded hillsides of the village were strewn with the garbage and junk of winter. The Depression was still evident, as was human misery. We were not impressed with what we saw. The months of isolation had classified us with those who prefer to live in the unspoiled wilderness. We decided to return to the cabin and spend the summer there.

Muskrat prices had improved. The buying price was now thirty-five cents a pelt. We sold the hundred-odd pelts and loaded up a meager grubstake. We stayed in town just long enough to enjoy fresh fruit, vegetables, and beer. As we embarked down Crooked Lake we were already laying plans for the winter.

4

SECOND WINTER

In the black earth between the big poplar stumps of the little clearing we planted a garden. Seeds brought from Big River and rhubarb roots gleaned from an abandoned ranchhouse were soon producing, but the garden became so overrun with woodchucks and rabbits that it was only partly successful.

Ab had long had the urge to make a dugout canoe fashioned after the models he had seen used by British Columbia Indians. Therefore, during the previous winter he had felled a great white spruce located near the Rat Lake shore. We had worked on the log from time to time, shaping it roughly on the outside and gouging at its insides with a homemade adze. When finally the log had been pared down in weight, we skidded it on the snow to the lakeshore. Soon after our return to the Rat Creek cabin, we floated the roughed-out canoe down to the cabin site.

We worked on it now with knives, axes, and the adze. We gouged until the thickness of the walls averaged under two inches. Carefully now we chipped and carved lest a crude stroke cut right through. Eventually, the canoe was completed, a sixteen-foot craft cut from one great log. She checked a little at the ends but Ab soon had these cracks sealed, and we found it well balanced and very serviceable, compared to our heavy wooden boat.

It was the end of June when we assessed our cabin as a summer home and found it wanting. The trees, now in full leaf, cut off any breeze, the poplars and the willows took on such lush foliage that the cabin was shaded most of the time. It rained a lot that year and the creek remained at flood stage all summer. The swampy area behind the cabin became a vast incubator for millions of vicious mosquitoes, for the humidity and stifling heat created ideal mosquito hatching conditions. These winged stabbers drove us indoors and we had to sleep under mosquito netting if we were to sleep at all. Underbrush grew up thick and green about the cabin so that we had a clear view from the cabin of only a few yards.

The poplars formed a solid wall, blotting out the spruce. The grasses stood three feet high at the creek's edge. The grey willows and the red willows with long waxy leaves so changed the appearance of the creek that we could have imagined ourselves in different country.

Now we had an invasion of bulldog flies. These flying butchers are similar in size and disposition to the horseflies I had known on the prairies; however, the bulldogs are more vividly coloured and have a blood-drawing bite that cuts from both sides to the centre when they are able to get at the skin of man or beast. They swarmed into the cabin and we were forced to make a door of netting.

The final and deciding factor occurred when a skunk dug under the outside wall of the cabin and took up residence beneath the floor. Ab was forced to shoot her because she kept us awake nights with the noise of keeping house. After she was shot she released her offensive weapon too close to the cabin so that the flour and rolled oats became tainted. Our cabin had become untenable. This moonshiner's retreat was not for us. We had to get to higher ground, with a view and a breeze lest we become victims of claustrophobia. We would relocate and build a new cabin.

The site we chose was a quarter of a mile upstream from the old cabin. On a rounded ridge wooded with tall mature white poplars we found a level area. To the north the land rose in a gentle slope while on the west the ridge fell off sharply to provide excellent drainage. On the east the downward slope was less steep. To the south we could see past the cattails and reeds all the way to the lake. We could feel the south wind here, and the sun shone through the leaves and dappled the ground.

Ab began to fell the poplars. His double-bitted axe sent them crashing to the ground. The trees were so tall and heavy that most of the limbs were shattered from the trunks as they came in contact with the ground. He taught me how to fell a log exactly where it should fall, how to "pull" a tree to one side or another to avoid getting it hung up on another. It was the season when tree bark is loose and we peeled each log with our axes simply by cutting a long strip and then peeling off great slabs of bark. Before the logs became dry we skidded them down the north rise, across other peeled logs so that with a minimum of effort we hand-logged enough prime timber for a cabin twelve feet by twenty-four feet in size.

Ab had had some experience as a carpenter's helper. He possessed an uncanny knack for making a saw cut that fit with precision. The cabin walls began to rise. We used all the board flooring, roof boards, factory windows, and the door from the old cabin. At last a new, clean, white cabin stood on the rise which overlooked Rat Creek to the lake. Lastly, we neatly trimmed all the log ends of the cabin and were a little proud of our new home. The site was cleaned up, the limbs and bark burned, and we moved into the new cabin, aromatic with poplar scent.

We were faced with a problem: we were broke. With our present supplies we could stick it out until autumn, but there was no money for food, clothing, and equipment to enable us to spend the coming winter at this place. It was decided that I would return home and work in the wheat fields during harvest in order to assure us enough cash for our needs.

Ab and I parted company a few miles south of Big River. We shook hands, he turned north and I south. Twenty-four hours later I had hitchhiked to Saskatoon.

In Saskatchewan's second largest city I viewed at first hand the effects of the Depression and I hated what I saw. The city was full of young men, all jobless, destitute, and with no place to go. I saw men lined up for blocks awaiting a turn at a soup kitchen. I possessed the fare and I was determined to ride on the passenger train the rest of the way, and I had a six-hour wait for my train. I walked about the city. I caught the looks of faces haggard with worry, pain, and misery. I saw once again the hopelessly crippled, the blind, the handicapped, and the weakening aged. This caused me to reflect on the many ills of mankind with which I had been out of contact; so that becoming suddenly aware of this after several months I was appalled and felt that the clean, free, and easy life up north was much to be desired in place of city existence. I wished with all my heart to return and as soon as possible.

Back at my home I found most of my friends interested in my experiences and they questioned me for hours. Some of my schoolmates had spent the winter on farms through an arrangement whereby the provincial government paid the farmer and the man each the sum of five dollars a month.

I had a good long run of harvesting with little delay for wet weather. In early October I was back in Big River with fifty dollars left of my earnings.

I hunted around for someone with a motorboat to run me to Crooked Lake Dam. I wandered down to the government dock next morning and, sure enough, there was Irvine loading supplies into his boat. Of course he would take me to Crooked Lake Dam. His father was operating a small pole-cutting operation ten miles down the lake and he must help him finish hauling out the poles to the lake, about two days' work. I could come along if I wished. I was delighted to come.

The weather was sunny, warm, and the winds light. Irvine, now using a smaller boat and a new outboard motor, had us out to the pole camp in short order.

I spent the next two days in a most delightful setting. It was that season that is free of mosquitoes, has warm sunshine and leaves showing their last blaze of colour. I sat on a sunny hillside and awaited each load of poles that Irvine hauled out to the lake by horse team. Then I assisted him at unloading one pole at a time and watched them roll down the hill into the lake where they became part of a large boom. The poles were about twenty feet in length and up to ten inches in diameter and could be used for fence posts, corrals, or the many other uses to which such logs can be put. If I became thirsty I walked back on the wagon road for a few yards where a sweet-water spring trickled through a little draw. The men had made a trough of two small boards so that the water carried over an ancient mossy log and cascaded from it in a crystal stream. It was the best-tasting drinking water that I have ever had.

The pole-cutting operation completed, we left for the dam on a bright, sunny morning. Our trip down the lake was a thing of great beauty, and something I cannot forget. The lake was a long narrow mirror which reflected all the colours of autumn, for the poplars and birch were painted a rich yellow. Each tree was duplicated in the water mirror to the finest detail so that the autumn colours were doubled. In contrast to our first cold and dangerous trip down the lake one year ago, this was sheer enjoyment. I have seen the leaves colour, flame, and fall many times since, but often the weather turns wet and cold with harsh winds that strip the leaves away even while yet quite green. The trip was completed by early afternoon with Bill Mahoney holding our gunwhale to the dock as we stepped ashore.

I hiked the seven miles to Rat Creek. Happy to meet again, Ab and I had a good visit. He had put all the finishing touches on the cabin, prepared the traps and cut the winter's supply of wood. We would be ready to start trapping with the first snow; but first we had to return to Big River for supplies and equipment. The next day we sailed the boat up Rat Lake before a fair wind. We ascended Stony (Delaronde) Creek to Stony (Delaronde) Lake and after two days made the landing from where we walked overland to Big River. We laid in enough supplies for two months, we bought a used 38.55 Winchester carbine for ten dollars to replace Ab's deer rifle which had proven defective. At the landing we loaded into the boat a 100-pound sack of vegetables bought from a homesteader for fifty cents. The good weather held and we made it back to the Rat Creek cabin without delay.

The trapping season was again at hand. We had shot a couple of mule deer to supply our need for meat so that our time could be spent at trapping. We went to work with enthusiasm but, alas, with little success. Somehow our traps would not work for us. Those placed atop the muskrat houses were warily skirted by fox and coyote. I must say here that our efforts were continually dogged by bad luck and outrageous circumstances. Old Bill Mahoney, out of pity, had shown me how to make a trail set at a place where a deadfall lay across the trail. He demonstrated how a fox or coyote, when travelling, would jump over the log and step on the concealed trap on the other side. I tried these traps at likely places and caught rabbits. One morning a coyote loped down one of the trails I had set. There had been one inch of new snow in the night. I trailed the coyote to my set. It had leaped the log—and continued on! Out of curiosity I lifted the trap and found that the animal had stepped on each jaw and not set off the trigger. We had several other near misses. By the end of November our catch consisted of a dozen weasels and one mink. Other than Mahoney's tip on trail sets no one had offered us any clues to successful trapping.

One day Ab and I had a serious talk and decided that we must reassess our position. Although we both enjoyed the life here we must be realistic and realize that we must make a living with enough surplus to purchase new equipment, clothing, rifles, even a canoe, and outboard motor.

The use of snares for taking fur animals was unlawful in Saskatchewan. We had accepted that law and so far had not violated it. However, on our travels we had seen many snares set by Indians and half-breeds and whites. We had heard of no one who had been charged for violating the regulation. Ab and I looked at each other for a moment, then looked at the three-quarter-inch cable hanging on the wall.

"Are you thinking the same thing I am?" I asked.

He grinned and answered, "I think so."

We set to work first cutting the cable into lengths with a hacksaw. Taking several strands of wire for each snare, we fashioned loops in each end by twisting the ends around the strands to form a small loop through which the end was threaded to make the noose. A similar loop was made at the other end to be used for anchoring. The wire worked into snares perfectly.

We began to experiment with the setting of snares. We were soon to learn that successful snaring is an art that must be acquired by trial and error. We hung a few in the rabbit runs and game trails and anchored each to a sapling. We set them wrong because foxes and coyotes either dodged under the loop or jumped through loops that we made too large.

The snows were growing deeper. One morning the new-cut poplar stumps about the cabin all carried fourteen-inch snowcaps. We realized that all our traps had been useless for fox and coyote. The coyotes, as usual, howled tantalizingly from quite close to the cabin, from the shadowy recesses of the thick woods, and faintly from far away swamp and muskeg.

On my rounds one morning I found one snare noose drawn shut and pulled askew. Close examination of the wire showed a few hairs caught in the ends of the wire windings. They were unmistakably the black-tipped coyote guard hairs! My pulse quickened. Here was failure once more, but probably the loop had been set wrong and the coyote had caught his tail momentarily in the wire ends. Ab showed great interest in this event and proceeded to string out a line of snares in the game trails through the grey willow flats all the way to Rat Lake and part way down the lakeshore.

It was a week before Christmas. Ab made ready for the long hike to Big River, this time south via Chris's cabin, Brown's abandoned ranch, across country to Craddock's ranch, Crooked Lake, and so on into Big River. He was to pick up the mail, tobacco, and such groceries as the proceeds of twelve weasels and one mink would bring. I saw him off in the early dawn and settled down to cleaning up the cabin, washing and mending my somewhat tattered clothing.

A couple of hours later I heard a whoop from down the trail. Ab, a grin of triumph on his face, walked toward the cabin, and atop his pack was a snared coyote. This was indeed cause for jubilation, a prime fully furred coyote was worth ten dollars.

What was more important, we had actually wrested a secret from this land, and our efforts were beginning to pay off.

Ab had found the coyote in one of his snares in the willow flats; he had looked over the snares on his way, just in case. The snare victim was frozen solid into a statue that caught in great detail the desperation and terror of the death struggle. The muzzle was frozen in a last death-defying snarl, the tongue lolling and bloodied, the teeth bared and threatening, the tail flailing, the legs straining desperately against an unrelenting foe to the very end—choked to death by a noose drawn taut by the tension of many willows pulled into a cone-shaped bundle by the wire which we had cut a little too long.

We were a couple of days thawing the coyote carcass, and skinning out, stretching, and drying the pelt. Just as a fur pelt insulates against the cold it also acts as insulation against heat and therefore fully furred animal carcasses thaw slowly.

Then Ab departed again for Big River. A similar scene occurred later that day; this time Ab bore another snared coyote and a snared red fox, both prime and full furred. We now had about fifty dollars worth of furs, enough to buy our supplies and clothing until spring. We felt that at long last we were on our way.

Ab got to Big River on the third try. He stopped in to visit with Chris. During the course of the conversation Chris declared that some good-for-nothing so-and-so was illegally setting snares—and in his territory! Ab made no comment, but puffed steadily on his pipe as Chris talked on. Finally Chris stated that the snares belonged to Ed Choquette, a white trapper with headquarters on Crooked Lake, due west of Chris's cabin.

We learned quickly that, although the use of snares for taking coyotes and foxes was illegal, according to the game laws of Saskatchewan, they were used by Indians who had done so from time immemorial and would use them as long as they hunted furs. The half-breeds used snares also, for wire was cheap and easily carried about. I once snared a coyote that already carried a crudely made loop of two strands of hay-baling wire. Oddly enough, while most white trappers used snares they would not admit it. Some whites failed to "catch on" to snares at all because they did not learn the craft and set snares with little or no success.

The craft of snaring, it turned out, was highly effective when properly applied. I found the use of snares more to my liking than lugging around heavy steel traps. A dozen coiled snares tucked into a parka pocket were, of course, much less cumbersome than packing a like number of traps in a packsack. I consider that a properly set snare is more humane than a trap, for if skillfully set a snared coyote or fox will hang itself. The trapped animal may live for many days unless it chews or twists off its foot. The fascination of snaring is that there may be some surprises in the catch from snares. I have caught a full-grown lynx in a snare set for fox. The best and healthiest animals are taken with snares, while traps catch the crippled, diseased, and undernourished. One of the pitfalls of using steel snares is that snares may be snowed over and lost, then when the snow melts they will reappear and catch fur animals all summer. The snarer takes on a greater responsibility and marks his sets well, carefully accounting for each one.

The 1933-34 winter turned out to be one of the severe ones that come along perhaps once in twenty years and is remembered for its severity. On a visit to Bill Mahoney's cabin he informed us that temperature below —60° F. had been recorded in Big River when he was in town in January. The village, set on bare hillsides with a northern exposure was bearing the brunt of a bone-chilling north wind that swept up the lake. Wildlife tracks were seen less and less as the animals kept to the shelter of the bush where four feet of snow covered all ground landmarks. At sunrise when the temperature of the day is often at its minimum, the trees crack loudly with the frost.

We travelled on snowshoes and had by now learned to use them. Bill Mahoney lent us one of his Indian-made models which we used for a pattern to make our own. We used birch for frames and crossbars, steaming the wood in boiling water to bend the staves into shape and for the upward toe binds. Raw moose hide was cut in strips and used in the centre section while deerskin strips were cut for weaving the end sections. We decorated them with gaily coloured woolen tassels. We learned the slightly spread-legged walk of snowshoers and to avoid contact with snags. We experienced *mal de raquet* the French Canadian term for the torturing pain under the toes caused by snowshoe webbing chafing moccasined feet.

In the beginning I found that I was no hunter. I had to learn how it was done. The first winter, when alone, I felt unoriented and lacked a sense of direction when in the bush. In the second winter I began to hunt alone; I followed the game trails into the lush poplar and birch stands where moose trails crisscrossed the whole area. I went back into the meadows where there was much evidence of feeding deer.

I did nothing right. One day I sat resting on a convenient stump and looked all around. Two dark objects among the trees less than seventy-five yards away drew my interest for a time. I decided that they were two uprooted spruce whose spreading roots had carried up black earth. Then I saw the dark objects move. A moose cow with calf were legging it for more distant parts. Another day, after a hard tramp, I sat on a log, resting. I heard a twig snap, then another. I watched in awe as a big mule deer buck walked neatly toward me, curiosity in his flared nostrils and wide eyes. At the same instant I stood up and shot at his neck, he wheeled and my shot whistled over his rump. I realized my error at once. Had I remained seated, I could have shot him in the eye at forty yards. These were bitter lessons. I later gained complete confidence in bush travelling and also learned to hunt effectively, contributing a share to our meat supplies.

With the heavy snows came the intense cold that invariably follows in this latitude of Saskatchewan. The coldest weather was characterized by the complete absence of wind. The thermometer was often in the low minus fifties. This grim cold seemed to crowd down and dull the ambition. The creek froze up tight and stopped steaming. We spent a good deal of our time in our new, clean cabin, reading, talking, or playing cribbage, a popular card game in the North. Our reading was augmented by a box of "pulp" adventure magazines, a popular newsstand item of the times. These had been sent to us by our former partner, Bob. We analyzed critically some of the Northland stories and picked out certain flaws with authority.

Late in February, Ab shot a mature doe back in the tall timber that stretched in a band from north to south just east of the cabin. The doe had been faring badly for she consisted mainly of hair, hide, bone, and paunch. Not a vestige of fat could be found on the meat which had an unhealthy pink colour. We rejected it for food. The snow had covered so much of the browse that the animal was starving.

Occasional milder days broke the monotony of winter. The coyote chorus was heard more frequently for it was their mating season again. We saw where they urinated at their favourite "posts"—the snags that showed above the snow along the creek.

Ab went north one day hunting for caribou in the Voisin Lake country. He was away all day and reached the cabin after dark. He had spent the entire day walking down a crippled coyote that had escaped from a trap. Back and forth through the wooded muskeg country the coyote had tried all his tricks to throw him off the trail. The moment came when the coyote moved from cover into the open for a few seconds and fell to Ab's rifle.

Once again the drumming of woodpeckers heralded the coming of spring and with it the muskrat-trapping season. We concentrated on our work and set all the push-ups we could find on the creek right down to the rapids and on the lake as far as Chris's trapline. We made many open-water sets in the open area of the creek. The yield was good and our pile of skins grew each day.

Indians from Green Lake appeared on the creek one day. They came in groups of three or four and set their traps alongside ours. Their dogs smelled out all the push-ups that we could not locate under the snow. These people waded up to their waists in the icy water to get at choice locations. We were a good deal nettled, but eventually adopted the philosophy that some of these people had probably trapped here before we were born. Later several white homesteaders came along to augment their meager incomes by trapping muskrats. We overlooked these also, for the game laws permitted each holder of a two dollar trapping license to operate where he chose on unrestricted lands throughout the province.

In prime muskrat country, on certain warm days occasional muskrats were to be found adventuring on the lake ice. One of these which I ran down had both front feet missing from previous trappings. I heard a story of one hunter who had trapped a muskrat by the tail since it had no feet at all, having lost them in traps.

The whole cycle of spring unfolded again, the vivid green of the spruce as the sap began to rise, the drumming of grouse, the return of crows, waterfowl, and songbirds. Some of the songbirds called with notes that could be compared to the sound of tapping on the finest glass goblet. We heard the din of frogs and saw the fish swarm up the creek, the small jackfish, and once in a while one so large that our eyes popped. Loons arrived and made belly landings on the creek. Bitterns thunder pumped in the backwaters and great blue herons rose silently and were airborne as we neared them around some bend in the creek.

One day we worked our muskrat sets out on Rat Lake where the ice did not cover a narrow stretch where the creek begins. Busily occupied among the dead reeds, cattails, and wild rice beds, we encountered a sudden storm of wind, sleet, and snow. Paddling the dugout canoe hard against the stinging sleet, we made it to the shelter of the creek. Here we surprised a flock of some fifty pelicans who had also sought the creek's shelter. These ungainly looking birds made a laboured take-off into the storm. The wind carried them back, now at a good height overhead. I noticed that one bird was having some trouble keeping up with its mates. Then a long jackfish squirmed out of the bird's great beak and with a resounding slap struck the mud among the willows. As the fish fell through the air, I judged it to be in the four- or five-pound class.

All the ice left the lake one day as a southwest wind ripped at the shifting mass. Before our eyes the ice shifted and moved to the opposite shore where it pushed up on shore for some feet. The wind and waves did the rest. The open stretch of water widened. By evening the lake was clear of ice, the only signs of winter's grip were the piles of ice on shore and on the sandy points that jut out into the lake. Chill breezes came from this area.

The next day I beached the dugout canoe on a small sandy beach. A pair of sandpipers waded just at the shoreline, calling each other. The male bird took to the air, circled back and forth, calling all the while. The female answered from the beach and performed her mating dance. Then I witnessed their mating as the male descended to her on gentle wings, as delicately as a falling poplar leaf in the still warm air of an autumn day.

One day Cyril Mahoney arrived at our cabin. Cyril was the son of our old friend Bill, the dam keeper. Travelling overland on foot he had come from the Little Rat Lake country where he had been muskrat trapping. He was on his way to Big River via Crooked Lake Dam. He had just completed a very successful season, for he had 250 muskrat skins in his big packsack. I recognized him at once for an accomplished woodsman by the neatness of his clothing and equipment. He looked like a capable man in the bush. The way he had prepared his furs was a revelation. Every trace of fat and tissue had been expertly removed so that the skin side, turned out, had a smooth, varnished look. From this we could see that our skins, although acceptably prepared, would not command as high a price as these expertly prepared ones. We thenceforth prepared ours in a like manner.

Cyril visited with us for half a day. We enjoyed his conversation. Once while discussing the merits of a trappers' life he remarked, "This is the only life."

A few days later Chris arrived with his sailboat. Chris was pulling out—moving to Cree Lake to rejoin his old trapping partner, Holgar Petersen.

Cree Lake! The name quickened my pulse and set my imagination to working. Some of the white trappers from that area were reportedly doing well, trapping many minks and foxes. Many a tale could be heard in Big River of the fabulous fur catches made in the Cree Lake country.

We bought from Chris some of his equipment, including the sailboat. He gave us his neat cabin halfway down the lake. We also bought his ancient radio receiving set that had two headphones. We wished Chris well in Big River when we parted. We were well established now, having enlarged our territory to twice its former size.

Muskrats were selling for seventy-five cents each. We found that we had enough money for a short holiday Outside.

5

L'ORIGNAL

THE FRENCH CANADIAN fur traders of old had a name for the moose that was aptly descriptive. They called him *l'orignal,* which embodies in its meaning grotesque, awkward, fantastic, and freak. So the name is fitting for the appearance of the moose, which under certain adverse conditions is anything but beautiful, while at his best he is nothing less than magnificent.

The Rat Creek country teemed with moose. The very first time that we walked overland from Crooked Lake Dam we encountered a majestic bull moose resplendent in his great polished antlers and shiny dark coat. We were all heavily laden with our bulging packsacks, Ab in the lead carrying the rifle in one hand. Suddenly the bull charged across the trail, and although Ab had time to get off one shot in the thick bush, he was handicapped by his heavy load and made no hit, for we tracked the bull for a good distance and could not find a single drop of blood on the yellow poplar leaves with which the ground was strewn. We were thrilled with the sight of such a huge beast which appeared to be taller than a horse.

Later that season, when the snows came, we observed with satisfaction the moose tracks that crisscrossed over our own trail and along the creek where the animals browsed in the red willow thickets. Any sign of a moose was a good sign, for it meant that fresh meat was available to augment our food supply. The heaps of glazed, rounded, brown, hard droppings were signs from which we learned to tell if the animal was young or mature and the trail fresh or old.

Ab had been spending his time moose hunting since we were

out of fresh meat. It seemed that when the larder was empty the moose were difficult to find. This occasion was no exception and he was becoming desperate. One late November evening Ab was much later than usual in returning to the cabin. I assumed that he was lost in the bush and camping out overnight. Just as it became quite dark he walked in, tired, pale, and sweaty. He had been hunting in a hummocky, wooded muskeg area to the north of the cabin when he saw his quarry. He could see only the paunch of the moose where it stood among the stunted spruce. Ab soon had the moose gutshot and moving. Through the two-foot depth of snow he dogged it for hours while it moved generally southward toward the cabin. The sky was heavily overcast and it looked as if it would snow. When the moose finally veered to the west Ab plodded on southward to the cabin.

It did not snow that night and we were on the move at daylight. We picked up the moose's trail in due course. It led through the most difficult terrain to be found, down crisscrossed timber that curtailed our progress. The moose, realizing that it would be followed, was making desperate attempts to slow us down. It shuffled at a steady walk and favoured its right hind leg, as we could see by its tracks. It emerged from the bush to the bank of the partly open Crooked River and waded across. From where we stood we could see its trail on the other side leading straight into a thick poplar stand.

It was now necessary that we build a raft large enough to carry us both across the open channel. This was accomplished by packing from the bush a number of large dry poplar logs. We placed them side by side on the ice, and fastened poles across them by nailing with ancient square-sided spikes gleaned from a long-abandoned logging camp nearby. The raft must be large enough to float us across the open channel and to float us back with the meat, should we be successful in finding the moose.

Up on a little poplar-covered ridge we found him where he had chosen to die, facing his back trail. The meat was unspoiled, for the moose had bled to death into the abdominal cavity.

After we had packed out the meat to our cabin, we no longer

carried our big rifles for we had all the meat for our needs for some time to come. On many occasions we were to observe these interesting animals at close range. From our new cabin on the hill, we often saw a lone bull crossing the creek, or a cow and a calf feeding in the red willows until they moved on, unmolested and with our best wishes. While on our traplines, we frequently encountered moose and, standing still, observed them feeding or travelling from one lush feeding ground to another.

The moon shone so brightly one early autumn night that we saw the cow moose across the creek, standing just beyond the willows. She called then, a sound rather difficult to associate with such an animal. She called again and again. The sixth time she vanished silently.

Ab shot a prime cow moose one windy afternoon, late in February. Our meat supply was once more uncomfortably low. The snow was four feet deep, which made travelling over new trails something less than a pleasure. This day it had warmed up considerably as a strong warm wind raked the Rat Creek country. The bush was noisy with the creaking of old poplars, and bare branches rattled against one another; coupled with the wind roaring through the trees, any sound made by a hunter tended to be obliterated. Ab ran onto a very large and very fresh moose track. The freshness was confirmed when he placed his moccasined foot into a track and found it soft all the way down, including the ridge of snow that is left between the imprints of the cloven foot. He now discarded his snowshoes and stepped carefully into each track as he moved forward. Bill Mahoney had instructed him carefully as to correct procedure in just such circumstances. Indians, said Bill, on a very fresh moose trail move very carefully and slowly, placing the feet very slowly into each moose track so that a minimum of noise is made. It was almost too easy. Ab, seeing that the animal had been feeding, stepped slowly, step by step around a large alder thicket. Suddenly he sighted the cow feeding peacefully in some scrub birch. So successful had been the stalk that he stood less than fifty yards from this huge animal that was in full winter hair, fat as a seal, and in

top condition. He felt as an elephant hunter might feel on suddenly encountering his quarry at very close range.

From the cabin where I was cutting firewood, I heard the roar of Ab's 38.55 Winchester. Soon there followed a second report and, after a few minutes, a third and final shot. From the timing of the shots I felt certain that he had made a kill.

At dusk Ab arrived at the cabin carrying on a forked stick an extra large moose heart. An almost unbelievable amount of prime fat meat lay just a mile from the cabin for the cow had run towards it as soon as she was hit. We later packed out all the meat in our big packsacks, real labour from which we rested from time to time by placing the load on convenient stumps or logs along the trail. There was the satisfaction of knowing that our meat supply was assured until spring, and further killing of big game was now unnecessary.

When we made a kill, we usually had a feed of fried liver which, when properly prepared, was found to be delicious. As the meat cooled out and aged we prepared steaks, chops, and roasts. We astonished ourselves at the amount of meat that we could eat. A two-inch-thick steak that covered the inside of the big frying pan disappeared between the two of us. We made hamburgers by the dozen, grinding the meat in our hand-operated meat grinder, eating with gusto, our young appetites whetted keen by outdoor living. In early autumn and early spring the hanging meat turned very dark, but we found that when the outside was trimmed away the meat was more palatable than ever.

"I am eating meat twenty-one times a week," said Chris Timson, in noting the abundance of big game in his trapping territory. This was frequently the case when northern dwellers lived largely off the land.

"A moose can carry a lot of lead," Chris also said to me. Explaining that the animal should be hit in a vital spot in order to bring it down, he stated that a moose might well escape the hunter even though riddled by bullets if they were improperly placed. The account that follows demonstrates the truth of Chris's observation.

It was Indian Summer, those last warm, sunny, and glorious days which forestall for a brief time any hint of the coming winter. Ab and I sat in the cabin, eating a noonday meal of three stuffed mallards. The cabin door stood wide open and the warm sun shone down onto the cabin floor, one of those fine days when it is a joy just to be alive. Suddenly from the creek we heard a crackling in the willows and from our seats watched in fascination as a prime bull moose came forward, twisting his great rack of antlers from side to side to negotiate his way through the willow thicket that bordered the creek. In a few moments he stood among the poplars just outside our door. Ab, meanwhile, had unlimbered the Winchester and taken aim. As the rifle cracked, the moose fell flat on its side as though slapped sideways by a giant's hand. Ever conserving our supply of cartridges (now numbering nineteen) Ab asked me to bring the .22 to "finish him off." I grabbed it from its rack on the wall and whirling around I saw the moose back on its feet and making for the screening bush. Ab pumped several shots from the Winchester at its vanishing rear but it did not stop. We tracked it for hours through the woods, but when it took to grassy swampland the trail was hopelessly lost.

After three hours, we returned to our now cold and gluey duck dinner. Our disappointment was great for two reasons: one, that for an unbelievable few seconds the moose had lain at our doorstep, which would have eliminated much backbreaking labour in packing out meat. The second was that the moose had been hit and would probably die and be wasted. In analyzing Ab's poor shooting, we concluded that he had shot too high; we hoped only grazing the animal causing shock for only an instant.

One hot sunny day in July we were visited by Harry, a Green Lake half-breed. He appeared at our cabin having arrived by his small hunting canoe, after a series of long portages. Harry, in pidgin English, informed us that he was making a summer moose hunt to feed himself, his wife, and eight children. In his canoe there was a small white-tailed doe, shot as he paddled up the creek to our cabin. At the conclusion of his visit we watched him paddle out toward Rat Lake, the canoe winding through the channel among the tall reeds and bulrushes until he disappeared from sight.

The next day Harry returned and asked if he might borrow our skiff. He informed us that he had killed two large bull moose about halfway down the lake. He had shot them from the canoe while screened by reeds as they fed in the water among the water-lily beds. The carcasses now lay on the west shore where he had horsed them by brute strength. The skiff was lent and he worked hard to freight all the meat down to a spot below our cabin where he dried it in the warm sun and wind and with the aid of a slow fire. He later had to portage the dried meat several miles to a wagon road where the trip home was completed with a team of horses and a wagon. He had to battle various insect pests all the while—blowflies, mosquitoes, sandflies, and bulldog flies—so that he had to endure great discomfort. This had been the way of life of his Cree ancestors.

Possibly his white ancestors had been slothful. One evening after Harry had pulled out I went pickerel fishing at my favourite bend in the creek just below the cabin. I pushed the bow of the canoe into the reeds and cast my lure into the creek. Then I saw Harry's small doe, discarded and floating in the reeds where he had dumped it. Evidently, after he had shot the two moose, he decided that he did not need the deer. He had not offered it to us, either, and we had no fresh meat since we did not hunt in summer, not yet having learned how to dry meat for summer use.

In our second winter at Rat Creek my trapping career almost came to an abrupt halt. The creek was still wide open in early November as I paddled the dugout canoe down the creek that I might inspect some traps without leaving the telltale tracks made by a trapper who walks. A few miles downstream I heard the snap of a dry twig, then another, and another, the unmistakable sounds of a moose walking or feeding. I let the canoe drift quietly into some reeds and it hung there, motionless. Carefully I reached for the Winchester and stood up, studying the place in a big willow thicket from where I had heard the sound of breaking twigs. I could see the head of a moose, the top of the head a greyish yellow and a darker brown as I looked down its face. I pulled back the hammer of the Winchester, raised it to my shoulder and sighted at the moose's head. I thought of the baseball-sized brains I had observed in moose skulls. I decided that a shot at a partly obscured head might not stop a moose, so I lowered the rifle and looked for the neck or shoulder where a more effective slug might be placed.

The moose head had vanished. I stood as a statue, awaiting

any sound or movement from which I might pierce the protective camouflage. After several minutes I stepped silently ashore and began slowly to circle the willow thicket. Sneaking around a sharp bend, I almost tripped over Harry, our visitor from Green Lake, who sat boiling his tea pail over a tiny willow fire!

Harry was dressed in a brown parka, the hood of which was trimmed with a coyote skin. He was trapping in what was considered to be our territory, so, Indian fashion, he had hidden his fire of dry willows which give off much heat but very little smoke. The cracking of dry twigs that I had heard had been Harry breaking willows for the fire. I explained to Harry how he had appeared to me from the other side of the thicket and that I had had him in my rifle sights. Harry's almost black face turned a sickly somewhat lighter shade. We were both shaken. I was nauseated and felt that I might retch. The experience taught me a very severe lesson: make sure of my target before shooting. It had a lasting effect on Harry also, for we never laid eyes on him again.

It was early May, the ice had just gone out of Rat Lake and we were camped halfway down the lake, trapping muskrats. In the long twilight I paddled the canoe up a small creek that meandered through muskeg, floating bog, and stunted, moss-draped black spruce and tamarack. In this grim-looking place, it was rumoured that a white man had been drowned some years before and the body was never found. The police and the coroner had come out from Big River, but no discovery of the body was made. There were rumours that it had been murder, and a more appropriate place for such a deed would have been difficult to find. The shoreline quivered at the touch of my paddle and I could push my paddle under it and feel nothing. Hiding a body here would have been extremely easy.

My mind occupied by such morbid thoughts, I paddled around a half circle in the creek that skirted a stand of black spruce. I then came upon the biggest bull moose that I had ever seen. It was feeding in the swamp and was unaware of me. I silently watched this great beast at a range of about seventy-five yards.

Here, indeed, was *l'orignal.* Against a backdrop of stunted spruce it appeared solitary, huge, grotesque, its long hair now bleached and ragged, its antlers long ago discarded, little resembling the popular conception of a bull moose. However, when September returned once again, this bull would become resplendent, majestic, and with great palmated antlers that might well be in the trophy class. I silently wished him well as I paddled out of sight. In such an area it is possible for a moose to live out its entire life span, for access is treacherous in the bogs in autumn, and the creek is not always navigable in low water and is seldom travelled by canoe. The deep snows of winter have a deterring effect on human travel in such a place.

We learned that, unlike white-tailed deer, moose are not apt to stay close to human habitation, but seek solitude. We found them in the most remote areas of our trapping territory.

A cow moose, with her small rusty-coloured calf, that stood facing us on a game trail one spring, was given a wide berth, for she showed no inclination to move out of our way and wagged her ears warningly and her ragged hair bristled. We offered no argument.

Moose are large beasts and at times appear to be not too intelligent. Most moose are taken by hunters on the chance encounter, by sighting a moose that does not see the hunter. Try to stalk a radar-eared moose and you have an entirely different situation. Since a moose is forever worrying about its back trail it often beds down on high ground, facing its back trail. A moose hunter's success is related to his ability to stalk moose.

I learned to do this with good effect. When we moved into the Cree Lake country we found that moose were not plentiful and the chance encounter almost never occurred. We had to stalk them successfully in order to obtain meat.

One winter morning I came upon a place where two moose trails cut across my trapline and led off to the west. I took up the hunt, feeling the tracks with my moccasined feet. I judged that since the tracks were frozen hard the trail was at least one day old. I tracked the pair for more than five miles until fresh tracks crossed the older trail. I was in hilly, second-growth jack pine country, the trees no taller than myself. I now followed slowly and carefully. One hillside had rather sparse tree growth; there I saw the two dark blobs which I knew were bedded moose. I crept very slowly and very carefully closer to the hillside. At last I crouched within 200 yards, effective range for my .30 Winchester rifle. A slight breeze must have carried my scent ahead for both moose presently stood up. I aimed just back of the shoulder of the larger of the two and squeezed off a shot. The moose fell back in its bed and I heard the sound of escaping air, a sound like a great sigh. When I dressed out the fat cow, I found that I had made a lucky hit for the bullet had ripped through the upper portion of the heart, the lungs had collapsed, and she was dead when I got there.

One man, dressing and cutting up a full-grown moose has his work cut out for himself. The shadows were gathering when I completed the task that day. I had to strike out due north for the river which would be my guide since it would be too dark to follow a bush trail. Later the moon rose and I walked on the frozen river, seven miles to the cabin where I arrived at 7 P.M., carrying a moose nose on a forked stick.

Ab mastered the art of moose stalking with as much ability as any Chipewyan Indian. He could track on bare ground in autumn and became an able stalker. He killed a fine bull moose one day in early October, picking up its tracks in the sand at the river's edge where it had stopped to drink. From his boat he could see that the track was new. He beached the boat on the sand and tracked the bull for a long mile through big jack pine timber. Then he heard a grunt. The bull stood motionless among the pines. He had seen the hunter first and as it was the mating season he had issued a challenge, probably mistaking the hunter at a distance for another moose. Ab killed him in his tracks with one well-placed shot.

Ab once tracked a big bull into a circular basin of second-growth jack pine. All around stood big jack pine timber. The basin was about 400 yards in diameter which he circled carefully to pick up the trail where the bull had emerged. When he arrived again at his own trail he realized that he had circled the moose since no trail led from the basin. On the second time around the bull was alerted; Ab saw the moving trees and heard the crash of broken branches as the moose charged into the timber.

At Cree Lake we discovered that since there was little else in the way of trees, moose fed on the tips of young jack pines, eating a branch down until it was as thick as a man's thumb. A moose shot in this country had stomach contents that looked much like chopped green oats and straw that I have seen in domestic cattle. It set me to wondering if it were possible to use the uncounted acres of young jack pine for cattle fodder by grinding, chemical treatment, and the addition of food supplements.

Winter was not far away that late autumn day when I made my first trip of the season by walking across country to my small outcamp on Caribou Lake. This new, tiny cabin was set in a jack pine grove only a few feet from the bank of a small creek that enters the western extremity of the lake. I had had a busy day; the long walk overland with loaded packsack, and putting the cabin into winter condition, tired me and I retired to my pole bunk early and immediately fell asleep. Sometime during the night I awakened, for I had to go to the bathroom, a common enough occurrence for a trapper who retires early after drinking several mugs of hot tea. The bathroom was located a few paces to one side of the cabin, and had the sky for a roof, the forest on all sides for walls, and the earth for a floor.

I had settled in my bedroll once more and was dozing off when I heard the sharp snap of a dry twig. Then I heard it again and knew that I was no longer alone. I lay quietly wondering what could be walking about out there. I had seen a good deal of bear sign on the way over. Are bears nocturnal? I asked myself. I decided that they could be, since Ab once trapped one after dark. No Indian, I decided, would be abroad at this hour if he were in his right mind.

The sounds which had come from the vicinity of my bathroom had ceased. The fog was rising from the creek, the sky was cloudy. With no moon and as yet no snow, a darker night was not possible. My Winchester stood beside my bunk, but since it was impossible to see, it was likewise impossible to shoot. The silence lasted for several minutes. I was listening intently and I knew that my visitor was doing the same. Then I heard the rattle of willows on moose antlers and was able to identify my visitor as he plunged into the creek and crashed off into the jack pines on the other side.

Many years later I learned that a birch bark horn is used not only to call moose, but also to lure him to his doom by dribbling a horn full of water into the lake from a hidden position. The resulting sound is said to be effective in making a suspicious bull come charging to the sound during the rut.

Bull moose play rough during the rut. We learned this while examining our kills. Among other injuries we found cracked shoulder blades, broken ribs, dented rib cages, punctured rumps, and splintered and broken antlers. This is evidence of robust gladiators who battle with no holds barred.

6

BROKEN SOLITUDE

IN THE spring of 1934 the muskrat hunt had been good at Rat Lake. We were astonished to find that muskrat prices had risen sharply over the previous year, so that we had enough cash to take a holiday at our home on the prairies. We found the wide open, flat, colourless land somehow foreign. We felt that we were not in step with this country. Economic conditions were, if anything, worse than on my visit of the previous summer. We could not get back to the north woods fast enough.

We returned to Big River in July and purchased a summer grubstake. We returned to Rat Lake in Chris's sailboat via Stony Lake and Stony Creek. Stony Creek, we found, was a fine navigable stream that ran through heavily wooded, generally flat country where we paddled past feeding moose and deer and where the songbirds sang us to sleep in the long twilight and where the waterfowl hatched their young in the backwaters and swampy grasslands at the creek's edge. Here ducks could be heard chuckling away in the reeds and talking it up with one another—one of the happiest sounds I know.

It was on this trip that we witnessed the phenomenon called will-o'-the-wisp or swamp fire. We paddled down Rat Lake by night while the waters were calm, having been delayed most of the day by unfavourable head winds. It was nearly midnight as we paddled along the west shore opposite a vast swamp. Suddenly we saw a light just above the swamp, a light that resembled a hurricane lantern seen at a distance. The light did not bob or weave but appeared to drift away and then vanish.

We spent part of the summer on Stony Lake where we worked

for Joe Sheppard, a squat, aging Englishman who had a history as a cook for the Hudson's Bay Company at some of its northern posts. Joe operated on Stony Lake, a stopping place for winter teamsters who travelled back and forth, occupied with hauling fish from as far north as Buffalo (Churchill) and Snake (Pinehouse) lakes. We remodelled his big log house. Ab, as ever, handy with tools, renovated the place to Joe's liking.

A few years earlier Chris Timson had worked for Joe and took as part payment two weanling pigs which he boated down to his cabin on Rat Lake to supply pork for the coming winter as a change from venison. He fashioned a pole pen for them and planned to feed them on ground oats he had brought along and fish from the lake. The shoats had become wary and wild, and as soon as they were released from the sack they climbed over the pole walls of the enclosure and vanished into the bush. Chris tried to call them back and even put out food to lure them in. As a last resort he set traps, but they never returned. He decided that they had been killed by coyotes.

The summer passed and early fall found us once more established on Rat Creek. All was as we had left it. Apparently no one had travelled the creek while we were absent for more than a month. At this time we set up the old-style radio receiving set purchased from Chris. We had brought in new tubes and the cumbersome dry batteries which were vital to its operation. We strung up a copper wire aerial on two long spruce poles and raised them to hold the wire strung across the clearing. It was growing dusk when the operation was completed. We each donned a pair of earphones and plugged them into the wooden box. I turned on the switch. We heard nothing. I moved the selector dial and right away we heard organ music, the familiar "Beautiful Ohio" came in loud and clear. Thereafter we spent the evenings listening to a wide selection of stations. Radio reception here was free of interference and static noises. The set would not receive during the daylight hours, but by nightfall we could pick up a range of stations from Winnipeg to Vancouver and stations in the central United States right down to the powerful transmitters on the Mexican border, particularly one used by a Dr. Brinkley to promote a health clinic.

We had the whole area to ourselves now that Chris Timson had moved north. However, we did have company in the form of several whisky jacks and a red squirrel that came into the cabin and took bits of bread from our fingers. A great, waddling porcupine scrambled over the sill of the open door one day and I had to chase him out with the aid of a stick. When we were no longer bothered by mosquitoes and sandflies we took long hikes through the woods to hunt and just enjoy ourselves in the October woods where the wet poplar leaves gave off scented vapours where they lay on the damp earth. On certain trails that skirted big muskegs the aroma of decaying vegetation resembled the smell of coffee, particularly where we stepped into the hummocks to pick red cranberries.

We began trapping operations a few days before the lake froze over. Ab in the sailboat plied the entire lake setting traps in the best locations. By freeze-up we had a dozen foxes and coyotes, for at last we were getting our traps to work, thanks to some conversation I had heard from a drunken trapper in Big River. We now knew something of how to bait traps and where and when to set them. We had all the meat we needed and a good supply of store food. We lived the life of Riley.

I laid out a new trapline. Across the creek through the bush east and north of the cabin, I blazed a trail through the trees, through country hitherto unexplored by ourselves. I skirted the big muskegs near Voisin Lake and in tall timber I climbed a great white spruce from which I could see the white expanse of Sled Lake in the distance to the north. From this point I circled back to the creek to make a big loop that completed a full day of travelling to work the line. I experimented with traps and with several snare nets.

From the cabin one day, I heard a tremendous coyote chorus to the east of the creek. Not only the usual howling, but interspersed were yelps and snarls as one might expect them to make around a kill. A few days later I came upon a concentration of coyote tracks in the snow which led me to a spot where they had killed and eaten a porcupine. Here was a bit of knowledge until then unknown to me, for I had considered a porcupine to be invulnerable to coyotes. Later on I trapped a large male coyote in this vicinity. When I took off the pelt I scratched my hand on something sharp in the black nose. I found a long porcupine quill imbedded just below the nostrils, two inches straight into the fleshy part of the nose, only the tip protruding. No swelling was noticeable, yet my tawny victim would have been in for a rough winter had his career not come to an abrupt end in my trap.

A few days later I gathered in a prime red fox caught by the hind foot in one of my trail sets.

Meanwhile, Ab was having considerable success trapping mink along the lakeshore between the cabin and Timson's old headquarters. A strain of off-coloured mink that resembled somewhat the colour of a groundhog were playing merry hob in the muskrat runs all along the shore. Each den had been systematically entered by these diminutive assassins who burrowed through the earth straight down into the access tunnels. Each entrance hole had been later sealed by the muskrats by pushing up mud through the hole. After Ab had trapped four mink all signs and tracks of them vanished. The full effect of their depradations, however, would be felt later on. Down on Rat Creek I caught a fine dark mink to add to our fur harvest.

Our larder was full of meat. Ab had shot two bull moose back of Timson's cabin and freighted in the meat by sailboat just before freeze-up. Walking my trapline I shot a four-point mule deer buck with my .22 calibre trapline rifle. Shortly afterward Ab brought down a yearling bull moose with one shot of his .22 rifle.

One cold, still winter noonday, I stood alone looking out over a wide expanse of open muskeg near Voisin Lake. I felt that I was utterly alone, for we had seen no sign of other humans for some months. It was such a desolate and forsaken place that I stood fascinated, looking out over this wasteland, while I rested from my long walk through dense woodland from the home cabin. Suddenly, I saw a band of eight woodland caribou emerge from some stunted spruce and begin to cross the open area—a fitting and likely wild setting in which to see these animals. The group was led by a magnificent bull with flowing white mane and an impressive rack of antlers. They passed within range of my rifle, I raised it to my shoulder and sighted just back of the bull's shoulder. Then I lowered the rifle. We had no need of meat. I watched them cross at a brisk walk until they blended with the snow and small spruce on the other side of the muskeg.

Then I looked at the snow at my feet. Timber wolf tracks! As big as saucers, I could see the imprints of pads, toes, and claws. Thereafter, we saw wolf tracks from time to time all winter. On later trips, I saw tracks of wolves where they had chased deer in the woods—the deer tracks bunched together as they had bounded away in terror, the wolf tracks scattered and open suggesting the race in pursuit.

A condition now existed in the territory that was seldom to be found even in more remote areas of the North. We were utterly alone. In this vast forested region, by some strange quirk of circumstances, no other person, white, half-breed, or Indian, chose to enter. Fur and big game were so plentiful that we had our grubstake assured for the rest of the winter. The weather was not unduly severe and the snowfall so light that we could range far and wide without snowshoes. We were already in the happy hunting ground where the Indian expects to go when he dies. The cabin was clean and comfortable, the radio received clearly in the evenings, and we had a supply of good books and magazines. We felt robustly healthy.

Christmas was nearly upon us when we walked to Big River. Since the snow was not deep we legged it down Rat Lake, crossed over frozen swamp and meadow and sparse tree growth south of the lake. We were tougher and more seasoned now. We crossed over to the westward and struck the Crooked Lake shore near Craddock's ranch. We made it to Ed's homestead ten miles out of Big River by nightfall.

We had met Ed the previous winter when he had freighted in by horse team and sleigh the winter supplies for Chris Timson and they had come up to our cabin to visit. Yes, agreed Ed, he would freight in our supplies from Big River. A deal was made and we rode the sleigh into the village next day.

We were aware of more than a little interest in the size of our fur catch by the fur buyers and the other people in the village. We shopped about and sold to the highest bidder. Our circumstances were changed now as we rode out of the village, the sleigh piled with flour, sugar, lard, and dozens of items to make life more pleasant for us in our already Utopian existence—Utopian for men who can adapt to this kind of life.

We were impressed by the warmth and friendliness of the homesteaders along the way when we stopped to deliver mail and a girl passenger from the village. All were interested in things farther north and they asked many questions. We were favourably impressed with this brush with civilization, although we both picked up severe head colds which were absent when we lived alone and out of contact with infection.

The weather for the return trip held fine and we found it most enjoyable to ride on the sleigh, getting off only when we felt chilly, to trot alongside until we warmed up. At dusk we pulled up in the little clearing on the hill in front of the Rat Creek cabin.

Ed was good company and a great talker. He stayed over an extra day to visit and rest the horses. It turned out that Ed was interested in cutting railroad ties. He questioned us closely if there might be a suitable stand of jack pines in the vicinity where he might set up cutting operations. We assured him that there was a likely spot just a couple of miles east of the cabin where my trapline cut through a narrow belt of mature trees. We timber-cruised the area with him and he undercut several big trees with his double-bitted axe. We found that certain trees showed what Ed called red heart, a sign that the trees are overage and subject to rejection by the railway company buyers.

Ed decided that enough prime jack pine and tamarack existed in the vicinity to warrant a tie-camp operation. He convinced us that we could make more money by helping him than we could from our trapline operations. The foxes were becoming "rubbed" and the pelts would soon be worthless. Ed and his two partners, Alex and Charlie, would supply the outfit and food. Ab would be hired for logging for he had had experience in logging. I would be camp cook.

The turning point had come. We gave up the unregimented life of the trapper and accepted the busy routine of the tie camp. Axes rang to the east of the cabin where Ab, Ed, Charlie, and Alex built a bridge over Rat Creek with big poplar logs and crossed the stringers with smaller logs to make a corduroy bed to allow the teams and sleighs to cross over. Next, a road was cut into the jack pine stand. Finally, a crude barn was built to shelter the six horses before the business of cutting trees could begin.

Ab took charge of felling operations. "Timber!", called out in the cold winter air signified that the treetop quivered as the tree was about to come down. The rest of the crew acknowledged that he was the most adept of the lot at felling trees.

Ed began to swing his broadaxe. This tool was fashioned, said Ed, after the headsman's axe used in olden times for executions. Ed, I discovered, was expert in its use, for, standing on a jack pine log, he slabbed off both sides with such skill that few score marks were to be found, and the cut surface resembled wood that had been sawn and planed in a mill. Back along the access roads the pile of ties grew as the days slipped by.

Charlie and Alex, although inexperienced in logging, were seasoned teamsters and at first assisted by cutting out access roads and piling the finished ties. Charlie, cutting out deadfalls from a logging road, sank his axe into a rotten birch. The outer bark was intact which deceived him into thinking the log was sound so that the axe blade cut through and plunged into the snow under his foot. Examination back at the cabin showed that the sharp blade had cut through his rubber, insole, sock, moccasin, and sock in that order leaving the last sock intact. He shrugged it off, but I shuddered to think of the consequences had the blade come up an inch or two! Sometime later, Ed in crowded quarters reached up with his sharp double-bitted axe to lop off an overhanging branch—and slit open the back of his leather cap.

The men had brought up the carcass of a prime two-year-old steer. Flour, sugar, rolled oats, and canned goods were stacked along one cabin wall. I rose each morning before daylight and prepared sixty sourdough hotcakes to which all had taken a liking. Along with small steaks, gravy, and coffee this was the usual breakfast. I was left on my own until the men arrived at noon for the next meal. Noonday meals ran strongly to fried steak or beef roast, sourdough bread, stewed dried fruit—prunes, apples, and raisins—or such pastry as I might bake. Pies were my specialty. A popular dessert was a slab of cake covered with a sweet sauce, maple flavoured and thickened with cornstarch. We all thrived.

Sundays found the men resting on their bunks, playing cards, or, at night, listening to the radio. I then ran my trapline, picking up a few coyotes that fell victims to my snares and the stray mink that I trapped. This was a welcome diversion from the demanding routine of tie-camp cook.

Ed announced one day that in order to cut the number of ties contracted for in the time left before spring he would have to cease using the broadaxe. His time would be better spent in cutting the logs the proper length and have the slabs sawed off at the mill in Big River. Although his agreement called for finished ties, he made this revision.

In early February the quota of cut logs had been reached. A road was cut through the woods six or seven miles west of the cabin to the shore of Crooked Lake where the ties were to be staged on shore and floated to Big River as soon as the ice was out.

Ab directed the men as to the best and shortest route, and the road became a reality. Cut through poplar stands, tamarack swamp, willow and alder groves, a strip of mighty white spruce, through birch and muskeg, it ended abruptly on the shore of Crooked Lake.

Hauling the logs began at once. The winter, moderate so far, descended on the land with a vengeance. New snow fell heavily and the temperature dropped. The teamsters, making two trips a day reported that the moose and deer had become so accustomed to the passing sleighs that they stood and watched as the sleighs moved by, not bothering to bolt for the protecting cover of the thick brush.

We made a trip to Big River at this time to replenish the supplies and clothing, leaving Ed to look after the camp. We outfitted with new parkas, socks, mitts, shirts, and woolen underwear along with food supplies—all drawn against the tie-camp operation from Godin's store which financed the entire venture. Loaded with our supplies, hay and oats for the horses, and another beef carcass, we arrived back at the cabin without misfortune.

The log hauling continued. The hours of daylight increased, but the cold weather returned. The horses, though fed adequately, were overworked so that they grew thin and occasionally stumbled and fell to their knees. I was concerned that some of them would die, but the last of the logs were sledded out by the end of February.

One day, just before the tie camp was disbanded, two horse teams with a number of Indian hunters arrived at our cabin from Green Lake. Suddenly, made aware by "moccasin telegraph" that a road had been cut through from Crooked Lake to Rat Creek, they had come to hunt moose. Next day another party joined the first group. Since the moose had accepted as harmless the moving logging sleighs, the Indians shot from their sleds the moose that stood looking at them. Then the Indians fanned out, and we heard shots ring out from several directions. Our teamsters were outraged. With a spirit of game protection often found in loggers they felt a responsibility for the welfare of these moose. Charlie told me that a big pile of meat lay at one point along the road. He was by nature a dour man and not given to making jokes.

"I should spread some strychnine on that meat," he said darkly. The Indians were safe, for we possessed no poison.

The logging operations ceased and Ed, Charlie, and Alex left with their equipment and the three teams for their homesteads. This date, March 1, coincided with the opening of the muskrat-trapping season. Now the people from Green Lake came in ever increasing numbers. They loaded the open creek with traps. Their dogs sniffed out all the push-ups that were snow covered, before we could find them when the snow melted. We discovered that the Indians were breaching the muskrat tunnels as the mink had done earlier. We realized that their numbers had been decimated by mink and would be almost wiped out by such extensive trapping.

Too late we learned that by cutting the road in from Crooked Lake we had done our trapping grounds irreparable harm. The area was now open to all and sundry for the game laws gave each Saskatchewan resident who bought a license the right to trap on any unrestricted lands in the province. The Indians, we knew, preferred to hunt and trap in any area they could reach with their horse teams. Each season would see a repetition of their hunting and we would be outdone in the trapping grounds.

We ended the month with twenty-five muskrat skins. To the west, we then set up camp on an unnamed lake and gathered another twenty pelts before two Indians arrived and competed for what was left.

After the ice had left the lakes, we boated into Big River with our meager muskrat catch. We talked to Godin in his store, and he indicated that the tie-camp venture would probably be a financial failure since many of the ties would be rejected for red heart and the extra cost of sawing the logs would likely put the operation in the red. At this point, he did not know if there would be any profit to meet the balance of our wages.

7

LOBSTICK LAND

We spent two weeks at Big River in a state of indecision. The realization that the Rat Creek solitude had been spoiled since the winter road had been cut through the bush had convinced us that we must move to another locality. I had long been fascinated by thoughts of locating at Cree Lake, an area of Saskatchewan of which detailed maps were yet to be drawn. Far north of the Churchill River the Cree lies roughly 150 miles as the crow flies from Fort McMurray, Stony Rapids, and Ile-à-la-Crosse, the nearest settlements. To spend a winter there would require a sizable outlay of cash for equipment and supplies.

We had heard ominous warnings about the dangers of going into this country to spend a winter. There were tales of trappers who had lost their outfits in the rapids. On the Crooked River there were said to be swamped boats and canoes in the "Bull Chute," a treacherous stretch of white water. Down on the Beaver River there was the formidable Grand Rapids. On the Churchill River the mighty Drum and Leaf rapids must be negotiated. Beyond that we had no knowledge of the hazards to be encountered. Stories went around of trappers who had caught little or nothing in the way of furs in an entire winter. Men who were starved out, and trapping partners who fought each other and parted mortal enemies were spoken of around Big River as were accounts of unsolved murders, suicides, and trappers gone "bushed" (crazy). Old Joe Sheppard had warned us against "the north bug" as he referred to the lure to go ever farther north. He stated flatly that no good would come of it. We gave such warnings no heed at all, for we were young enthusiasts.

With the same enthusiasm we considered the location of Cree Lake. In this country Fred and Ed were making big catches of fur. Somewhere east of Cree Lake they travelled a remote land which they referred to vaguely as the Poorfish Lake country. Poorfish Lake could not be found on any published map of that time. Regnier Johnson was doing it big at Reindeer Lake. We felt that we now had enough experience, know-how, and seasoning to make the venture successful.

The deciding factor appeared in the person of Frank Fisher. We met him one morning busily building a boat near the government dock. Frank was short and powerfully built, with a heavy Austrian accent, a disarming grin, and a keen sense of humour. We liked him right off. He stated that he had spent last winter at Cree Lake and was now in the process of making ready to return.

We held a very important conference. Frank suggested that we travel together, he would lead the way. Our queries about the dangerous rapids were answered by assurance from Frank that he knew all the channels. I quizzed him about the terrible Bull Chute on the Crooked River. He grinned and said it was dangerous but could be run by experienced rivermen.

The problem of money was discussed and considered from every possible angle. After a serious talk with O. P. Godin regarding the balance of our tie-camp wages, he finally agreed to compensate us by supplying enough food and equipment to cover our equity. Then at Joe Freedman's store, we obtained credit in the amount of fifty dollars. We were over the financial hurdle.

The sailboat was lying on shore, but another craft was needed. Since the purchase of a canoe was financially impossible, we picked out and paid a few dollars for clear white spruce lumber from the sawmill stockpile near at hand. A fine riverboat was built; about sixteen feet long and pointed at bow and stern, she was painted standard canoe green. After a few days we were ready to depart.

We loaded our supplies at the government dock. Although our food supplies could be sufficient only to supplement living off the country and to give some assurance against starvation, we appeared to be well loaded, for the boats rode low in the water. There were case lots of raisins and dried apples (Ab refused to freight prunes, arguing that the stones constituted unnecessary weight). A case of lard, 100 pounds of rice, 120 pounds of beans, sugar, flour, tea, salt, and all the essentials that we knew must be available in winter made up the balance of freight.

We pulled away from the dock on a fine day in late June. Frank was to be delayed for a day or two but would join us on the Crooked River at Rat Creek Portage, the same trail used by Harry the moose hunter, and near the spot where we had once built the raft to find Ab's wounded bull moose.

Favourable winds and fine weather assisted us down Crooked Lake and we made the landing at Rat Creek Portage in three days. We walked across the trail to Rat Creek and followed it to the cabin, now deserted and forlorn looking. The dugout canoe was launched and loaded with all the gear that would be of use to us. To cut down on weight, we left everything that was not essential, limiting ourselves to one set each of knife, fork, and spoon, enamelled plate and mug. We took the guns, traps, snares, and tools. Left behind were the accumulated gatherings of three years—cabin furnishings, books, the cast-iron stove, extra utensils, and wooden fur-stretchers. We paddled away without looking back, the whisky jacks called as usual and the mudhens scurried and clucked away among the reeds. We packed across one load each before turning in.

Just after dawn the next morning I made a trip across for a load; coming around a sharp bend in the trail, through dense alders, I came face to face with a large, woolly, round-headed brown bear. We were but twenty feet apart when we both halted abruptly and stared at one another for a moment. It turned out that the bear was more startled than I, for in a few great leaps it vanished into thick cover and I could hear it crashing on its way and grunting at each gallop as pigs do when alarmed and running.

Frank joined us, paddling his trim riverboat which he had

painted red. By this time all our equipment had been portaged across and stowed in the boats. The cargo was covered with waterproof tarpaulins and we backed away from shore and pointed northward with the river current. I paddled the new boat and she rode the river well. Ab rowed the sailboat, looking over his shoulder to get his bearings. Frank took the lead and we followed in a line with my boat last in line. We soon encountered riffles and small rapids. Frank would stand up, find the channel by "reading" the current. This was my first experience travelling through white water and I worried about the dangerous Bull Chute farther downstream.

The river was high as the result of heavy June rains. We passed the mouth of Rat Creek which seemed small and narrow now that we were on the broader Crooked River. The current was steady and we passed through many small rapids where suckers darted from the shallows as the boats passed over. After many miles we entered a stretch of deep quiet water, and after a long journey we entered Beaver River late the following day. I suddenly realized that we had run all the rapids of the Crooked, including the infamous Bull Chute. If such a treacherous rapid existed, we had not seen it! I now understood that this was one of the north country jokes for the benefit of greenhorns.

As we paddled down the Beaver, we ran many lesser rapids. Many had winding channels where the line of our boats formed an S or a C or even a Z as we followed one after the other down the rapid to straighten out the line again until the next rapid showed ahead.

In some rapids we saw where channels had been "improved" by government-sponsored work. Most of these channels had been dug when the water was very high and were now high and dry while the natural channels far from shore ran in deep water.

We ran the Grand Rapids. By far the wildest water encountered thus far on our trip. We followed Frank down the channel with confidence, thrilling to the speed with which the boats glided down the long channel until we rested in the quiet water below the rapid. We could hear its roar for some distance as we paddled on.

Near Beauval, at that time a Hudson's Bay Company post, we stopped for a noonday meal. Here we were visited by a Royal Canadian Mounted Police constable and the game warden, Fred Redhead, from Ile-à-la-Crosse. They checked our food supply, explaining that some trappers had nearly starved to death last winter because of too little food brought in. They left in their motor-driven canoe.

We paddled on toward Ile-à-la-Crosse Lake. Down the now

placid Beaver through thick stands of poplar and spruce, the river widened out and had many large backwaters. Frank urged us on and we travelled into the night. Once we passed a dozen Indian tents on the riverbank. All were lighted even though it was well past midnight. Frank figured the Indians were playing poker all night so that they could sleep all day.

The weather had been ideal each day since we had left Big River. Sunny warm days with little wind had helped us to travel steadily through the long hours of daylight and well into the night. Frank was worried lest we meet with head winds on the open river and kept us travelling by night since there was little wind.

Another day brought us to the big lake. I saw it first in the misty dawn, the water broken by waves, yet pulsating along the shore from ground swells of the waves rolling in the day before. The sun rose and burned away the mist. We could see water in all directions and places in the distance where the water blended into the horizon. We saw the white-painted Hudson's Bay Company buildings on the western shore at historic Ile-à-la-Crosse. It was the largest lake I had ever seen—there is one mighty stretch that runs over fifty miles from south to north. Since we had no business in Ile-à-la-Crosse and our overloaded boats were not intended for traversing wide expanses of water, we hugged the east shore which is relatively straight and lies nearly north–south directly toward our immediate destination—the Churchill River. Frank pushed ever northward since the lake was calm. I could well imagine what seas might be created here by strong winds that raked the lake from end to end.

We encountered many pelicans resting on lonely sandy points of land where they were not disturbed—massive and awkward looking birds with bills that seemed out of all proportion. They alternately flapped six-foot wingspreads and soared in flight. Terns and gulls were everywhere so that we felt that we might be paddling along a seacoast.

We made steady progress down the lake, hour after hour, with Frank as usual setting the pace and hurrying us along, ever fearful that the wind would get up and make the waters too rough for our loaded boats.

The wind did get up late that afternoon. It bore down on us from the exposed side, the northwest, down the great Aubichon Arm and whitecaps beat on the east shore. By now we had beached the boats and unloaded the supplies on shore. We were pinned down here for three days and nights, resting, eating, and sleeping while the surf beat upon the beach.

I awoke early on the morning of the fourth day. There was an unusual quiet. The wind was down! I roused Ab and Frank. We made a quick breakfast, reloaded the boats and proceeded eagerly on our way after the long delay. We were not long under way when the wind rose again, but from the south and slightly offshore so that we were not hindered in our travel; but we did spend some anxious moments crossing some small bays along our course when the waves crested and splashed into the stern of my boat.

We paddled past poplars and spruce-covered land without misfortune all the way to the Churchill River, the trip broken once when we met a party of Chipewyan Indians from some far northern trapping grounds, now on their way to Ile-à-la-Crosse. We shook hands all around, they smiled a great deal and uttered a few words of welcome in English and French. We parted and waved to them as the distances between us grew. At last we rounded a point of land and pointed the boats eastward. Almost at once the lake narrowed and we were drifting with the current into Shagwinaw Rapids, a mighty sweep of fast water over rocks buried deep in the high water. Frank piloted us confidently straight down the middle. We saw a group of white-painted buildings on the south bank along with many Indian tents. We were entering the trading post called Patuanak.

At a spot among some great grey willow thickets we made camp on a grassy flat. Ab and Frank left me to guard the outfit while they crossed the river in one boat to make last purchases.

Patuanak was the last permanent human habitation which we were to encounter on our way to Cree Lake. Last items were purchased such as tanned moose hide and needles with three cutting edges so that we could make our own moccasins and mitts. Here we mailed last letters to the Outside. Patuanak was situated on a slope of the riverbank, denuded of every tree. A cluster of small buildings formed the Hudson's Bay Company post then managed by "Blooch" Belanger, a colorful and well-known figure throughout the North. A Roman Catholic mission had been established there headed by Father Moreau, small in stature, bearded, and referred to as "Little Jesus" by those who would minimize his efforts in a difficult, lonely, and unrewarding parish. On this day the jumble of Indian tents buzzed with activity for most of the Chipewyans of the area were gathered here for the summer. From my lookout on the north bank, I could see men, women, children, and dogs milling about. I saw one black-shawled squaw belabouring a dog with a large club while the most distressing howling could be heard along with a good deal of shouting from the children. All the sleigh dogs, now a nuisance to one and all, joined in the racket with their howling in sympathy for one of their number caught red-handed stealing food from a tent for they were all by nature the greatest of thieves. These were all typical sounds at an Indian summer meeting place, I was to learn.

We were happy enough to leave this rather depressing place and our swampy camping spot the next morning at dawn. The wind was calm all the way to the north end of Shagwinaw Lake where we reentered the Churchill.

In this latitude we first noticed the great hard rock outcroppings that mark the southern rim of the Canadian Shield. Never before had I seen such massive rocks. Here is the storehouse of much of Canada's mineral wealth which then as now was largely undeveloped. In some areas the entire countryside seemed to be made up of one continuous rock.

We were on the Churchill again and travelling with a strong current. Soon we heard the boom of Drum Rapid somewhere ahead. Frank piloted us in to shore at the head of the rapid where we unloaded some of the heavy goods to lighten the boats.

Then we ran the rapid. Somehow I misjudged the channel. My boat passed through great white-maned waves which clubbed the boat from all sides. Luckily I made it to the bottom after taking a good deal of water aboard.

"You just about did not make it to Cree Lake," said Frank gravely.

After packing over the goods we had unloaded, we ran the Leaf Rapid, a long stretch of white water over which the river drops twenty-seven feet. Too far to portage, we ran her fully loaded—and with complete success. Here again Frank demonstrated himself a skillful riverman and pilot. Below this rapid there was the smell of fresh fish on the water and undoubtedly there was fantastic sports fishing here, had we taken time to throw out our fishing lines. However, we were interested only in travelling and passed on down the river full of small eddies as the whole mass of moving water gathered its forces and, picking up the flow from the Deer (Mudjatik) River, plunged the entire accumulation into the Deer Rapids nearby. Our entrance into the Deer River was not impressive. Leaving the mighty Churchill, we ascended a much smaller river whose waters were clear and of a light amber colour that we had not seen before. Our boats became stuck on a great sandbar at the river's mouth so that we had to wade the boats about until we found the main channel which was not more than knee deep. Unimpressive as it may appear the Deer River drains a tremendous acreage of pine-covered terrain that reaches far to the north and whose headwaters almost meet those of the Mackenzie River that flow northward.

Thus began the ascent which was to last for twenty-two days. At the beginning Frank tied up his boat along shore near a stand of tall slim spruce where he cut and peeled three poles, about ten feet in length. Then we had to stand up in the stern of the boats and pole upstream, hard and steady work against the current every inch of the way. Much different from the downstream travelling we had done so far. We forced our way upstream with such effort that after each day's travel we found the bottom of the poles had broomed out, so that they had to be trimmed off until the pole eventually became too short and had to be replaced.

The southern half of the river is so crooked that continuous S-curves made it necessary to pole around bend after bend in the river. We came to places where we could see across a ridge and find a spot in the river which we had passed fifteen minutes before. Frank taught us to negotiate these loops by approaching the bend from the eddying side where the current was not strong, poling quickly across the current at the bend and approaching the next loop again from the eddying side and the whole process repeated countless times in a day.

We were now in sand country and were frequently reminded of this fact by finding sand gritting between our teeth while eating our food. Careful as we might be the wind would whip a few grains of sand into the frying pan or any uncovered container around our campfires.

The poplars were fast disappearing and jack pine predominated with black spruce and scrub birch along the river's edge. Reindeer moss became more noticeable as a ground covering. We found many ideal camping grounds at which to set up our tents at evening where the moss-covered ground was free of underbrush, in country green, clean, and unspoiled.

The weather held fine. Bright, sunny days helped us in our work poling around the endless bends of the river. Frequently, we bucked heavy winds so that our labours were doubled. The country was so green and fresh that we were enchanted. When we suddenly entered fire-blackened country, we felt depressed until we reentered green country a few miles farther on.

We had poled, waded, or lined the boats up several rapids including Bear Rapid and Old Woman Rapid, and one still night we camped at a spot where we heard the roar of a distant cataract far to the east which Frank said was a rapid on Porter Creek.

At Grand Rapids we portaged everything including boats, and later repeated the process at Little Grand Rapids. We were in solid jack pine country now, parklike in mature stands where the trees stood further apart and were stunted in comparison to the jack pines at Rat Creek. The river flowed more gently, the sharp bends were no more and the riverbed ran straighter between jack pine-covered hills.

Day after day we poled on. We became lean and bronzed by the sun reflecting its light off the water. Arm and leg muscles became hard and strong. We reached The Forks where the Gwillim and Deer rivers meet. Ole Jacobsen's cabin stood there silent and deserted for Ole was still Outside on his summer vacation.

We passed on and reached marshy open country where great blue herons rose in flight at our approach. Long grass waved with the current where it was anchored to the river bottom. The main river channel became vague. Frank took to his paddle and stood up very often scanning the distant riverbank. Eventually he found and pointed out a single black spruce trimmed of limbs except for a tuft left at the top, transformed into a lobstick and marking the channel. The swamp widened and we stowed the poles and took to the paddles. The river bottom was made up of several feet of decaying vegetation, which is called in the North by a common term that signifies loon excrement. Our poles had become discoloured, green, slimy, and stinking.

We passed through Sandy Lake and Little Sandy Lake, secluded and in solitude and a welcome change of scene from the monotony of the river. We entered a narrow waterway called Snag River for its thousands of fire-killed pines that had fallen into the stream. These had been axed out to let the river traffic through but we cut hundreds of new ones that had fallen since the last traveller had gone through.

Progress, of course, was painfully slow. Frank announced one morning that we were nearing Highland Portage but it was late afternoon when we made a landing at the place. Three miles overland would put us on the shore of a small lake from which a navigable stream led northward, then joined with a larger watercourse that led to Cree Lake.

At the portage we pitched camp and rested. We cut each other's hair with the hand clippers—cut it all off. We bathed and washed our clothing. Before we turned in for the night and in the long twilight that blends into the dawn we made one trip across the first portage with heavy loads of traps about a mile to a small lake.

Early next morning the packing began in earnest. We carried over all the freight and dragged the heavy waterlogged boats across. Plodding loaded through soft pine sand, the sun scorching hot, the humidity high, the sandflies and mosquitoes attacking frenziedly at any exposed portion of our overheated bodies, we completed the first stage in one long day, crossed the small lake and got a start on the second stage, a short carry over a few hills into a second lake. After two more days of packing over some wicked topographical features, we camped at the edge of the final lake, exhausted, sore, but happy in the thought that our heavy labour had ended.

Near at hand, in a tiny emerald-hued, cup-shaped lake not twenty-five yards in diameter, we swam leisurely in the warm sunshine for a time to cool our aching muscles and lave our insect bites. The tiny lake was about twenty feet deep in the centre, the water so clear that we could see stones on the bottom at the deepest part. The water, we found, was too cold for prolonged bathing as are all lakes this far north.

Our boats loaded once more, Frank led us down to the lake and into a small creek where we paddled downstream, through swampy terrain until we emerged into Cree Lake's South Bay. At once I marvelled at the clearness of the water and the absence of plant growth along the lake bottom when we encountered shallows. This was not a country for muskrats for there was little feed. The fact that we had not sighted a single big game animal on our entire voyage from Big River gave us some concern. Perhaps we would be starved out before next spring.

At Stony Narrows we discovered that Martin Brustad had arrived a few weeks earlier and was busy building a cabin of squared logs as a base for his trapping operations for the coming winter. We made his acquaintance, a reserved, slim Norwegian and a seasoned outdoorsman.

We now parted company with Frank. He would follow the

east shore of Cree Lake to his cabin on the American River. Ab and I would follow the west shore until we found a sizable river at the mouth of which we would build our cabin. We had no map of the lake, the only thing we could do was follow the shore and search out a river.

We struck out northward of the narrows. For days we paddled in and out of great bays along the west shore, finding nothing that resembled a river. We were stormbound by gale-force winds from the east that kept us on shore for days on end. One day when the wind was down, we rounded an exposed rocky point. I threw out a fishing line. Immediately I felt a tug and thought I had snagged on a rock, but it turned out that I had hooked a lake trout that we estimated at ten pounds.

Coming out of a long bay, which we later named Long Bay, we turned abruptly around a high rocky promontory and there it was! We saw a long, clean, sandy beach dead ahead. From the centre of the beach flowed a big stream of clear water into Cree Lake. We entered the flow and found a mile-long lake at the far end of which the river entered.

A small rapid appeared on the river at this spot. We beached the boats and looked around. Jack pines large enough to build a cabin stood in abundance. We looked at each other and smiled. We had arrived home.

8

BESIDE FLOWING WATERS

WHERE THE river flowed into the little lake was the site chosen on which to build our home cabin. The area was heavily wooded with black spruce standing tall and thick at the river's edge while jack pines of suitable size for cabin walls grew all along the slopes of the river valley. The ground was covered with caribou moss so thick that when we walked among the trees there was the feeling that we travelled on a vast grey-green, deep-piled carpet. The absence of underbrush, the fine green forest unmarked by humans, the fresh, clean appearance of the countryside gave us a sensation of enchantment so that we decided at once that this was where we wished to build our cabin.

The presence of a small rapid in the river near the cabin was more than coincidental. We had become accustomed to the idea of living beside the flowing waters at Rat Creek where the current kept the ice from forming so that our water supply could be obtained very easily. We had learned that at a rapid there is always an easily accessible water supply. Even in the most severe winter weather a tap of the axe will collapse the covering ice shell and a pail can be lowered for swiftly moving fresh water. I have felt some compassion for people I had observed living in cabins on lakeshores in the grip of winter when they must break through as much as sixty inches of solid ice to get stale water.

Our rapid gurgled and murmured and tinkled, depending on its mood and the season of the year. The breaks were not so great that a roar could be heard and there was no white water. It was what we termed a lesser rapid. The sounds it made were pleasant to hear and a relief from the profound silence of the wilderness. We knew well that its muted tone would be quieted completely by the winter frosts.

The jack pines, in this latitude, rose only half as high as the Rat Creek jack pines of equal butt diameter. Consequently, the logs tapered more sharply, but by laying them alternately top end over butt end we put up a neat twelve-foot by eighteen-foot one-room cabin. A pole roof covered with moss, sod, and sand completed the main structure with materials that we found at hand. A large window facing east and another on the south wall were made by installing sheets of roll celluloid purchased at Patuanak, an item usually available at the northern trading posts. Logs were carefully hewn to make a clean level floor when placed side by side. The top row of boards was removed from the green boat and made into a door. A stove box was built and filled with sand on which the stove and stovepipe oven were placed. Bunks were built of very slender, straight spruce poles that served as springs for our beds on which we hoped to place caribou hides for more warmth and comfort as soon as these animals might be shot.

A small dock, built in deep water at the foot of the rapid proved to be a most convenient and oft-frequented place where we went daily to dip our drinking water, to clean fish or to wash clothing on a warm day. Here one might contemplate the fast-moving water and assure himself that this was the link by which he would eventually return to civilization.

We had another direct line of one-way communication. A new radio receiving set, bought in Big River, functioned with awesome clarity and volume as soon as darkness descended on the Northland.

It was mid-August when our cabin was completed. We rested and relaxed and took note of our new surroundings. Our old friends the whisky jacks were with us, as numerous as they had been at Rat Creek. We saw kingbirds, robins, and crossbills in large numbers. Loons, apparently in their true habitat, called weirdly among the islands of Cree Lake. Mallard ducks fed on the river, but their numbers were few in comparison to those at our former location. Spruce hens had been seen in small flocks and snowshoe rabbits had been flushed out of the thick cover along the lakeshore. Red squirrels were everywhere.

We were concerned with the complete absence of big game. Weathered moose-droppings were seen back of the cabin as were caribou droppings on the game trails that were torn through the moss but that now held no tracks of any kind. Study of the long sand beaches on Cree Lake showed occasionally a single fox trail on the smooth sand. Frank had described to us very vividly how the barren ground caribou migrated to this country so that the land swarmed with game and, yet, some years came not at all. Had we erred in coming here? Time would tell.

At this time cold rain showered down for three days, followed by sleet and enough snow to whiten the ground. These signs were taken as a warning of the weather to be expected this far north.

We prepared to ascend the river as far as possible on an exploration trip. On a still, sunny evening we had previously hiked the four miles to the falls whose roar could be heard from our cabin. Here the river fell ten feet from a flat rock ledge across its entire width as from the edge of a table. On this expedition we portaged our green boat around the falls over an old but well-defined trail.

Progress upstream was easy since we were poling against the firm sandy river bottom a good deal of the way. The terrain was always the same long rolling hills and sloping valleys all covered with millions of jack pines. Black spruce grew in the swamps and rimmed the muskegs. An exceptionally high hill rose to the south of the river. After securing the boat, we climbed the hill to look over the countryside. As far as could be seen to the horizon in all directions in the clear air were the green pines with small blue lakes gleaming like gems between the hills with Long Bay of Cree Lake lying smooth and deep blue to the south.

Sandflies drove us back to the river. These bloodthirsty and diabolical creatures inflicted stinging bites on the face, ears, and neck so that we attached sheets of cloth to the backs of our caps in the manner of the képi worn by French Foreign Legionnaires. The sandflies grew more and more voracious each day as summer drew to a close. I observed that they were present as long as the sun shone warmly by day even though the previous night had brought heavy frost.

A large lake was discovered in the late afternoon of our first day out. Here two days were spent building a fine small outcamp where the river entered and where there was again a lesser rapid. When the structure was completed Ab carved neatly in the log over the door the legend "Albert's House."

The lake lay shaped like a large hook and curved south-eastward so that we reckoned that a great circle could be made to join Long Bay to make up a circular route back to camp as a winter trapline.

The expedition continued up the river. About ten miles up, and after portaging around rapids, we entered a second lake, much larger than the first. Here we built outcamp number two. Although some hours were spent in an attempt to find where the river entered the lake, we were foiled by an extremely ubiquitous shoreline which led us in and out of dead-end bays. It was decided to continue the search on the ice after freeze-up.

Then we withdrew. Travelling with the current, running the lesser rapids and portaging where rapids could not be run, we made it back to the home cabin in one day of travel.

We had seen no big game. Other than a few fox tracks and one bear track no sign of large animal life had been observed at all.

But there *was* sign of animal life about the home cabin. Discovered by a medium-sized bear the place had been well looked over. Bear tracks covered the sand on the roof and the door bore several scratches. A large tin can that stood by the door showed teeth marks. It had spent some time at the windows, but these had been barred by spiking several poles across them before we left. We did not like to think of the havoc that would have been created in the cabin had the bear been able to enter and entertain itself with our provisions!

It was September. Down at Rat Creek the poplar and birch leaves would be turning to autumn yellow. Since the only deciduous trees here were scrub birch that grew along Cree Lake shore and on the islands, we missed the autumn colour show. However, the low brush along the river, made up of willows and Labrador tea, turned crimson.

Still missing till this point were any indications of big game. We had lots of fish for the taking, but were thoroughly fed up with fish.

One day our hopes soared. Just beyond the main cabin I saw the fresh tracks of a large moose where it drew up sharply as it came upon the cabin, looked for a moment and then bolted down the game trail that paralleled the river. Its big hooves had splayed out and bitten deep into the sand leaving a trail that was well defined. The tracks led off to the northwest into country that we were not ready to explore.

There was other work to be done. We made a foray overland to the north. We walked past pine forests, muskegs, lakes, and hills to a place where a hill rose about two hundred feet above the average land height. Scanning from the crest the country to the north, we again saw the vast reaches of forested hills, the small lakes, and away off to the north, a large lake. After a long hike we came out on the shore of this body of water amid a fine jack pine stand, bordered on the shore by a heavy cover of small spruce.

Here outcamp number three was erected. Set on a steep slope the site overlooked a large expanse of the lake. I pictured myself circling the lakeshore on the ice in winter and ascending the two creeks that entered the lake at right angles to one another at its western extremity. In this beautiful green country the woods were again free of underbrush and travelling in the woods was easy and enjoyable.

Except for cutting the wood supply for fuel, we were ready for the coming winter. What did the future hold for us? The country, to all appearances, seemed still to be almost without big game or fur animals. Frank Fisher had suggested that foxes migrate to this land at freeze-up. We would just have to wait and see.

Our first diet had been heavily augmented by the eating of fish. Soon after our arrival we had set a gill net one hundred yards long off a point of land on Cree Lake which we visited each day unless high winds prevented it. The net yielded large pike, lake trout, and whitefish. We prepared fish grilled, roasted, boiled, and in the form of fish cakes. After a month the thought of eating fish became almost revolting. We found that big slabs of jackfish fillets were more appetizing when dried for a few hours in the sun and wind. We craved good, red, fat meat.

As September passed Ab left one morning at dawn to tour his proposed trapline. As usual, he took with him his long-barrelled .30 Winchester rifle. All day I busied myself at the woodpile. At dusk Ab returned, grinning, and carrying on a forked stick the big heart of a moose.

Always, when Ab made a successful hunt, he recounted the event in every detail. It was the same on this occasion. Poling his boat on a stretch of river above the falls he saw the big tracks on a sandbar. His breath sucked in a little quicker as he noticed that the tracks were so fresh that the edges crumbled and slid into the depression as he looked. Beaching the boat, he grabbed the loaded rifle and ran on moccasined feet, silently on the wet moss, into the woods, tracking the moose as he ran. The trail was easily followed for the big hooves ploughed deeply into the wet sand. After a mile of tracking he saw the bull and killed it in its tracks with one shot.

It struck me suddenly that Ab was becoming something of an authority on moose hunting.

Our position was now a good deal more secure. We rejoiced that our meat supply was assured for at least two months. Our time could be devoted to trapping.

The big-boled jack pines near the cabin were felled for firewood. Easily cut into stove lengths with a Swede saw, the wood was split and piled in neat long rows for seasoning. The fuel contained much resin and dried quickly. It gave off plenty of heat but burned more quickly than the white poplar formerly used for stovewood. The importance of cut fuel was well known to us so that enough was made available to see us through the winter.

One day I looked down the trail from the cabin door and saw an undersized, starving dog come fawning toward the cabin. We recognized it as a typical Indian bitch, starved, abused, deserted, and lost. After a few days of good feeding it began to fill out and its coat became shiny. Thereafter it remained close to the cabin and made a fine pet for it was clean and well behaved.

We had known for some time that Indians were about. From cabin number three, from my little lookout on the hillside, I saw their tents across the lake. A Chipewyan hunting party, the tents had disappeared on my next visit and I saw them and their owners no more that winter.

Blueberries grew everywhere. In the big pine groves the fruit was small, but in the burned-out country where new tree growth had already started, the berries were large and grew in great profusion on the hillsides. Here we stripped them from the low bushes until we had all that we could eat. Made into deep pies or eaten with sugar and milk, blueberries proved to be a significant part of our diet from August to early winter.

Temperatures had been gliding downward at night for some time now. Out on Cree Lake, when I went to unload the fishnet, I found ice on the branches that touched the water, so that the swells made them tinkle softly as they touched each other. One morning in late October, we found all the lesser lakes frozen over.

It was time to set our traps. Working our own traplines, we went our separate ways stringing out the steel traps, blackened by a minute coating of paraffin wax that helped to prevent rust and covered man-scent. Likely-looking places were set along the river, on the shores of Cree Lake, Long Bay, and the lake to the north where my outcamp stood. This lake, we discovered from the ice, was the northwesterly extremity of Cree Lake, joined to the main water body by a very narrow channel.

Our bait was lake trout. Hacked into convenient chunks these were buried in the sand, a V-shaped pen fashioned from weathered dead tree limbs, and the trap set at the entrance or on top of the bait, all camouflaged with caribou moss. We hoped that foxes would be lured to the putrefying fish which, even when buried in frozen sand, soon deteriorated into a green gangrenous mass that stank as an abomination to the highest heaven. Light snows covered all traces of the sets.

The foxes migrated to our country. For a time fox tracks could be seen almost any place foxes frequent or on the ice. These tracks crisscrossed the countryside in a great pattern that eventually led past the river and far to the south. They were not planning to stay, for, coming to open channels in the river, they plunged into the water, shook their fur dry on the other side and continued on their way. Soon the tracks diminished so that their fresh tracks were only occasionally seen. The big move had lasted for about two weeks.

Our trapping success was beyond our fondest hopes. We "lifted" foxes until Christmas by which time we had collected thirty-seven foxes, five mink, and two coyotes. The awful-smelling bait attracted foxes from afar—for their tracks could be seen diverted from their normal course of travel—mesmerized so that they stupidly stepped into the traps. The sly fox of the children's story book had been discredited.

We were financially stable for the next year.

Adding to our good fortune, the barren ground caribou arrived in their thousands, in November, assuring us a glut of meat, along with warm and thick-pelaged hides for sleeping comfort.

The time for our prearranged rendezvous with Frank Fisher was upon us, the place, Cree Lake Outpost. We hiked the twelve miles across the lake ice which we judged had not frozen solidly until mid-November. Following Frank's directions of last summer, we skirted all the islands we encountered until we made for a larger island near the east shore.

We had no trouble finding the outpost. This Hudson's Bay Company establishment was under the charge of Jim Buchan, an Orkneyman, capable, congenial, and well chosen for his lonely charge. He made us welcome in true northern style, plying us with good store food, hot coffee, and boiled caribou. Alex, his big assistant, was half Cree, half white from Ile-à-la-Crosse way, a great talker and entertainer, with a fine sense of humour. We all spent a leisurely and most enjoyable two hours over the meal. We had not had the company of our fellowman in nearly five months!

Just before dusk Frank arrived from his cabin on the American River. He was fully bearded now, but with his ever-present grin and we greeted each other warmly for we were all genuinely glad to see each other. The evening and most of the night was spent in lively conversation and good fellowship. Towards morning we rolled into our bedrolls and were so late in rising next day that we were persuaded to stay another day.

Ab and I had brought along all our furs in a large pack which we took turns carrying on the lake since our one dog was well loaded down pulling our bedrolls on a small toboggan that we had made. Our foxes were about sixty percent reds, the balance crosses and one silver. Jim, we figured, would give us a fair deal which he did. With part of the proceeds we bought an excellent nineteen-foot freighter canoe that Jim had lying on shore, and even after paying for the trade goods we bought, we still had a few hundred dollars to spare.

Alex had a buff-coloured male pup for sale. Though fully grown, with a thick woolly coat, it was still too young for heavy pulling. We bought the dog for ten dollars and named it Snuff. When we took our leave Alex gave us a spare dog harness. When the dog was hitched behind the small bitch, we set out for Frank's cabin. The pup took to the trail like a veteran and after fifteen miles we arrived at Frank's place—without a stop.

Frank had a snug little cabin, with everything neat and clean. However, he had not done so well at trapping for he had gathered only a dozen foxes, even though he worked hard and travelled far. Somehow there had been no big movement of foxes through his area. It turned out that Ab and I had made the best catch at Cree Lake that winter, according to Jim Buchan.

In two days the time for visiting ended. With two dogs to pull everything the whole distance to our cabin was made in one day's travel after a brief stop at the outpost.

Well into the season of long nights and low temperatures, we took a good deal of interest in reading our thermometer. A good-quality Fahrenheit thermometer hung on a spruce near the cabin. This instrument was graduated down to —60° with a blank space above the ball. One morning I stepped outside, pursed my lips and blew a breath into the tremendously cold air. The sound was similar to that of a sheet of paper being slowly torn in two. Curious, I went over to read the thermometer. The red mercury column ended well below the graduation marks. I estimated that the reading was —72° or over 100 degrees of frost! Prince Albert, far to the south, has recorded a low of —70°.

We knew that it was dangerous to travel in such weather. Fur-bearing animals knew it, too, and their tracks vanished altogether for a time; holed up to keep from freezing. We likewise remained in our cabin. We rested and ate well from our store supplies and the flesh of caribou. Books and magazines had been swapped with Frank and Jim Buchan and were now read and reread. The radio receiving set continued to function flawlessly on cold, clear nights. We tuned in weekly to the "Northern Messenger," a program beamed to the North and by which we received many personal messages from our relatives in the south. Dr. Brinkley still exhorted us very loud and clear on the virtues of his medical clinic from his powerful transmitter just across the southern United States border in Mexico. In this weather our dogs were allowed at large, but they did not stray from the cabin.

The cold lessened after several days. Now the snow fell steadily until it lay four feet deep in the bush. Affected by an almost complete absence of wind, the snow clung in great blobs to the pines all winter long for rarely did we experience a winter thaw. Average temperatures were well below that of Rat Creek area.

We were greeted by the croaking of ravens as we travelled our traplines. The big black birds were ever present on the cold desolate scene of midwinter. They eyed us while flying just above the trees and sometimes lit on nearby trees for a closer look. One day as I worked on a fox set, a raven glided silently over and perched on a dry snag almost at arm's length, looking me over with black beady eyes. I was reminded of Barnaby's raven, but the resemblance was in appearance only, for this one was probably viewing its first human, possibly having mistaken me for a sick caribou and hoping that I would lie down and die so that it could pick out my eyes. As I travelled on I saw the bird rise and disappear over the hills. We had to cover our meat well, for one caribou carcass, hastily covered and left for two weeks, was stripped to the bones by ravens although the meat was frozen rock hard. I have watched their flying antics which include the "loop-the-loop." I will always associate ravens with this land in the dead of winter—a country of wild and desolate beauty.

Ab was showing an increasing interest in something new appearing on the river. Small open holes in the ice showed the snow had been pushed back by some animal. Many springs fed the river and we saw tracks and mud along the edges of the open holes. Then we found two sets of tracks where animals had come from overland and entered the river. The newcomers were otters.

We had no idea of how otters could be trapped. Having seen the remnants of an old otter set in the Deer River the previous summer, Ab built one of a similar nature. A circular pen built by driving pointed spruce poles into the river bottom to make a small circular enclosure about twelve inches in diameter with a six-inch opening facing the river centre. A fish was secured within the pen and the trap set at the opening. Lying on the ice and peering under cupped, mittened hands the set was visible in great detail under two feet of water. One day the trap was sprung and the bait stolen. Ab then reasoned that the trap must be placed to one side of the pen, for the otter must spread its front feet wide when pulling at a tied bait. Next time around he found the otter neatly caught by its front paw, very wet and drowned. He had discovered the key to successful otter trapping.

All winter long the ptarmigan fed in the willows. Since we did not want for meat, we rarely bothered to shoot them except when we wished to eat fowl for a change. We would then roast one apiece in the stovepipe oven. Spruce hens were flushed from time to time as we travelled in the bush but were not often taken for food.

We discovered that foxes remained in good condition much longer than at Rat Creek, due in part to the absence of underbrush in this area and consequently the fur did not become "rubbed" until late winter.

So the winter drew to a close. In mid-April we heard crows for the first time. The south wind brought warm air and the thermometer reading was above the freezing mark for the first time in many months. The trees became unburdened as the great blobs of snow slid off the tortured branches of the conifers. The sky gave off a soft blue light. In a few days the north wind was back and out on the Cree Lake ice it was bitterly cold once again.

Caribou began to drift northward on their return migration. We wished them a safe return next winter; we had fared well because of their presence. Small herds passed by the front of the cabin and we had no need to shoot them; passing so near that we could hear the peculiar clicking sound of the foot bones. As the weather warmed they plodded through the heavy wet snow, sides heaving in the unaccustomed warm temperatures.

The spring season was spent trapping otters and muskrats. This was poor muskrat country, but a few were found in places where plant food was available.

Early May saw the river mouth open into Cree Lake. I strung out a short net in ten feet of water. Next day I had some three-foot-long trout and a longer pike. Fresh fish tasted delicious after six months of eating caribou.

It was May 15. A crude sled had been built and shod with iron strapping brought with us from Outside for this very purpose. Loaded on the sled was all the gear for the trip Outside. All traps and tools had been cached in an open muskeg, safe from fire.

The two dogs trotted effortlessly on the rough spring ice, the sled sliding easily on its iron-strapped runners. Travelling in a direct line to the outpost, the dogs remembered the way and needed no guidance. Here we sold our furs, the big canoe we bought at Christmas time was loaded onto the sled and we headed south toward Stony Narrows. There we found Frank and Martin preparing to leave for the south and civilization. We would all travel together.

The mode of travel to the river was to transport the loaded sleds over the ice until they were as near as possible to open water; launch the canoe, load everything into it including the sled and dogs; paddle across the open water and pull the canoe out onto the ice on the other side where the loading process was reversed from canoe to sled. Finally we reached the river and open water all the way to the Highland Portage.

The river had wide, marshy areas between its banks so that it was alive with migratory waterfowl. Among those present were ducks, geese, mergansers, herons, gulls, terns, loons, mudhens, sandpipers, and bitterns, with a good deal of noise of quacking, honking, calling, whistling, peeping, and piping, with the bitterns working their thunder pumps overtime in the twilight.

A flock of Canada geese flew high overhead. Ab laid down his paddle and fired at them with his deer rifle. We heard the projectile tick an outstretched feather but the flock continued northward with no change in number.

Highland Portage was just as long and gruelling as before, but we travelled light now and found the big freighter canoe to be much lighter than the waterlogged boats that we brought in. Where we had toiled up the rivers for weeks we passed quickly in days, downstream with the current, running most of the rapids, now running wild, deep, and strong with the spring thaw. We passed through Snag River, Sandy Lake, the long and twisting Deer River to the broad and powerful Churchill River. We poled up the Leaf Rapid and portaged the Drum, visited briefly at

atuanak, paddled down the now glassy Ile-à-la-Crosse Lake to ıe Hudson's Bay Company post on the west side. Here we ought a second-hand "kicker"—an Elto outboard motor. With it 'e crossed the lake, towing Martin and Frank in Martin's canoe, the Beaver River, all the way to Crooked River, to Green Lake, ıd hired an Indian to transport us overland by wagon and horses Crooked Lake Dam, and so we got to Big River. We arrived ırly in June.

Everything looked a bit unreal and Cree Lake seemed a long 'ay off. Big River had changed little since we had last seen it. he sawdust burner stood as solidly as before. A small sawmill 'orked steadily all day. Snipes waded on the lakeshore almost nderfoot. We settled our account with Joe Freedman, the merhant, who did not bat an eye and accepted payment as if the ebt had been incurred last week.

We found that we could afford to take a vacation to our old ome in the south.

This was to be the pattern of our lives over the next three ears.

9

TRAPLINE HARVEST

ELSEWHERE IN THIS BOOK I have mentioned the trade secrets of trappers and their reluctance to give information about methods by which furbearing animals could be taken. By now we had learned some things from experience. We had also heard a few trapping secrets dropped in drunken conversation. We knew that various scents could be used, aniseed oil, peppermint oil, catnip, and asafoetida which will lure some animals. At Cree Lake it was the same. Trappers discussed everything under the sun, but were mighty closemouthed or misleading about their trapping methods.

The big secret of fox trapping we discovered for ourselves.

By the time we had spent the first winter at Cree Lake one basic principle had been learned. There are certain locations to set traps; and there are big areas where no traps need to be set for the animal you are after rarely frequents such an area. The places that produce furs we call naturals, and it is a favoured spot frequented by animals of the same species year after year. There is, of course, no object in setting a trap at a place where no fox will come in the course of a season. Strangely, we made our best fox catches in the same places, year after year, while a spot a few hundred yards away might never be visited at all by a fox in an entire winter.

The naturals for fox trapping were certain stretches of sandy beaches on Cree Lake shore, along certain trails, especially at the top of certain high-cut banks on the river's edge, in a defile between certain hills, and on some point of land that juts into a lake. As the years passed it became quite clear to us where the

naturals were and we picked them out easily when travelling into new country.

Otters were found to favour certain creeks and rivers and areas where moving currents kept the water ice-free. Mink had special hangouts about some islands in Cree Lake and on certain grassy creeks where crustaceans abound to serve as food. Beavers, of course, left so much sign of cut trees that their presence could be detected most easily of all the furbearers. We found a stretch of hilly country that abounded in marten. These agile animals that successfully hunted red squirrels in the jack pine tops were found not far from our main cabin but nowhere else in the Northland did we ever see their tracks.

The principle of the natural holds for the big game hunter and the fisherman.

Trapped animals, if alive, were dispatched as soon as we came upon them. We took no pleasure in the actual killing of these creatures. The thrill of catching the animal was somewhat marred by the utter cruelty of the steel trap and the snare. There are unpleasant memories of the mounds of debris built up around the base of a tree where the trap was anchored, clawed in a heap by the animal reaching vainly with a free front foot to escape and dragging dirt, twigs, brush, leaves, and snow into a sickening monument to its pathetic struggles. There are recollections of broken swollen legs of animals far too long in a trap.

We reasoned that if there were no trappers, these animals would become so numerous that they would die of starvation and disease—equally appalling sights.

There is a wealth of information to be observed in a bundle of fox pelts when examined by the initiated. An expert can tell, on examining a fox pelt, the month of the year in which it was taken. The skin side, if black or bluish signifies October or November. A full-furred pelt with creamy white on the skin side means December; rubbed area on the fur, January and February. The skin side tells if the animal was trapped, snared, or poisoned. The skin shows red discoloration on the leg caught in the trap. Snare marks can be seen or felt on the skin at the neck, and a vivid red tinge on the skin indicates strychnine.

Trapping success was measured by the number of pelts taken and, in foxes, the percentage of "coloured" fur—darker colour phases in the same species which were much more valuable than the more common red foxes. Our foxes ranged in colour from light sorrel red, to deep rich red that gleams wickedly in certain lights, to cross foxes which varied from a touch of black underfur in a red pelt to the superior cross fox which had a small touch of red colouring in an almost black pelt and contrasting white guard hair, to the silver foxes that varied from almost black with few white guard hairs to the full silver whose black pelt is liberally peppered with white guard hairs from the tip of his black nose to the white tip of his tail.

There were foxes that were off-colour so that they could not be classified as red, cross, or silver, and were referred to by trappers as bastards. Normal in the length and texture of fur, however, they brought the same price as a red fox.

On rare occasions we caught nature's jokes. These are runty foxes, with short, dark, woolly underfur and no guard hair at all and whose pelts are worthless. They have the appearance of being singed and are called Samson foxes after the Bible story that tells how Samson caught foxes, set them afire, and drove them into the camps of his enemies.

A story went with each pelt. Since no two skins are identical, each could be segregated and the story told by the trapper of how it was taken and when and where and under what conditions and peculiarities; an interesting subject at evening, after a long trapline patrol, in the home cabin recounting to one's partner the circumstances of each catch.

The proper preparation of pelts was learned through observation, trial, and error. Foxes are relatively simple to skin by splitting the hide on the inside of the hind legs down to the vent, and the tail skin is split to the very tip. The hide is then pulled off with as little cutting as possible so that the hide comes down over the shoulders, the front legs, and to the ears which are cut, and so on down to the nose which is cut off with the pelt. This is called case-skinning. There is little cleaning on the skin side of an average fox pelt when placed skin side out on a wooden stretcher. When partially dried the hide is reversed to place the fur side out and again put on the stretcher until dry. As soon as the drying process was complete the pelt was removed from the cabin and hung in cold storage in our small warehouse; here it was frequently checked for damage from mice which can create havoc if they get into a fur cache.

Trappers make good use of needle and thread to hide flaws in long-haired fur pelts. When the pelt is freshly skinned, small rubbed spots may be removed by cutting out, the edges sewn together, and the pelt dried so that the mend is difficult to detect. I used the needle on many occasions to sew up cuts and rips in the hide. I have sold to some very shrewd fur buyers but I was never caught at it. I reasoned that there is a good deal of cutting and sewing together in a fur garment factory, and so I deceived with a clear conscience. A trapper told me that he had once stitched together the best parts of two damaged fox skins to make one good one.

A fur buyer usually spends some time shaking and whipping each fox pelt to judge its value. This procedure consists of holding the pelt at the base of the tail, head end down, fingers gripping well into the pelt so the tail will not tear off. The head skin is gripped with the other hand and the pelt whipped until every hair stands straight out so that the texture, lustre, hair length, and colour can be exactly determined.

Muskrat, mink, weasel, and otter were also case-skinned, but dried with the fur side in and never reversed after being dried. Proper cleaning of these skins is essential and all traces of flesh and fat are removed, leaving the skin side an off-white or light amber colour. Beaver pelts are difficult to prepare for the fat is intergrown with tissue especially in the area covering the shoulders, hips, and the base of the tail. Beavers are skinned open, that is, the skin is split from the chin to the base of the tail, the legs are pulled through and the skin cut at the wrists and heels, so that the finished product is oval shaped and skin side and fur side can both be examined.

"And so, as it must to all men, death comes to King George V of England," announced the news commentator as we switched on the radio one evening. Aside from its interest and news value, this fact was to have a favourable impact on fur prices for we were happy to learn that in the year of the coronation of King Edward VIII, fur prices suddenly turned sharply upward. Fur became so much in demand that Alex Ahenakew chartered Cecil MacNeal's plane for a trip to our cabin where he bought our catch up to early December for well over $900, a tidy sum in those days—about the price of a new car in Regina at that time.

We will take you on a typical trapline patrol in the Cree Lake country in mid-December. We will follow Ab's trapline on a routine trip. Come with us.

We are up and stirring by 5 A.M. Mountain Standard Time, according to Ab's very dependable pocket watch. Except for the starlight and the pale light from the moon already set it is very dark outside. The sun does not rise before 9 A.M. at this season—it sets by 3 P.M. Everything was made ready the previous day. Now we have our usual breakfast of sourdough hotcakes, caribou steaks and gravy, topped off with a big helping of stewed raisins, several slabs of sourdough bread with canned butter, and a couple of mugs of hot tea.

I step outside and shine the flashlight on the thermometer. It reads −33°.

The toboggan is now taken down from where it had been upended and leaning against the cabin wall so that the frost would not roughen its slick finish and cause it to pull heavily. We are moccasined, mittened, and parka-ed in light, serviceable clothing that will insulate us against the cold. Rifle, snowshoes, bedrolls, axes, traps, baits, tools, and cooking outfit are loaded, along with frozen fish for the four dogs we now own who, having finished a snack of frozen whitefish, know exactly what we are about and are yelping and straining at their chains at their kennels, eager to be off. They are brought to the toboggan, one by one, their heads poked into the little leather collars that are factory made and look exactly like miniature horse harness collars except that they are circular in shape. Bellybands are buckled and we are ready.

Ab legs it down the trail at a brisk trot, without snowshoes, for the trail, though half full of new snow has a solid base of packed frozen snow and he moves swiftly on nimble, moccasined feet. The dogs bound off after him and I jump on the tailboard for a long glide downhill. I grip the two handles fastened to the backboard which somehow remind me of handles of a walking plow that I recall seeing farmers use, and that are pulled by a single horse as they plow furrows to plant potatoes.

The first fox trap is undisturbed where it sits atop a river-cut bank, a mile west of the home cabin. I shine the flashlight over it from a distance and see no fox tracks about. The trap has not been too deeply buried by the snowfall, for although six inches of new snow has fallen recently the trap was set under a big jack pine whose branches are carrying most of the snow.

There is a bit of daylight showing over towards Cree Lake. There are long dawns and twilights in this country. Ab has slowed his pace to a brisk walk now and the dogs trot along easily. We come to a place in our own toboggan trail at which we can see in the snow where a fox has just entered the trail and is following it ahead of us. My heart beats a bit faster when I remember that last time out we set a snare in our trail not far ahead of this point. It is a secret we had learned: foxes and also wolves will follow our trail for miles and we have snared some fine foxes in our own toboggan track. Alas, just before reaching the snare, this fox turns off to investigate some snowshoe rabbit trails. Ab moves the loop aside, we pass through and reset. We had been told in Big River that snares were useless north of the Churchill, but we had brought them along just in case the information was wrong.

We had now reached the falls. We have an otter set in an open hole nearby and I look it over while Ab continues on above the falls to look at a mink set. The otter bait is intact but getting old and rotten looking, with brown threadlike fungi trailing from it in the current. I replace it with a trout head before I rejoin Ab, who has nothing in the mink set.

Right away, we spook a big herd of caribou; the dogs become insane with excitement and dash full tilt down the trail, heads up and tails curled upward and over the back, and me riding the tailboard and steering the toboggan so that it will not be smashed on a tree or rock. After a short, wild ride the caribou herd has vanished and we travel on at a normal pace.

At the next fox set the bait has been stolen. We see the tracks coming from the north as he is drawn to the bait, his tracks circle the set, advance and withdraw a number of times, finally setting off the trap, taking the bait and moving off to the south. I lift the trap, shake off the snow, and reset in a quick movement of depressing the big springs with both hands while shoving sharply downward on the trap that rests across my knee. Ab says I have a strong grip. The trap is rebaited and camouflaged. We move on.

We take nothing nearly all the way to Albert's House on the first lake. As we come within sight of the cabin I look at the otter set where the river just leaves the lake. I chop a small hole in the thin ice and peer down into the water. The trap is gone! I call to Ab who comes over, takes a look and enlarges the hole with his belt axe. We see the chain and ring, still anchored to one of the poles that makes the pen. The chain leads downstream and out of sight under the ice. I pull out the pole and see the trap with the otter's foot neatly caught. I drag to the surface a full-grown male, fat and heavy, rich brown in colour, drowned, stiff, ice cold, and soaking wet. It has torn away part of the pen in its struggles. The pen is rebuilt, the trap reset and we ride on the ice to the cabin for the sun is going down and we are hungry and tired and ready for a rest.

The sun sinks out of sight behind a big hill off to the south as we pull up to the cabin. The fire is soon crackling in the little tin stove in one corner, improvised from a discarded five-gallon oil tin. Grub box and bedrolls are taken inside. Spruce boughs are cut to make beds for the dogs who are chained to the small spruce trees a few yards from the door. Four large whitefish are brought in and stacked near the stove to partially thaw before feeding the dogs. We do not like to feed dogs on fish frozen so hard that they sound like two rocks when struck together.

I skip down to the rapid nearby and dip a pail of water from an open hole. The water is clean, clear, sparkling and sweet tasting for it has run fast all the way from the second lake, eight miles away over rock, sand, and bounding rapids, under ice all the way down. There is no human contamination or pollution here. I am thirsty from my long hike and take a drink. The water is so shockingly cold that my front teeth ache like they did when I was a kid eating an ice cream cone.

I light a paraffin candle. We prepare the evening meal of caribou steak, gravy, and bannock. The tea pail is filled and put on the stove to boil. We eat with appetites that, as always, astonish us, consuming a great deal of meat. Then we sit back and rest, light our pipes and smoke; our conversation is to analyze the day's events.

The dead otter is hung from the ridge pole and has dripped and dried off. Ab case-skins it expertly. The brown pelt is carefully rolled up, tucked into a bag and placed in the coolest corner of the cabin. We wash up and clean the cabin and roll out our sleeping bags, ready to turn in. Ab's watch tells us that it is 9:30 P.M.

I take the otter carcass outside and drape it over a pine branch. The whisky jacks and ravens will feed on it. The night is still, very cold and the waxing moon is up over the hills. The sky is so clear and the moonlight so bright that I can count the jack pine needles against the sky on a branch just over my head. The white vapour and wood smoke rise straight up in a thin column from the tin stovepipe chimney. There are many caribou in a lush feeding ground to the south for I can see vapour from their bodies rising above the stunted spruce. The dogs are curled up tightly on their spruce bough beds. One lifts his head and howls and is joined by his mates, mournful notes that are the natural night chorus of these beasts. They become quiet. I look out on the white expanse of this as yet unnamed lake. It lies empty, silent, startlingly white in moonlight with dark green backdrop. I reenter the cabin.

We retire to immediate sleep that is dreamless and restful. Toward morning I am awakened by the low growling of the bitch and I know that timber wolves are prowling about, for she always sounds a warning when wolves are within scenting distance. There is frost rime on that part of my bedroll near my face as I prepare to rise. My bullet-shaped "Kaschie" lighter is used to ignite jack pine shavings cut the night before. I drop them into the stove, pile on more wood and very soon I can feel heat. We roll out of our beds and make breakfast.

This meal is a repetition of last night's supper, but we eat heartily as usual. We are again on the trail before daylight, heading for camp two which lies ten miles generally westward, up the river.

We take no furs at all on our journey to the lake. There are tracks of foxes about, but they have missed going near our traps. When we arrive at the lake itself we pull over to a spruce-covered point on the north shore. We look at a fox set and discover a full-furred red fox caught well up on the front paw. It has been freshly caught and is full of fight. As we approach it slinks back against the snow, lays its ears back and snarls. I lay it out with a solid head blow from the handle of my belt axe, then kneel on its chest until the heartbeat flutters and then stops.

The night is spent at camp two. Located on a hillside it is in the green timber but overlooks a vast burned-over country where the young jack pines have only grown a couple of feet tall. This view is somewhat depressing, for as far as we can see to the north there is nothing but bare hills with a few dry snags still standing here and there and downed timber everywhere. In the cold winter twilight we are aware of isolation and depression as the intense night cold builds up. However, if we look to the south we see fine green country once again.

At daylight it is so cold that we decide to return to the home cabin and await a warmer trend in the weather. We are back at camp one for a noon meal, for the dogs have travelled well on the new trail and seem even more anxious to move on as we discover fresh wolf tracks on the trail. We have taken turns at riding the tailboard all the way down.

The weather has moderated slightly. We decide to circle down the hook of lake one and return to the home cabin via Long Bay, for we have traps along the way that require attention; but it is the long way home. As we head far down the lake the dogs stop where the fresh tracks of three otters cut across our trail. They are travelling over the ice and we follow the tracks for a long way. Otters are sometimes encountered far out on the ice where they can be overtaken and killed. The trails veer off to the west, where we know there is a small creek and good otter country. We have no time to investigate further but will check on the next trip around.

Where we turn off the ice and into the bush to get to Long Bay the trail runs through a thick stand of second-growth jack pines. Now a fox track appears on the trail. Our hopes are up for there is a snare set in the trail just ahead. We hurry the dogs along. As we round a bend in the trail the dogs lift their heads high for something black is on the trail. A half-silver fox had been neatly snared, then having jumped over a tree limb it had hanged itself. It is a beautiful specimen, heavily furred with black guard hair to its shoulders where the white guards begin and increase down the back and sides. We clap each other on the back and laugh for the pelt will bring sixty dollars.

We pass through four or five miles of woods with no further incident. It is growing dusk as we emerge into Long Bay. As we round a point we see seven timber wolves crossing the Bay and heading north. They stop and stand surprised for a few seconds. This gives Ab enough time to unlimber the Winchester rifle and he fires rapidly three times. The wolves are streaking back from whence they came in full retreat. The ice is clear of wolves and we are disgusted and chagrined for they were within range. An inspection of the snow where they stood reveals an ivory-white broken fang and we know that we were very close to gathering a wolf pelt. I have never been so close to wolves and am a bit surprised to note that they were of different colors, tawny, grey, and one coal black.

Now we reach the spot where the bush trail takes us overland to the home cabin. The moon is up to light the way as we pull into the little clearing in front of the cabin.

After we have eaten and done the evening camp chores, we sit on our bunks and rest. Ab flicks on the radio. Dr. Brinkley is exhorting us again on the benefits of his health clinic in Mexico.

We laugh for we do not need his services. We are healthy, hard, and strong.

There are other trapline trips that are made alone. Some of these are not productive and there are long, cold, and lonely journeys that produce nothing at all and make us feel useless and depressed. There are other trapline trips in which our fortune is so fantastic and such strange things happen that no one Outside would believe if we tell of them, so we keep the information to ourselves.

10

CARIBOU TRAILS

I SAW THEM COMING from a long distance away. As I stood in front of my little outcamp, high on the hillside that overlooks the big lake I saw three tiny dark dots on the ice. It was mid-November and the lake ice was covered deep in winter's white mantle and in this white world, edged in green by the forest, the three dots quickly loomed larger. Strung out in a thin line they drew nearer at a relentless mile-eating trot, travelling in a straight line from north to south. They passed a long way west of where I stood and vanished into the snowy swamps. There could be no mistake. From Frank's description during our first trip to Cree Lake I recognized the newcomers as the advance guard of the great migration of barren ground caribou to the Cree Lake region.

Frank had talked a great deal about caribou. He referred to them simply as deer, as did all northern residents. In great detail he had told us what he knew of their migrations, habits, and characteristics. He told of their movements from their summer range in the Northwest Territories to the timbered country. He stated that sometimes they came in such numbers that the snow in the woods was packed hard by their big hooves as they moved about their feeding grounds, so that one could travel there without snowshoes. Their small black droppings were everywhere and defiled the clean snow on the lake ice. They became so concentrated in favoured areas that the woods actually reeked with a goatlike stink. Unhappily for residents of this country, there were winters when there was no movement of deer into the area at all.

Frank had not lied.

Next morning, on my way back to the home cabin, I came across many fresh caribou tracks in the snow, all leading generally southward. The tracks were literally everywhere, and I saw caribou in the bush and on the small lakes that I crossed. As I neared the cabin I shot a young bull for camp meat. Ab, on his way home from his trapline up the river, left Albert's House at dawn and observed no caribou tracks at all until he met a small herd head-on and shot three of them. By the time he reached home he was walking among their trails as I had and he had seen dozens of caribou on the river ice. We were elated. We could now be assured of all the fresh meat we would require that winter.

Out on Cree Lake, a few days later, Ab and I spent some time just looking at caribou that dotted the lake in all directions. We counted, on one open stretch between two islands, in excess of six hundred animals, which, in moderate, calm weather were wandering leisurely about or just resting since there was nothing to molest them. We passed within rifle range of a good many of them. As we neared some groups they raced away in an amazing burst of speed while others raced towards us before suddenly veering off in another direction.

In the woods the deer did indeed pack down the snow so that we walked about on their trails without snowshoes. They fed all winter on the lush caribou moss that carpets the sand country where the big-boled jack pines grow. I found that caribou browse a great deal in the low brush that borders the muskegs. I found them to be very adept at pawing away the deep snow to get at the browse; in no time at all, it seemed, they could paw their way down into deep snow so that just the top of the back could be seen.

Cast Caribou antlers became very common back in the bush. Close examination revealed that these were being chewed by caribou in their quest for salt and by spring, with some help from squirrels and foxes, they were almost chewed away. The pursuit of minerals led them to our traps; they pawed up and dug out our baits and chewed or sucked the frozen fish. We had to put diverting poles over our snares so that they could not blunder into the loops and cripple themselves.

Caribou meat was now our main item of food. Since there was no shortage of meat, we ate all that we wished and varied its preparation from stews to steaks and roasts. Hides were fleshed, dried, and trimmed to make insulating pads under our sleeping bags. These insulators became part of our equipment and were lashed over the sleeping bag rolled up for travel. Bill Mahoney had told us that barren ground caribou babiche is without equal for snowshoe webbing; this, too, we found to be true. The finished product was light amber in colour, translucent, and had a professional appearance.

Out of the inhospitable barren lands the herds had now moved into the jack pine forest and the lush feeding grounds. Large herds were seen everywhere we travelled. After their journey from the hard windswept tundra they prospered in the friendly bush country. In this immense area, almost uninhabited by humans, they were not molested at all, save by an occasional wolf pack. Here they stopped in their migration and grew fat as winter progressed. The meat of the cows and younger bulls soon became interlaced with fat and it covered the region of the loins and hindquarters, just the thing for hungry trappers. We fared well.

As with cattle, most of the day of the caribou was spent in feeding. It seems that caribou moss must be at least as nutritious as grass, for I did not notice the grossly distended bellies on caribou that I have observed on cattle feeding in the ranchlands of the south.

By now the few moose that frequented the area were absent and we reasoned that they had probably moved south to get away from all the caribou visitors. We saw their tracks no more until the following summer when again the rare track appeared and once more we saw the single trail of a travelling bull moose as it moved up the length of one of the long sandy beaches on Cree Lake.

As we skinned out the meat of the caribou that we had taken, we found that they were infested with warble-fly larvae in varying stages of development. These large grubs establish themselves just under the skin along the back. Some animals carried only a few; all had some worms. Occasionally we took an animal that was so loaded with the parasites that the meat was used to feed the dogs. I have seen Indian-tanned caribou hides that were so riddled with larvae holes that they appeared to have been hit by a buckshot blast from fairly close range. I once opened a freshly killed bull and found the respiratory and abdominal cavities so covered with lumpy growths that I left the carcass where it lay in the bush. Dogs fed on raw caribou meat were seen to pass large tapeworms.

We stood in bright sunshine on the snow-covered ice of a small unnamed lake deep in the interior bushland in a country where the watershed divides the Cree Lake country from the Clearwater River drainage. A herd of some forty caribou suddenly appeared on the far shore and raced across the lake at full speed, in typical fashion as they do, not necessarily away from danger. In this case they were coming nearer to where we stood. Because we were in need of fresh meat, I grabbed the rifle from the toboggan and lay prone on the ice while Ab held the dogs. I shot into the speeding herd at about two hundred yards. As the rifle cracked, one animal was seen to go down and slide on the snow. A geyser of powder snow knifed high in the air. On examination we found that a lucky hit had severed the spine just back of the withers. The caribou was dead when we walked to where it lay. This was the kind of shooting that we liked: a well-placed fatal shot knocked the animal dead.

The shooting of caribou can be a grim business. It was, however, as necessary to us as cutting firewood or carrying drinking water from the river. When not properly hit the first time it seems that the animals were anaesthetized to subsequent hits. A shot-off leg, for instance, did not slow them down appreciably.

Ab picked off several deer from a big herd one cold winter afternoon on the lake ice. At long range a low shot ripped open the belly of a racing yearling so that its entrails fell down among its flailing hooves where they were kicked off, the pieces showering in all directions until the animal completely disembowelled itself and mercifully died before we reached it. We cursed such happenings.

I shot a young cow out of a small herd that I encountered in the bush on a trapline patrol. As I was skinning out the carcass and working intently I saw a movement out of the corner of my eye. Her calf, almost white and nearly as tall as its mother, stood at my elbow! I shooed it away, but it would yield no ground at all until after a few minutes it paced away in the direction the herd had gone.

Timber wolves had followed the herds down from the barrens to enter the range of the wolves born and bred in the region. It was a common sight to see wolf tracks interspersed with those of the caribou. There was weird and mournful howling along the ridges on certain moonlit nights when the hunting pack was organizing the activities for the night. Once in a while we came upon the remnants of caribou carcasses, pulled down by wolves. These creatures, whom I consider the wiliest in the land, preferred to travel down the centre of the river away from our traps and snares.

Sometimes we took caribou in such remote places that we could not freight out the meat at once. The meat would then be piled on logs, covered with the hide and the edges well weighted down with other logs and snow to keep off ravens and whisky jacks. Wolves never came near our meat caches, but if the meat was left for long foxes occasionally burrowed beneath the hide and ate it.

The caribou fed all winter long, frequenting the moss beds in the jack pines and the mossy swamps and muskegs. As the days grew longer, loosening winter's grip with a warming sun, the caribou were seen to move northward. The return migration was not as spectacular as when they had come; they drifted off in small groups so that we were not aware that the main migration had taken place until only a few stragglers remained.

During the second winter I trailed a big moose in the country west of the home cabin. Here I encountered the first caribou herd seen that winter. The return was not as heavy as the migration in 1935, yet many caribou wintered in our region and we did not want for meat.

In the winter of 1937-38 we waited in vain through the month of November for the return of the caribou. A number of Indian families, aware of the glut of meat in the two previous winters, had moved to Cree Lake from Ile-à-la-Crosse, wintering about thirty miles up the lake from our cabin. Alas, they all but starved and found it necessary to return south in midwinter. The Chipewyan Indians from Lake Athabasca brought word that caribou herds were wintering sixty miles north of Cree Lake. They came no farther south that winter.

In October, previous to freeze-up that season, we had shot two moose so that we did not lack meat. The dogs, however, were kept on a fish diet. In February, back of the river in an area we had never penetrated, Ab, while tracking a moose, came upon a tiny herd of caribou and by some pretty good shooting knocked down three animals. Next day, coming in with the dog team I sighted another and was able to shoot it. This small band had evidently wintered here and had not ranged far for we had not previously sighted their tracks. We were of the opinion that these animals had possibly slipped down from the main herds but more likely were laggards that had not returned with the main herds in the previous spring.

Occasionally, at some unfrequented small lake in summer and autumn, we found very small bands or even a single caribou which for some unknown reason had not returned with the great herds to their normal summer range out on the tundra a thousand miles farther north. Thus, at Cree Lake we took barren ground caribou in May, August, September, and October in various years. These were animals that had failed to migrate, but were healthy and normal in appearance.

In the dead of winter, when we had no need to shoot more caribou, I often stood very still and watched them in the clearing in front of the home cabin as they fed on caribou moss or browsed at the river's edge. There were occasions when they thundered away at my slightest move. At other times they almost ignored me and came to within a stone's throw if I stood very still. When alerted, they sometimes ran towards me before changing course and racing in twos and threes, heads back and keeping their interval spacings just like the accepted version of Santa's reindeer racing in a string of four or five pairs.

I realized that it was a privilege for me to have witnessed the sight of the great herds on the move, a phenomenon that relatively few white men had seen up to that time. I know that the herds had already dwindled considerably from thirty-five or forty years previously when the J. B. Tyrell expedition had first entered caribou fawning grounds near Dubawnt Lake, Northwest Territories. Current estimates in 1935 were said to be around one million animals down from two or three million in 1900. I realized that, as more people entered northern Canada, the herds would shrink more and more. The decline would be gradual for the Northland would not be overrun by settlers as the prairies had been. For many years there would be those vast empty regions where humans do not settle, but where people pass through once in a while as trappers, prospectors, and adventurers. Even then I knew that the herds were being thinned out by repeating rifles and human greed and waste. We had witnessed the great treks of these animals and would always remember it. The herds would one day shrink to a trickle, yet would likely not become extinct in my lifetime, considering the kind of land that is their habitat.

I will never forget the appearance of a certain mature bull. I am standing near the shore of a small lake, looking out toward a point of land two hundred yards away. The sun is so bright that the reflection of light from the snow makes me squint as I watch something moving on the point. Then a prime caribou bull steps out of the black spruce on the point and walks boldly out onto the ice. He is in fine November pelage and his coat is not yet ragged or faded. He has a massive rack of antlers that towers high and wide above his head. His coat varies in colour from grey to light brown to very dark brown. The long ruff on his neck is startlingly white. As he turns and comes toward me he looks like a man all dressed in dark suit and white vest. He advances a few more steps and stops. A slight breeze brings my scent to his lifted muzzle. Suddenly he rears almost straight up and turns at right angles to his previous course. As his front feet come down on the snow they are pacing in unison with his hind legs as he turns his head to look at me over his shoulder. Then the head is held out straight, the great antlers are laid back and he breaks into his full stride. He is in the classic position of the racing reindeer now as he enters the dead run down the entire length of the lake. Then he vanishes into thick spruce in a shower of powdered snow, for as he entered he gave no hint of breaking his stride.

11

SPRING HUNT

IT WAS FEBRUARY OF 1937. Since we had completed our fox trapping for the season, we were becoming a little bored with midwinter inactivity. One day Ab slipped over to the Hudson's Bay Company outpost to see if any mail had arrived there for us and to have a chat with John Lawrie, successor to Jim Buchan of the previous winter. He returned next day with startling news. Our legislators away down the Saskatchewan map at Regina had seen fit to open the season on beaver! The take was to be rigidly controlled, however, with a limit of ten pelts to each trapper and each pelt to have affixed an official tag. Ab had the necessary permits and tags tucked in his pocket. Due to the extreme scarcity in the northland, the Saskatchewan Government, a few years earlier, had closed the trapping season on beaver. We were astonished that it had been reopened so soon and we assumed that pressure groups had prevailed upon the authorities to do so.

It would be necessary that we seek out the beaver. In all our travels in the Northland thus far we had never discovered a live beaver lodge. Occasionally a well-aged beaver-gnawed stump was found along the river. In the three winters spent down at Rat Creek I had seen a single old beaver-cut stump. On the lower Deer River, in the previous summer, we had seen our first and only fresh beaver sign. That was all.

We had heard the story that was circulated by moccasin telegraph around Cree Lake of how Black Alex, the Chipewyan hunter, had shot a lone beaver near our home cabin that first spring after we had left for Outside. Since there was no fresh sign about, we reasoned that this beaver had travelled downstream from the headwaters of the river that emptied into Cree Lake where Black Alex had shot it to feed his wife and several children. Ab and I now made preparations to make an extended exploratory expedition as far as necessary to locate beaver.

A long day of travel by dog team put us into fine green-timbered jack pine country south of the great desolate burned-over area northwest of lake two. In a secluded bay we pitched our tent not far from the extreme south end of the lake. Here, where there was a southern exposure for daytime warmth from the sun and plenty of wood and shelter, we prepared a base for our operations. Using snowshoes as shovels we cleared a space slightly larger than the perimeter of the tent by digging away the four-foot depth of snow right down to the reindeer moss. Here the tent was raised among the jack pines and tied to the trees for rugged support. The tent walls were weighted down with logs and sealed to the earth with packed snow. Selected spruce boughs were laid carefully a foot deep to cover the entire tent floor except for one corner where a small sheet metal stove was installed, the smoke pipe was stuck through the metal pipe support that had been riveted in the canvas. Over the spruce boughs we laid a large tarpaulin. Quarters were made among the trees for the dogs before we retired to our bedrolls for the night. We doffed our outer clothing; the stove gave off plenty of heat and its sides glowed for a time. As the wood burned out we slept the night through as usual without awakening.

Next morning we trekked to the southern limits of the uneven shoreline of lake two. As at the north end, the lakeshore here led into many small bays and backwaters, through narrows and past small islands and around points. We were seeking the elusive river mouth which we thought must be near the south end of the lake. We discovered a small creek but the flow of water was too meager to be the main stream. We would return here later because fresh otter tracks were visible below a small open rapid just a short walk upstream.

We found the river mouth late that afternoon. Hidden by screening willows the river flowed through a small swamp and

joined the lake. Here, too, a large beaver lodge was discovered. It was covered with frozen black mud and towered seven feet above the ice. There was much evidence of freshly gnawed wood all about the vicinity. Two sets were made under the ice before we returned to the tent at dusk.

Now that the river had been located, together with the large beaver lodge, we became highly enthused with the possibilities of gathering our limit of beaver. We were off at dawn to ascend the river to wherever it might lead. The travelling was easy for the many caribou trails had packed down the snow on the river ice. We followed its winding course and found it free of rapids and slow of current, so that there was no danger of breaking through the ice. The river had a swampy shore with much willow and other brush—prime beaver country.

A few miles up the river I spotted a cabin back in the bush and almost hidden from the river. From the state of weathering of the newest axe marks, we judged that it had been unoccupied for three or four years. The structure was of moderate size but crudely built and the builders appeared to have been neither skillful nor careful. The cabin was empty save for a small notebook stuck between two logs of one wall. I read it with interest from cover to cover, a day-to-day diary of only a few words for each day. The author, it seems, had been almost illiterate and his spelling was so bad that some entries were unreadable. One day's notation of three words read, incongruously, "pig bred today." I had no trouble in interpreting the true meaning as "baked bread today." The diary's owner had not signed his name.

It appeared that the cabin's occupants had been the last humans in the area until our arrival, for nowhere had we seen new axe marks. The beaver, left unmolested in this interval, were making a comeback, and continuing on our way we located another, much smaller lodge. As the day wore on we snowshoed on upstream until we reached a small lake. By sighting our position according to the direction of the sun, we judged that we had made a great half circle and could cut off some miles by striking back through the woods, taking a direct line back to the tent. After breaking trail for a couple of hours, we arrived "home." We camped that night in high spirits for prospects were getting better every day. Ab even played a few renditions on his mouth organ.

Out early next morning, we doubled back over the newly broken trail, the dogs making good time on the packed frozen path until we reached the small lake. We found the river mouth along the north shore and followed its winding course. The river was becoming smaller by the mile now, being little more than a small creek at this point, but still navigable by canoe in summer.

From a long way off we saw the felled and peeled jack pines that littered the entire sloping side of a hill that formed the riverbank. From a distance it looked as if a gang of loggers had been at work. Trees up to eighteen inches at the butt had been knocked down to form the food supply for a beaver colony. The lodge stood near the riverbank.

Strangely, the lodge had a steaming hole at its top. We examined this carefully and found that the occupants of the lodge had opened it from the inside. Although it was winter weather the river ice was covered with water, for the spring-fed stream was flooding the ice in this section of the river. The beaver had made an escape hole to avoid being drowned by flooding. Ab widened the hole by chopping it out with his belt axe. The hole exuded a dank and woody odour. Ab peered intently into the hole for a few minutes. Then he whispered, "Hand me the twenty-two rifle."

I passed it to him, loaded and cocked. Deliberately and slowly he shot into the hole four times. Then he put his mitt back on his hand, reached far into the hole, and dragged out one after the other two very large and two medium-sized beaver, all shot neatly through the head. We gazed dumbfounded at the brown furry heaps, the first beaver we had ever seen. We would sell the four for eighty dollars.

The fat, heavy carcasses were rolled onto the toboggan. The dogs strained with the dead weight as we made for the sheltering bush to skin out the pelts. Neither one of us had skinned a beaver before. We knew that a beaver is skinned open, but we made the error of splitting the skin of the legs as a deer is skinned. This brought a hearty laugh from Harry MacDonald, Hudson's Bay Company factor at Ile-à-la-Crosse, when he bought our skins that spring. He sobered as he examined the balance of our catch for we had recognized our mistake right off.

"You sure learned how to do it properly," he then commented.

We had discovered the large castoreum glands near the anal region of the beaver as we skinned them out. This was the source of the heavy woody smell that is reminiscent of the scent of crushed buds of poplar and willow, a blend of the scents of various woody plants on which a beaver feeds throughout its life. We knew this was the scent that had lured beaver to the point of extinction even in the most remote areas of the country, for a set doped with the castoreum is sure to attract any passing beaver. So heavy is its scent that it is used as a base for expensive perfumes.

Now we lived in excitement and with the expectation that the farther we travelled upstream, the more beaver we would find.

Next day was spent in travel far up the dwindling watercourse, the entire way through swamp, willow, black spruce, and various kinds of brush, all excellent beaver habitat. After a full day of long hard travel, we camped amid a desolate tangle of snags in muskeg country where there was not a single beaver sign. The area was flat, swampy, and given to casual water that flooded the swamps so that a great many trees were dead or unthrifty in appearance. It was decided that we were on the wrong track. In the morning we backtracked to the tent.

If there were more beaver in the country we must locate them away from the river. On one of a string of small lakes, we found another big lodge and still another on the last small lake. The perimeter of our operations was thus established. Rounds of the five known beaver lodges were made at regular intervals while we took turns every ten days to drive the dog team to the home cabin more than twenty miles distant to get food and inspect otter traps on our other regular traplines.

In all, we took fourteen beaver that season. We deliberately did not take all the animals of any lodge, for we recognized this to be sound management if we were to continue to operate in the area. We also knew by now that the opening of the beaver season by game authorities had been a stupid blunder. In this region, a country of excellent beaver habitat, the beaver was only beginning to make a comeback. Here had been the seed to repopulate this land with hundreds of busy rodents which the land could easily support. We were destroying this seed, yet if we did not take them someone else surely would. This fact was demonstrated to us very dramatically.

On a bush trail of our beaver trapline one day, our dogs picked up their ears and began to yelp with excitement. We were then met head-on by two dog teams. Oscar Petite and Art Olson, trappers from far-off Ile-à-la-Crosse, while hunting likely beaver country, had come upon our trail in the swampy headwater country of the river and had followed it all the way down to locate us.

The visit was memorable and unique. The element of surprise and being suddenly brought face to face with strangers had a singular impact upon us, for we had been isolated from other humans. I experienced a certain shyness and self-consciousness which was not completely dispelled until, right there, we kindled a blazing fire and boiled the tea pail. As we all squatted about the fire and relaxed, our tongues loosened and we had a very cordial and good-natured visit. We exchanged information about mutual acquaintances and inevitably the reason for us all being there was discussed—the beaver. I questioned them closely as to their success at beaver trapping. They indicated that in the hundreds of miles they had travelled they had not seen enough sign of beaver to establish a camp. After a couple of hours they rose, shook hands, and departed the way they had come. We never saw them again. They had left with an unspoken message which we understood. In withdrawing from the area, they were showing the standard courtesy that one white man usually showed to another in those days. It was our territory, but had we not been present they would have taken the beaver that were there.

Chance encounters did not always end as had this one. Sometimes a ranging trapper located where other men were active. The resulting competition ended in the annihilation of beaver in vast areas, for he was the most vulnerable of all fur animals. For this reason I had advocated registered traplines as early as 1938.

We knew well the possibilities had the season remained closed for beaver for a few years longer. By that time lodges would have mushroomed all the way down the river to the home cabin. This, of course, was not possible under the game regulations of the day.

As if this were not enough, incredibly, the season was reopened the following year. We made one long sweeping foray as far as the headwaters of the Clearwater River, cruising new country of lakes and streams where countless beaver could have thrived. We found so few scattered lodges that we decided to stand up and be counted for fur conservation. We withdrew and took no beavers at all that spring. In the next year we discovered that as many lodges existed as when we began our activities there in the year of the first beaver hunt.

That first beaver hunt had some profitable sidelights. In the small creeks we trapped three otters and Ab, lying in wait at a creek rapid on a bed of spruce boughs, shot two more with his usual deadly aim from the screening bush.

The numerous timber wolves that kept us under surveillance were my particular target and I set good snares for them, sometimes in my own trail which they chose to follow from time to time. They always eluded me and I never learned the secret of taking them. One chance encounter surprised a small pack as I drove the dogs from the bush onto a small lake. They streaked for the trees on shore with a smooth effortless gait.

All the traps were lifted on a warm sunny day early in May. The snows had been settling in sodden masses all along the southern slopes of the hills. Camp was broken and everything was loaded into the worn and battered toboggan, the curved hood of which had been split on striking a rock and had to be reinforced by wrapping with rawhide. The toboggan had encountered many a tree and rock that winter, but being made of tough native birch was still in fair condition. Our snowshoes were worn of frame and patched of webbing. The long hair of the dogs was bleached now from the combination of bright sun and reflecting snow. Our own faces were as tanned as any Indian's except for a bar across the eyes from the dark glasses we had constantly worn to avoid snow blindness.

With parkas shed and shirts open at the neck, we waded through soft snow and onto the now snow-free surface of lake two. That night we camped on a tiny island, not much larger than the base of our tent and containing a few trees for firewood.

The night was very mild; we rolled out our bedding under the stars and slept in comfort until we were awakened by mosquitoes that had come alive and hungry even though the island was locked in solid ice. We were quite unprepared for them, so we were on our way at daylight after spending a rather miserable night listening to their whining wings and feeling their sharp stabs.

We crossed lake two from south to north on the solid ice until the lake narrowed and formed the river. Since our old trail led over rotten sections of ice and into open water a new trail must be made through the bush and the safety of solid ground. The toboggan dragged over bare ground and rocks at times but we made it to Albert's House before night.

This small outcamp stood strangely tall now because the deep snow had all melted away; the outcamp stood on a southern exposure of a hill. I saw mallards swimming happily and stretching their wings in the open reach of the river just below the cabin. We camped at evening to the sound of quacking ducks and the whistling of their wings as they passed overhead.

During the winter Ab's short fishnet had become frozen in the ice where he had set it in the eddies below the rapid. We retrieved it now that it was melted free. Surprisingly, it contained two large and very lively whitefish. We enjoyed a large fish fry that night, a most welcome change from our steady diet of caribou meat. These two very fresh fish taken from water very near 32° were among the best and choicest fish that it has been my privilege to eat.

We reached the home cabin before noon on the following day. Time was taken now for hot baths, laundering clothes, darning socks, sewing up ripped outer garments. We fished at the river mouth and once again enormous pike and lake trout were taken.

After a few days' rest we strung out a line of muskrat traps. We caught thirty and then the traps would not produce.

It was that time of year once more when we loaded our gear for the long trip Outside. The way led far down the Deer River to the trading posts at Patuanak on the Churchill and to Ile-à-la Crosse to sell the spring catch. Then through the commercial forest country until we encountered the first settlements, to the small towns and the cities of Prince Albert, Saskatoon, and Regina to be reunited for a short while with relatives and old friends.

12

THE DOGS

Our longest nonstop trip by dog team was to Cree River from our home cabin one cold clear January day. Estimated at forty-four miles the road led in a slight curve northeastward among the islands on the lake ice within sight of Cree Lake shore, all the way to Henry's Trading Post. The time of departure was 3:30 A.M. A decrescent moon lighted our way as the journey began.

Of course such a trip could not have been possible without a stop for food and rest if we had not had the help of our sleigh dogs. Footing was exceptionally good on the snow-covered ice because the snow was hard enough to carry the dogs, toboggan, and ourselves on light trail snowshoes. So good was the travelling that we took turns riding on the tailboard. At sundown, as we neared our destination and twilight settled over the frozen land, I stopped the team to inspect the feet of the dogs, looking for ice that can pack between the pads of the foot and which will freeze the foot if not removed. When I lifted the front foot of our big wheel dog he made as if to play, as a puppy will by drawing his head down between the shoulders and peering mischievously into your eyes. Considering that he had been pulling steadily for twelve hours, I could not help but admire that dog. I patted his head and we continued on our way.

Our dog team had begun very humbly in the first winter at Cree Lake when Meg, the small bitch, had wandered to our cabin from her Indian owners. With the acquisition of Snuff, the buff-coloured pup, we had a useful pulling unit. As the winter progressed, Snuff gained in weight. He proved to be a worthy performer and a steady worker. Later he developed into a capable lead dog and although he was somewhat small for a sleigh dog, we never knew him to shirk on a long hard pull.

In the second year we added Cap and Duke, two half-grown pups, bought from a Chipewyan Indian at Patuanak when we stopped at the trading post on our way north that summer. These dogs were jet black in colour with decided Labrador breeding and just enough husky dog ancestry to be noticeable.

Cap was heavy, thick, and bearish in appearance even to the white patch low on his throat. He was a natural puller from the day that I first put harness on him until the day that we parted. I placed him at wheel position, or last in line and next to the toboggan. When he threw his weight into the collar he could break the loaded toboggan loose from the frost by himself. His black, shiny coat was so thick that every hair seemed to stand straight out from his body in cold weather. Wide chested and iron-legged, he was by far the strongest dog of the lot. I could sit on his shoulders and he could bear my weight for a short time. Good natured and playful, he never growled at me on any occasion.

Duke was a four-flusher, a sneak, and a malingerer. Long, rangy, and black as raven, with beady slant eyes, he required supervision much of the time. Whenever possible he trotted loose in the traces, a cardinal sin in a sleigh dog of the Northland. I should have shot him in the beginning, yet he was a noble-looking beast; but born to be a laggard, a showoff, and a playboy. A troublemaker of the first order, he fought with the other male members of the team. He led the howling of the dogs at night. He did not take a well-deserved whipping without showing his wicked-looking, long, white teeth. He had been born a shirker and would never change. I have noticed similar traits in horses and, of course, in humans.

So, at the beginning of the second winter at Cree Lake with Snuff in the lead, Meg second, then Duke, and Cap, we owned a four-dog team which was the usual number for a white trapper although occasionally a man drove three or five dogs. With them we transported our trail gear: bedroll, axe, rifle, traps, bait, and grub box, and other essentials for life on the winter trail that

often included a tent and small stove. They hauled the heavy loads of meat from where we had shot it, often out of hilly, difficult terrain where a great deal of energy must be used up by both the driver and his dogs before reaching the cabin. They hauled the unskinned carcasses of fox, otter, mink, lynx, beaver, or other furbearer that was taken on the trapline. They hauled fish from the nets set in Cree Lake. They sometimes hauled firewood into camp and our mail to and from the trading post. They were the means of transporting our big, heavy canoe, outboard motor, and gasoline across the ice in springtime and they pulled one of us where the trail was good for then the added weight did not make much difference, and the actual weight that these dogs could pull astounded us on occasion as the toboggan skittered across the frozen lakes and bush trails.

Snuff and Duke were enemies from the beginning, always growling at one another. I kept Meg between them while in harness for she tolerated no nonsense from any of the others. The two enemies fought savagely with each other, standing on their hind legs and battling toe to toe. We made it a point never to let them run at large simultaneously for we feared that one might well kill or cripple the other.

Their enmity reached a climax one bitterly cold January day when I drove them far into jack pine country in order to transport caribou meat back to camp. On the way I shot a standing caribou. I had wedged the toboggan between two trees to hold the dogs down before I shot. In the resulting excitement Snuff and Duke were at each other's throats and tangled in the harness. Cap tried to get in the fray, but being anchored to the toboggan was unable to wreak the havoc he might have. Meg also got in her share of fight. Snuff and Duke were locked in a death grip. I parted them finally and strung them out by chaining Snuff to a tree and tying the toboggan to another. I make an assessment of damage. One of Snuff's gleaming, long, white fangs had snapped off at the gum line and the skin at the side of his neck hung down in an empty bag, not torn open but pulled from the flesh of his neck. Duke had a three-inch-long gash above his nose from which his breath plumed out on the frigid air. One ear hung crookedly down the side of his head. There was a great bloody rip in it and the white cartilage had been exposed. There had been no winner.

While I dressed the caribou, I planned punishment. I loaded the toboggan heavily and since the dogs apparently had had energy to spare, I rode the entire way home. All were subdued and penitent by the time I arrived at the cabin. Both of the aggressors were terribly stiff and sore for some days but healed and recovered quickly.

I have heard it said in the North that dog drivers learned to swear with more authority than did the mule skinners of pioneer days in the United States. Many times the activities of our dogs so aggravated and exasperated us that we were prone to agree with all our hearts.

Only four spoken commands were given to our dogs: "Mush"—go forward, "Whoa"—stop, "Gee"—turn right, and "Haw"—turn left. These directions were understood perfectly by the dogs and at most times they were obeyed. On the occasions when profanity became involved, it was the result of the ignoring of one or more of the commands.

Sometimes there were runaways. This situation developed when a lone traveller trotted behind the toboggan on the lake ice and ahead of the dogs there suddenly appeared a herd of caribou. This was the signal for each dog to prick up its ears, curl its tail up over its back and break into a gallop. A shout of "Whoa" might slow them down a bit, but as the traveller, on the dead run now, almost reached the backboard handles, the toboggan spurted ahead again, and the process was repeated until the caribou fled into the bush and the excitement subsided. Our dogs were trained to stay on the trail, but we never broke them of the habit of breaking into a dead run every time caribou were sighted or scented.

Sleigh dogs, the same as dogs everywhere, answer the call of nature and this quite frequently. On harnessing the dogs in the early morning and striking off down a bush trail, the leader stopped at the first bush, cocked his leg and urinated. Each male dog now stopped in turn at the bush and did likewise, causing three stops. This performance could be tolerated as a necessity, but when the process was repeated at the next bush, and the next, and the next, despite determined shouts of "Mush! Mush!" which we knew they understood, it took a good deal of self-control to keep from cracking the skull of each dog in turn.

The outrage most often perpetrated by sleigh dogs occurred when one was hunting caribou. Rounding a point of land on some remote lake, a herd of caribou is suddenly sighted and the hunter wishes to shoot one or more animals. The dogs cannot give chase since the hunter has hold of one trace in order to keep the dogs off-balance. But all the dogs are lunging forward, yelping with excitement, jumping up and down, so he wrestles the big wheel dog to the ice, sits on him, digs his heels into the snow as a brake while trying expertly to pick off a racing caribou. I saw one full-grown man so enraged at his dogs for causing him to miss while shooting at caribou that he attempted to choke his big red dog, the chief noisemaker of the team. He was not at all successful, for it became almost impossible when the dog pulled his head back into his beefy neck—and when released did not even look worried. It immediately began to look around for more caribou at which to yelp.

Our dogs were of different sizes, colours, markings, dispositions, and personalities, yet one factor all had in common. Their wide skulls and slanted eyes indicated timber wolf ancestry. They were never heard to bark, but frequently they whined, yelped, or howled. The howl was initiated by a single dog, then joined by all. These weird quartets occurred usually at night, led by Duke, and the others joining in the final chorus, then it subsided and was heard no more that night. We considered this another wolfish trait. I have never heard the like of such howling except by sleigh dogs of the North, beside lonely campfires, at remote cabins, and Indian camps and trading posts or wherever sleigh dogs are chained to their quarters.

All their food was wrested from the country. All spring, sum mer, and fall they were fed fish, most often the whitefish mos frequently caught in the big gill nets used in the lake. Lake trou and jackfish were used for dog food on occasion when whitefisl was not available. The dogs ate fish with relish so that the thrived and their coats were shiny. In winter the frozen fish wer thawed slightly for it made for easier eating. I have watche dogs prop a frozen fish between the forepaws, head end up, an eat it down as a small boy eats an ice-cream cone. By spring th dogs were passing large tapeworms, so that we forced them t swallow patent capsules purchased Outside, after which the gained in flesh and assumed a thrifty appearance.

When the caribou appeared at Cree Lake the dogs were fed good deal of meat in the form of trimmings and the entrai which normally were waste. On a long lone journey they wer fed caribou meat since enough dog food could not be carried fc a long stay. The dogs much preferred meat to fish and once on meat diet were difficult to feed on fish until nearly starving.

I have never known any of our dogs to eat duck. They wer terrified of a duck's head and refused to eat any part of a ducl I asked an Indian why this was so. He said that a sleigh dc would not eat duck unless starving but he did not know why.

At various times our dogs ate rabbits, the carcasses of muskrat, beaver, fox, and coyote, but these are starvation rations for dogs and were offered only during the few times when fish or venison was not immediately available. In summer you might see the dogs eating blueberries on some favoured hillside where the fruit grew in such profusion that a blue tinge covered the ground.

Whenever possible, sleigh dogs eat human excrement. It seems that in the wilderness there is no cure for this horrible trait. We laid the cause at the door of diet deficiencies in the dogs. In a land where no indoor plumbing existed we took great pains to keep them from committing this revolting act and was one of the reasons why we kept them chained to their kennels much of the time.

Martin Brustad was justifiably proud of his three beautiful dogs. They were from a strain of tall, lean, sharp-eared, long-faced, heavy-coated, black and white animals, well trained, well fed, and expertly handled. Martin was a lone trapper and his three dogs were adequate for his purposes. A quiet, well-behaved bitch was an intelligent beast and an experienced lead dog. Martin arrived at our home cabin one day in early spring on foot; he had tied up his remaining two dogs a mile away so that they would not contact our dogs. The bitch was dead of distemper picked up from travelling Indian dog teams that passed his camp at Stony Narrows. This dreaded scourge frequently wipes out the dogs of whites and Indians alike.

On a summer return journey to Cree Lake we overtook Harry Jones at Grand Rapids on the Deer River. Harry was on his way in to his home cabin, situated near the source of the Deer River in desolate and seldom-frequented country, well off the main artery of travel. Harry owned no sleigh dogs. He had packed most of his provisions over the Grand Rapids Portage before we arrived. As we began to unload our canoe Harry made another trip over. Then we heard his big game rifle boom just once. On arriving at the other side with our first loads, we saw a large, yellow dog lying dead beside a ripped-open bag of flour.

This had been one of the lost dogs of the North. Allowed to

run along the lakeshores and riverbanks while their Indian owners are travelling by canoe, they frequently become lost from their owners. To keep alive they scavenge the dead fish that they find on shore. Not able to hunt as do their wild ancestors, they lead a lonely and miserable existence of creeping starvation, not wandering far from the rivers for they know that their owners are likely to return someday. So they frequent the rapids portages where there is sign of man. A man's grubstake left unattended becomes vulnerable to their depredations which was what had happened when Harry shot the gulping derelict through the head. There could be no question that Harry's action was justified for his grubstake was his life insurance and no pilfering could be tolerated.

Harry had no other choice. Many a white trapper has harboured a lost dog belonging to Indians, has fed it well and begun to use it as a sleigh dog come winter. The first time the dog is seen by its Indian owner it is claimed and nothing can be done but hand it over to a life of starvation and overwork. The same situation developed when an Indian claimed Meg, the bitch that had wandered into our camp. In this case he demanded payment. We paid. Frank Fisher once picked up a fine white and tan dog at the Highland Portage. He kept it until midwinter when a Chipewyan trapper claimed it. He was left with an empty harness in his dog team.

These lost dogs are skulking, cringing, unhappy-looking brutes that most likely will keep well out of sight of travelling strangers, but only so far away that one's every movement can be watched, and if a chance to steal food presents itself, it is acted on at once.

We were a mile out from Cree Lake shore as we approached the home cabin by canoe and outboard motor after a summer trip Outside. Cap and Duke, lying in the bottom of a new hunting canoe we had purchased, decided to mix it up. Two big dogs lunging about in a small canoe are destined for trouble, which soon arrived as they both rolled out and into the lake. Ab left the throttle wide open and the dogs were allowed to swim for it.

Of course all animosity between them had vanished. Both dogs were powerful swimmers and their Labrador blood became more apparent than ever as they struck out for shore near the river's mouth. They had fallen a long way behind as the motor roared on. As we rounded a point, they were seen to be swimming strongly and steadily, cutting down the distance to shore. As we tied up to the dock and made an inspection of the cabin, the dogs arrived, tongues out, weary, sheepish-looking and unusually quiet and docile. The one-and-one-half-mile run through rugged bushland had not helped them to get rested. We had not acted out of malice. Retrieving them out of the lake into canoes heavily loaded with our grubstake would have been rather dangerous, cumbersome, and apt to wet precious cargo. We knew the mettle of these dogs.

In midwinter, it was unusual for the wind to blow strongly when the temperature dipped down to —30° or —40°, yet it happened that January day. We were pinned down at Cree Lake Outpost by intense cold and high-velocity winds. Snow swirled about and a grey white, murky cloud covered the lake. Toward sundown of the second day the winds abated. In the twilight, we set out for the home cabin, twelve miles across the ice on the open lake. Four miles away from the outpost the winds, incredibly, rose again and soon the snow cloud enveloped us. The descending darkness contributed to the gloom and our island landmarks became obscured, then disappeared. With our parkas tightly buttoned and their deep fur-trimmed hoods pulled down over our faces, we trotted steadily into the wind. When we no longer could see a landmark, we gave Snuff his head and both of us followed the toboggan. The cold was beginning to seep through our usually adequate clothing and the road seemed a good deal longer than usual. We began to think that Snuff had lost the way. Then, as the cold was beginning to bite more deeply, he hit the bush right on the trail beside the river mouth. The sheltering spruce broke the wind as we crossed the little lake and climbed the hill to the cabin. The door was flung open, we drove dogs and toboggan into the cabin and lit the fire. As the wood crackled and the cabin warmed the dogs licked the packed snow from their fur. Their faces became free of the powdered snow that had whitened their heads as we travelled. Snuff lay dozing by the fire for some time before I reluctantly turned him out to his kennel.

On our first beaver hunt Cap and Duke were lost to us for four days. We had turned them loose one day and they vanished. On the fourth day they returned as suddenly as they had left. When I later mushed the dogs down to the home cabin twenty odd miles away, I saw their tracks in the vicinity of Cree Lake. Why they did not blunder into some of my wolf snares I will never know.

The jolting collar when the toboggan hood collided with a tree trunk or rock, the ice pellets that formed between the toes and froze the footpads on long cold trips, the steady straining into the collar all day long, the weary uphill climbs with heavy loads, the eating of frozen fish, the gulping of snow on the trail to combat thirst were all part of a hard life which our dogs did not protest. They did not mind sleeping in the snow, chained to a tree through the long cold nights and there were periods when they did not get as much food as they required. They were always eager to go when preparations were being made to start on a winter trail. Excitement gripped them so that they yelped and jumped expressing glee as a dog can: with a big smile.

I sincerely believe that our dogs revelled in the sleigh dog's life and to them it was all one long enjoyable game.

13

TIMBER WOLF COUNTRY

In our third autumn at Cree Lake, Black Henry, a lone trapper, came from the south and established a trapline upon a series of small lakes and the river that connects them to the main drainage artery which winds its way through swamp and muskeg into the south end of Cree Lake. Henry's home cabin was located so far from the canoe route to Cree Lake and the winter trail to Ile-à-la-Crosse that he had no communication with anyone. Ab and I had learned all this, even to the general location of his home cabin, via moccasin telegraph, the news passed on from one lone traveller to another on the infrequent occasions when one meets other humans in this vast wilderness. We reckoned that Black Henry's cabin lay about fifteen miles southwest of our home base.

In the following February Ab and I decided to pay Black Henry a surprise visit and thereby make his acquaintance. We planned to find him by travelling south through the forest until we reached the river where his snowshoe trail would be located, and which we would follow to his cabin.

We crossed Long Bay and struck off into the bush early on a clear cold morning. We took turns at breaking trail for the dog team, travelling toward the sun through dense bush, swamp, and rough terrain all that day. We passed from the sand country of our area into decidedly different topography for here there appeared great outcroppings of Precambrian rock, in rough country not unlike mountain terrain near timberline. On one particularly rugged section our trail led to a sheer drop of some fifteen feet onto a great level slab of rock below. The dogs were unharnessed and persuaded to jump down into a deep snow cushion. The toboggan was let down on a rope after which we scrambled down over great boulders on one side of the drop. The land levelled off considerably after that.

At sundown we came upon a small creek. Following its course downstream, we passed through a land of many high wooded ridges. Two sets of moose tracks were seen here, the first noted on this trip. Quite numerous, however, were the big tracks of timber wolves. I remarked to Ab that we were in likely wolf country. He nodded and said nothing. We were in some of the wildest and most desolate country we had yet travelled.

Black Henry's snowshoe trail was discovered where the small creek joined a much larger stream. Following it along we reached his cabin just as darkness came on. Henry flung open the door. Tall, well built, and with a full black beard, he looked the part of a storybook trapper. He stared blankly as we shook his hand and introduced ourselves. We allowed him some time to get used to us, for we understood the impact on one who is surprised by complete strangers after months of isolation. After we had eaten our evening meal and lighted our pipes the conversation picked up. Black Henry's tongue loosened. He talked until he was hoarse. He talked a long way into the night, and he told us the story of the timber wolves.

Black Henry was not a man who operated a trapline in the conventional manner. He owned no dogs, and snowshoed his long trapline in utter solitude. He packed all his trail needs in a big packsack, striding strongly across lakes, up and down the rivers and creeks, and through the woods. He took his chances, asked no favour from any man. He used a large number of snares and frankly admitted to using poison baits for foxes. He said that he had freighted in a coil of barbed wire, which when the barbs were removed could be used for snaring moose, all in defiance of existing game laws. His philosophy was that a man did not come this far north for the good of his health and he must make the most of the opportunities as they were discovered, to take all the fur animals he could in one season and then move out.

Our host told us that shortly after freeze-up seven timber wolves had moved into the area. He knew their number for he had counted their beds in the snow one day as he had passed along the top of a high ridge while on the hunt for a moose. He was not particularly interested in the wolves at that time. He did not know too much about taking wolves, he said, and besides their pelts were of similar value to a red fox in those days. So he spent his time setting for foxes, mink, and otter since he knew how to take these.

As winter wore along Black Henry became aware by certain signs that the pack had become interested in his movements. He knew that they watched him from the ridgetops as he patrolled his lonely trapline, for wolf howls were frequently heard coming from the hilltops as he passed by.

Black Henry had noted that the timber wolves never went near his fox baits or the snares hung in the game trails for they were uncanny in their knowledge of a set. He knew, too, that they felt the scarcity of food since moose trails were few and far between in the dead of winter. There were no caribou at all this winter. The land was in the state of great cold and food scarcity that settles over vast areas of northern Canada in midwinter.

In this section of grim rock ridges there existed an aura of desolation and a feeling of isolation that we did not feel in the parklike sand country where we conducted our operations.

The signs became more ominous. As he snowshoed on the frozen river he observed that the pack frequented the river also, and their trails became more numerous and tracks were present near his outcamp cabins. Then he noted that wolf tracks were on his own trail and had followed it for miles. Black Henry sensed that the wolves were growing bolder each day.

In the last days of January the cold was most intense and in the gathering dusk as he neared the home cabin, several times he saw wolves crossing the river far ahead, and at right angles to his trail. Sometimes they came within rifle range but he did not shoot; he had only a handful of cartridges for his bastard .25–.36 rifle, and he doubted very much if more of these cartridges existed between the Churchill River and the Cree Lake country. He needed each cartridge desperately to guarantee his meat supply. He had squandered too many when moose hunting.

One night as he lay on his bunk, he felt that wolves prowled near the cabin. At daylight he found wolf tracks just back of the big woodpile.

It was time for Black Henry to make his move. He possessed in his pack a small bottle of strychnine–innocent-looking white powder, given to him by a trapper friend at Ile-à-la-Crosse, along with a genuine secret as to its use on wolves grown bold. From his lean-to warehouse, Henry took the whole head of a cow moose and packed it out on the ice of a small lake, not far from the home cabin in an area that the wolves favoured. The head was laid on its side on the snow-covered ice. Under the head, Black Henry had placed ten scraps of moose brain, each loaded with lethal strychnine.

Black Henry recounted the following details: In the beginning, his trapper friend had explained to him that the Canadian timber wolf is a wily beast, difficult to trap, snare, poison, or shoot. He is not likely to take poisoned bait readily, but through long experience the trapper had learned that the wolves have one inherent weakness. Under certain conditions timber wolves will become so interested in, and curious about a moose head lying on the ice that they will approach it and turn it over. Any small scraps of meat found under the head will then be bolted without taking time to become suspicious. Indeed, this was exactly the pattern of the events that actually happened and as Henry related them to us on that cold night in the lonely cabin in that starkly forlorn country.

It was on the third night after the bait had been set. The night was a flood of bright moonlight and the black speck lying on the lake ice so fascinated the watching timber wolves that in spite of their natural fears and suspicions they drew nearer, stopped, and drew nearer still. They were very near now but stopped again, circled about and stopped as before. Then a big tawny male wolf approached the head and turned it over. He snapped up one bait

before the others snatched away the other nine baits, some swal
lowing more than one, some having none of the poisoned brain.

The tawny one made his way into the jack pines where he die
in his tracks. He was at once disembowelled by some of th
others. A silky female was repoisoned from the entrails and fel
silently on her side without any struggle for both the front an
hind paws were crossed. Some of the pack had been suffering th
effects of strychnine for they had rolled and retched upon th
snow until their vomiting cleared them of the poison. They the
withdrew and their fresh tracks were not seen that winter agai
nor were their howls heard in that wild country where they ha
ranged for so long.

To substantiate his story of the previous night, next mornin
Black Henry took us out to the little lake and showed proof. Th
poisoning had taken place a week before our arrival; no ne
snow had fallen in the interval so that the evidence lay open t
the bush-educated. The moose head lay a hundred yards fron
the shore on the ice, unmolested except for two whisky jacks tha
shuttled back and forth from the woods to pick tallow from th
raw end of the neck. Wolf tracks were everywhere. Henry led u
into the bush where the tawny one lay—a great ugly brute col
oured like a coyote except that the hair was coarser and th
mane darker. The carcass was held together by the backbone an
a strip of hide, its belly had all been eaten away and the pe
ruined. This timber wolf in frame, weight, and size of foot wa
considerably larger than Cap, our big sleigh dog. Henry pointe
out where the poisoned bitch wolf had died. There was no ev
dence of a struggle, just the depression in the snow. Yello
frothy stains were on the snow where the others had vomited an
the snow was all packed down in room-sized areas where the
had rolled in agony. Finally, back at the cabin, Henry showed t
us the silky grey pelt of a bitch wolf. I turned over the leg ski
The flesh side was shot through with vivid red streaks, the u
mistakable evidence of strychnine poisoning.

Martin Brustad related to me how he had once been traile
by a pack of six wolves. On a wintery afternoon he patrolled h

trapline along the east Cree Lake shore, working his way down to his home cabin at Stony Narrows. They had been following him for some miles, keeping out of rifle range, as he snowshoed alone, until the sun sank below a row of high hills off to the southwest. As darkness descended and it became too dark to shoot, they came so close that he decided it would be prudent to make for shore and climb a tree, whereupon the wolves split into two groups of three and circled the tree from opposite directions. They hung around for a half hour before they moved on. He saw no more of them when he continued to his cabin.

At the time of our first beaver hunt we were continually under surveillance by timber wolves. We were soon aware that a pack of seven or eight ranged all through that country and we frequently saw their big tracks. They lived in a wolf-Utopia. The land was overrun with barren ground caribou. Several partly eaten carcasses were found on the lake ice. Other wolf kills were marked by mere bones for the foxes and ravens were doing a good clean-up job.

For all the available food, on several occasions, the wolves prowled close to our tent at night. Meg, the team watchdog, would begin to growl softly as soon as she became aware of them. Once we were alerted just at dawn. We sneaked out to the lakeshore, but although we saw their shapes in the murky light, we were unable to train rifle sights upon them. At another time, as we returned to the tent after a week-long absence to the home cabin, we found timber-wolf tracks all about the tent. No attempt had been made to get inside.

When the days grew longer and warmer, I hit the trail at daylight one morning to patrol the beaver trapline on the frost, before the trail softened under the warming sun. The first set was near a beaver lodge built in a swamp about one hundred yards from the nearest timber. My head was down, peering into the water to study the trap set on a log that slanted into the depths. Then I heard a wolf howl, loud, clear, and very close by. I looked up in time to grab the turning toboggan, as the dogs bolted back down the trail leading back to the tent. I stopped them and

turned them around with some difficulty. This had never happened with our dogs before. All that trip the dogs were uneasy
the only occasion I had known the dogs to be worried by wolves
I had never heard of wolves actually attacking a man in the wilderness, certainly never an authenticated successful attack
Whether we were in danger of attack at this time I do not know
but I can say that the dogs were worried and uncertain and
had to respect their judgment in such matters. I saw or heard no
wolves for the rest of that trip.

Far out on Cree Lake I explored a number of islands, looking
for mink sign. As I walked alone over the ice I came upon a
large number of animal tracks which from a distance looked to
be caribou tracks in the snow. On close examination, they proved
to be fresh tracks of timber wolves. I counted more than thirty
sets of tracks, spread out and travelling eastward. I had never
heard anyone talk of packs of such size, the usual number being
about seven. I got to thinking about my position should I suddenly encounter such a number of wolves. I carried a .30 Winchester carbine with only six cartridges. I decided that I would
certainly be at a disadvantage. I suddenly remembered a paint-
ing I had seen when I was a boy—a lone hunter at bay on the ice
encircled by perhaps fifty timber wolves. With smoking revolver
in hand he looked wildly about. Two wolves lay dead upon the
ice, the others looked very much alive and not at all discouraged
Had the artist's inspiration been founded on an otherwise unre-
corded incident that had happened somewhere in Canada's
Northland? I felt a good deal more secure when I reached the
timber on the shore of Cree Lake that day.

Our chance encounters with timber wolves were always of a
similar pattern. We surprised them when they traversed the frozen lakes or as they lay on the snow in some sheltered bay in the
warming sun and out of the cold wind. They fled into the bush
the moment they saw us, showing little of the curiosity that leads
some animals to their doom. I have several times watched, from
some vantage point, a lone wolf cruising leisurely upon the ice
until it vanished into the woods on the opposite shore.

I spent a weird winter night in my tiny cabin over on Caribou Lake. It was a night of low temperature and the full moon's light, reflected from the deep snow, lit up the surrounding hills so that detail could be seen almost as though it were daylight. The night was calm and the winter silence so intense that I was startled when the wolf howled—one long-drawn, awful cry, full-throated, and with all the range of which an adult wolf is capable. The howl was answered from the hill just north of the cabin, and then another close by just to the west.

As I lay in my bunk I tried to picture the scene as viewed by the wolves from the surrounding hills. The little cabin was almost completely covered by deep snow. The moon was on the white smoke column that rose from the tiny tin pipe that protruded through the roof at one corner. The wolves were looking down from the heights, muzzles pointing towards the cabin, until one wolf howled, its muzzle pointed straight upward. Then a white plume of its breath rose against the sky.

When the howling ceased the silences were again unbroken, as was my sleep until dawn.

I have heard the wolf howl many times and I have read vivid descriptions of the sound, yet it must be heard when you are entirely alone, at night, in midwinter under the moon, when it can be appreciated fully.

A few miles back of our home cabin there was a long narrow lake which when frozen over and snow-covered lay as a silver rapier, nestled between high wooded green hills. I named it Needle Lake. I had observed that each winter without fail, sometime during the season a pack of wolves travelled the lake from end to end, just once, as they travelled a natural trail leading through a defile between two rows of hills.

From a trapper friend I had acquired a small vial of strychnine. He had purchased the parent bottle in one of the Big River stores. When he offered the gift I accepted, thinking to experiment with the possibility of poisoning the wolves that I knew would travel the lake once more in the coming winter. I had refused to use poison for the taking of foxes for I had been told that too many foxes die far from where the bait is taken and are not recovered, but are eaten by other animals who form a link in a chain of death.

I performed the experiment as soon as the lesser lakes became locked in ice and when it would bear my weight. I took a whitefish from the net and prepared the bait by slitting open the belly and cutting through the flesh along the backbone to the skin of the back, taking care not to cut through the skin from the inside. I now spread open the fish and dusted a fine line of poison along the inside of the skin, folded all carefully together and froze it solid on a beam in the warehouse.

Next morning, out on the ice of Needle Lake, I cut a trench in the ice with my belt axe to hold my poisoned fish so that the back protruded a couple of inches above the ice. I broke the ice to the water, after which the trench filled with water which would soon

reeze and hold the fish where the wolves would gnaw at it until hey died there.

From a hilltop on my trapline, I could look down the length of Needle Lake and see the bait. On my first and second trips around, the bait was intact. A two-inch fall of snow covered the ce and the bait on the third round. A spell of unseasonably warm weather in November melted the snow from the ice and on my ourth trip the bait was gone! I discovered the reason. Found by whisky jacks, the softened fish had been torn away bit by bit and he meat hidden away where the whisky jacks hide surplus food.

I now had poison scattered about and not under my control; an undesirable condition, to say the least. I did not set another poison bait, ever.

The wolves used the route, just once, later that winter when wo feet of snow covered Needle Lake. From the hill I saw their racks, six sets in all, entering the lake from the east end, fanning out in six trails and converging at the spot where my bait had been. Here there was evidence of a good deal of interest, for all the snow had been scratched away to the bare ice and the snow was packed down all about the area for the smell of fish was there still. Then the tracks collected to a single file again and led to the lake's west end where the trail entered the bush.

I never killed a timber wolf. Although I set for them many times they never came near my traps and snares. I classed them as among the most wary of all the furbearers.

14

NIGHT AT THE PORTAGE

ON A MILD EVENING in late summer, we sat around the campfire, seven white trappers, at the embarkation point on the north end of the Highland Portage where the canoe route is reentered to Cree Lake and on the great Mackenzie River watershed. We sat there relaxed and weary for we had all just completed the portage. All freight and the canoes had been laboriously lugged over from Snag River. The freight now stood in tarpaulin-covered rows on the lake shore, ready for loading into the canoes in the morning. Then we would disperse to our various locations in all directions from Cree Lake.

The moon had risen above the jack pine-covered hills and was shining down on the lake where the surface was perfectly calm. From time to time loons called while passing in the night from one peaceful and secluded lake to another.

This was a unique gathering. It could only happen in such a place, that we could all meet together. Bunched here at this long portage, we had gathered by chance and worked through the portage together. At last the gruelling hot work had been completed. Once again, plodding heavily laden in sand where we sank ankle deep, the sandflies and mosquitoes attracted to our overheated bodies had tortured us without mercy. The waterlogged canoes had been particularly burdensome and I had wrenched a shoulder when I had tripped on a jack pine root while packing one end of the big canoe. Now we took time to sit and talk and smoke together and have a friendly visit and exchange news. Seven lean, craggy men, they represented a cross section of all the white trappers in northern Canada.

I sat across the fire from Holgar, a tall, spare, rawboned Dane. In a gathering where the conversation ran along the well-known topics of the North—dogs, fish, fur, women, and things such as religion and politics—Holgar was the greatest conversationalist that I have ever known. Holgar was old enough to have sailed on sailing ships in his youth. A real spellbinder, he talked long and well into the night. Soft-spoken and kindly by nature, he was a man who spoke candidly and truthfully. He was listened to with a great deal of respect by all.

Holgar was expounding on the desirability of blueberries, fish, and caribou meat as a diet. A veteran of the North, he knew what he was talking about. Provoked by some devil, I pointed out to him that this was the season of new potatoes and sweet corn Outside. He looked at me owlishly, grimaced, and allowed that this was so. Then he continued on his topic. His conversation was enriched by a heavy accent and a robust sense of humour. His eyes twinkled from time to time as he recounted one anecdote after another. He chain-smoked hand-rolled cigarettes and declared that he had been smoking heavily since the age of six. When I asked him if smoking had harmed his health in any way he assured me that there was no evidence of such harm.

Chris Timson, his partner and countryman, was as tall and lean as Holgar, but Scandinavian blonde, who wore long hair and a beard in winter. This was the same Chris who had been our neighbor at Rat Lake. All his front teeth were gone—knocked out in a fight in Big River the story went. He had served in the German army under Kaiser Wilhelm in World War I as a machine-gunner. He told one war story after another to anyone who would listen. He was full of his own exploits, but I never heard him speak ill of any man. He was accident-prone, dogged by ill fortune and had lost his outfit by fire at least twice. A wizard mechanically, he could do wonders with an outboard motor and distinguished himself by packing along on a trip such as this, the most complete tool kit in the North, which included such items as a blowtorch, soldering iron, and pipe cutters and threaders. He was later instrumental in transporting by riverboat the motor and chassis of a Model T Ford from Meadow Lake to Snag River where it was used on this very portage to transport freight. Twenty years later he drove a Model A Ford on the tractor-train winter road from Meadow Lake to Stony Rapids. He was finally to marry a Chipewyan woman and help establish a school for his children at Stony Rapids. Chris had hawklike eyes that always searched for new horizons, never finding one to his liking. He later trapped in the Black Lake–Selwyn Lake country and as I write he lies buried on Lake Athabasca's shore where the horizon to the west is very far away indeed.

Ed was the very best example of a successful trapper. Powerful of build, he was perfectly at home in the bush in any season. His unfailing sense of humour sparkled the conversation among the group. Ed was rugged. He told us how he had lived entirely on the flesh of caribou for three months on his lonely and extensive trapline in the taiga country far to the northeast of Cree Lake. He said that he grew fat but had little stamina so that he followed his dog team with difficulty. His home cabin was somewhere between Cree and Wollaston lakes and he referred to it vaguely as the Poorfish Lake country and the Waterfound River country. The land was at that time unmapped so that we didn't know the lay of the land or how access thereto could be obtained. The story was that it was an area shunned by the Chipewyans for they were decimated there by influenza in the year 1919 and considered this the land of their devil—the Dishlini.

It was said that Ed owned a farm somewhere down south. The lure of the North was so great that he rented his land to others and followed the trapline. He and his partner had already been in the country for twenty years and would be there for at least twenty more. They had traplines that extended to the fringe of the Barren Grounds and each year were known to take some white foxes. Their catches ran strongly to mink and they were by now well-off financially when one considers the purchasing power of a dollar bill in those days. The partner was not with him but would join him by chartered plane later in the season.

Old Michel was the senior member of the little group. Of medium height, and over sixty years of age, he had the agile physique of a man half his age, a result of his long and active life in the bush. He was almost bald and his clipped beard and remaining fringe of white hair, all about one inch long, contrasted startlingly against his skin—as brown as an Indian's. A great talker, he still had a marked French accent. Alas, he had already lived so long alone that some of his talk made no sense at all. In great shape physically, his mental strength was on the wane. He was travelling along with Ed, for he was still a good man in running white water, expert with the paddle and pole. Ed would leave him and his outfit at Michel's cabin up an unnamed river that chuckled down out of high country into Cree Lake's east side.

Michel was famous throughout the country for his method of cooking white navy beans. His was a slow process over a slow fire as he sat for hours tending the bean pot. When cooked they were always fine-flavoured and delicious. He sat up half the night cooking his beans, and I heard him mumbling to himself a couple of times long after we had rolled into our bedrolls for the night.

Martin was there also and he was already close to his home cabin at Stony Narrows. An immigrant from Norway, he had knowingly picked his cabin site where there was an abundance of fish. From the cabin he plied his traplines far and wide. Just before freeze-up he travelled Cree Lake with his big freighter canoe under sail across wild water and before strong winds. He had the cold blue eyes and blonde hair of a Viking and surely his ancestors were seafaring men. One cold day in late October he showed up at our cabin sheathed in ice from the spray created by a strong autumn wind. His outer clothing thawed and dripped dry near the roaring stove as he spent the night with us. Next morning he set his sail under a fair wind for Stony Narrows. I paddled out to Cree Lake with him and watched his canoe disappear under leaden skies into the mists rising from the lake. A lone operator, intelligent, shrewd, and given to dry humour, he would have made a successful businessman.

Ab sat here, also. From time to time he filled his pipe with tobacco which he shaved off the plug with a sharp jackknife. He was, at that time, only twenty-five years old and had been in the bush for seven years. Six feet tall, and 180 pounds in weight, he had a whipcord quality that fitted him well for this life. A superb axeman, mechanic, and logger, he was a good man to have around in an emergency. It cannot be denied that much of our trapping success was due to his abilities and ingenuity.

Some men are born hunters and Ab was such a man. He had hunted since he was a boy. A sojourn in mountainous British Columbia had stimulated an interest to hunt big game, and his years in Saskatchewan's wilderness areas had made him deadly on the track of a moose. In summer he practised by shooting flies on the cabin wall with a .22 rifle. I have occasionally seen him bring down ducks on the wing with a rifle, for he was willing to take a chance that it could be done. I have never seen another hunter who could get such constant results at long, long range, bearing in mind that the telescopic sight was not part of our equipment.

Ab was a walker. He could cover more ground per hour on foot than any man with whom I have walked. This includes a great many men in the Canadian infantry in later years.

A real tower of strength Ab could make a paddle, a toboggan, or a pair of snowshoes as well as an Indian could. Among his faults, it could have been said that he was sometimes too serious, and a bit short of temper. Among his talents, he could make the right decision in a split second when in a tight corner.

This group, counting myself, made up the seven who talked long into that unforgettable night. Here was a fountain of information as to how the pulse of the North was beating. The talk encompassed the full range of gossip and fact and downright lies—the North has its full quota of liars. The lies gave spice and colour to the conversation, for in what was told there was much of grim truth upon which one might ponder.

Some of the talk was ribald. Someone asked of another, "Did you get your annual dose this summer?"

"Sure," he answered, "but it was no worse than a bad cold."

"A damned bad cold," someone else said.

We talked of the prices of furs last season and the prospects for the season coming up, of the abundance and disappointing unproductiveness of parts of the country, tales of hardships and misfortune, of love and laughter, and wine, women, and song. There were tales of other days, and other places, and other faces, stories of the homelands, the new lands, the mountains, and the valleys, and the bitter winters of remote Canada.

And it became evident too, that trappers in the North are subject to the same ills as are all mankind. Over on Buffalo Lake, Karl had committed suicide in his secluded cabin last winter. In his home cabin on some secondary watercourse, Oscar had lain alone on his bunk for many days. He was dying of some unidentified malady and suffered such fever that, being unable to move off his bunk, he finally slashed his wrists and drank his own blood.

Jake had married a Cree woman at Patuanak and had been caught in a trap common to all whites who married Indian women. Jake now had all his wife's relatives come to visit whenever he shot a moose. They returned home only after the meat was all gone.

The conversation covered news items concerning all known white trappers from Big River to Black Lake. These men the Crees term *Monias* and their feelings towards them are a mixture of admiration and suspicion.

Someone said that Harry (Cockney English and late of His Majesty's Imperial Army in India) was back in the area of the upper Deer River. Elmer, from the State of Washington, would winter near Old Woman Rapid, one hundred miles south of where we sat. There was talk about the activities of Otto, Henry, and Pete who had a trading venture going at Cree River. Somebody had talked with Regnier who was on his way back to Reindeer Lake. I told of visiting with Ole on his arrival at Patuanak after eighteen lonely months near the headwaters of the Haultain River. His eyes had a peculiar stare that suggested that he had come very close to going mad.

Big Nick, who had been born in interior Russia, somewhere north of Mongolia, with skin as yellow as a Chinese, but with Caucasian features, was back in his trapping territory on the lower Cree River. Slavic John, who ate raw meat and fish raw from his net like a wild animal had to be flown from Black Lake to Edmonton to be treated for an infestation of tapeworms.

Ab and I had met all these people at one time or another. It was a fact that we knew personally almost every white man in this vast section of wilderness. We met some of them in places as varied as Prince Albert, Big River, and the northern trading posts. Chance encounters such as the one at Highland Portage or deep in the wilderness were the occasions when we got to know each other well.

We all had several things in common. The most predominant was an active sense of humour without which we could not have accepted our hardships and misfortunes as readily as we did. Loud laughter was common among us and the unwary became the butt of practical jokes. Ed, Michel, and Holgar, on their way Outside one spring day, paddling south of Stony Narrows, lifted a fat goose, accidentally caught in one of Martin's muskrat traps. Martin, coming upstream met the party boiling a big kettle on the riverbank. Holgar's greeting to Martin whom he had not seen for nine months was: "Your goose is cooked!"

I never heard of heart conditions or cancers among these men. There were none with paunches or excess fat on their bodies. I noticed that most had bad teeth, probably due to diet deficiencies.

None of us respected the game laws of the country. It was generally agreed among white trappers that strict adherence to existing game laws would result in us all starving to death. I saw some practical evidence that many practised conservation, especially when they located for several years in one place. Where two partners worked together, sometimes only one trapper's license was taken out.

All gave some thought to dying alone and helpless back in the wilderness. We shrugged it off with the simple logic that many people die Outside. Although there existed dangers here that are unusual, certain Outside hazards did not menace us. There is little chance of contracting a contagious disease when you live away from humans. You will never be the victim in a car accident in a land where there are no roads.

Once Monias has established himself in the wilderness and spent a year or two, he is, with few exceptions, dedicated to this way of life, with its absence of the shackles that burden people Outside. There is much to be said for a life where one can do just as he pleases, with no one to tell him when, where, or how to do a thing. One does only the kind of work he wishes, he exercises every day in the outdoors, drinks water that is crystal clear and free from pollution. He fishes and hunts to his heart's content!

All of these men had proven abilities. Any one could have made a living Outside even in the state of depression of the economy that was a byword of the times. The North lured them back year after year until old age or some sudden catastrophe caused them to be absent from their wilderness haunts. The lure of the North is ever with those who have returned to the Outside.

The discussions of that night were finalized by Holgar's opinion that man, alone in the North, does not fear the elements or the wild animals. He is not unduly concerned about what will happen to him through misfortune or misjudgment on his part. He is, however, concerned about and fears his fellowman. He sometimes worries about him and what he can do to the land and its resources. Carelessness with fire can burn him out, together with his entire trapping grounds. Indiscriminate killing can wipe out the animal resources.

Perhaps he fears and mistrusts himself most of all.

15

CREES, CHIPEWYANS, AND BREEDS

OLD RED IRON was a Swampy Cree. I first met him on a cold sunny day in midwinter when he snowshoed up to our cabin on Rat Creek. He had killed a moose down creek, he explained, and wished to borrow some salt.

Red Iron was a very old Indian of medium height and lean of frame. He carried himself very straight and erect. His skin was deeply lined and the colour of an old spruce root. His beard consisted of a few dozen coarse grey hairs, about six inches long, which were scattered about the face and more concentrated on the chin. His grey hair hung well down to his shoulders. His eyes were bright and keen and expressed the dignity and pride of his race. His outer dress was entirely of tanned deerskin and he wore moose-hide moccasins and mitts, light, warm, and serviceable in cold dry winter weather.

Red Iron was among the last of his kind. He spoke only a few words of English and French, reverting to the Cree language as soon as English or French failed him so that a sentence might have parts from three tongues. He had accepted practically nothing of the white man's ways. I have reason to believe that he had never accepted Monias—the white man—at all. He lived as had his ancestors before him. I once accidentally came upon one of his winter overnight camps—a primitive hovel built of logs chinked with moss, and with a flat earth-covered log roof. Inside, a baked mud and grass fireplace had been built at one end. A thick bed of spruce boughs lay on the earthen floor at the other end. Entrance to the hut was effected by crawling through a hole cut in one wall at ground level, after which the hole was plugged from the inside with a hay-filled sack to keep out the cold. So small was this hovel inside that it was impossible for me to stand up; I must kneel, sit, or lie down. Yet old Red Iron could live here, dragging long poles through the aperture that served as a door, burn off the ends in the fireplace and replenish the fire by merely pulling the logs forward so that chopping and sawing fuel was eliminated. He could sit in front of the fire, make tea and roast his moose meat. He could roll into his rabbitskin sleeping robe and sleep in comparative comfort on his spruce-bough bed. This was all he now required of life, therefore he did not aspire to things that he did not use. His pipe was filled with *kinnikinik,* the inner bark of the red willow which grows profusely along Rat Creek.

Red Iron had long ago learned to use his resources to the full. Examination of one of his moose kills revealed that he had packed away everything except the contents of the alimentary canal and a piece of skin that hangs from the neck which on a moose is called the bell.

Red Iron possessed most of the ancient skills of his people. He could build a fine birchbark canoe using only the birch tree for ribs, planking, and the outer bark covering all secured with fibres of spruce roots and the seams sealed with spruce gum. Only a few primitive tools were used. The canoe parts were secured with wooden pins, rawhide, and sinews and there was not one metal nail in the finished product. Measurements were made using the breadth of the hand, the length of the arm from elbow to wrist, and so on. He made excellent Cree snowshoes, paddles, and toboggans, all with a fine craftsmanship.

On an April day while trapping muskrats on lower Rat Creek, I saw Red Iron suddenly appear at the creek bank from out of the bush. Then he forded the creek up to his waist in icy water. As he stepped ashore on the opposite bank, with one fluid motion he gathered up a large handful of the coarse dry dead grass at the creek's edge and as he sat down on a dry log the grass took

fire from his match, so that all he had to do was to pile on some of the dead branches that were scattered about and thus make a campfire.

Old Red Iron is dead. Never a man to talk a great deal in life, there is buried with him a wealth of information of the Cree people in this part of Canada and certain secrets of the woods, the birds, animals, and fishes that as yet may be undiscovered by white men. Since even at that time the younger generation of Crees would not revert to such a primitive and lonely life as was Red Iron's they did not learn all his knowledge and his crafts and consequently these were lost when he died.

Red Iron was at his best in summer when hunting moose on some secluded lake. Sitting in the centre of his small slim hunting canoe, he screened himself among the rushes, reeds, and wild rice, paddling very close to feeding moose in lush water-lily beds, so that his battered old Winchester carbine barked only once. With a supply of fresh moose meat, his wants would be met for some time. His only purchases at Green Lake Trading Post consisted of minimum amounts of flour, sugar, lard, tea, and occasionally a box of cartridges for his Winchester.

"I wish I knew what that old rascal knows about the bush," remarked Ab to me one day.

At Cree Lake Outpost one day I saw the man they called Long-Haired Cree. This Indian wore his hair in braids that hung far down his back. By this token he told the world that he had not accepted Christianity and was, therefore, considered to be a pagan in the eyes of the cropped-headed Indians and those of mixed Indian and white ancestry who were all Roman Catholics.

Long-Haired Cree was a loner. He had little to do with white men and took no part in the discussions of the other Indians present that day. He was the most striking in appearance of them all for he was tall and straight and dignified. When he spoke or you spoke to him he looked you right in the eye.

Julian was a middle-aged Chipewyan, short, stocky, and wrinkled, and looked more like an Eskimo than an Indian. He was by far the most effective hunter among a band of Chipewyans that ranged generally northward of the Cree Lake country. Usually in such a group there is a man of outstanding hunting ability to whom the people look to provide meat. Such a man was Julian. A dead shot, he used a rifle with a slide action for he could manipulate this weapon much more effectively than a lever- or bolt-actioned rifle on account of his handicap. His left hand was off at the wrist, the result of an accidental shotgun blast. The accident had occurred when Julian had been a young man. It was said that Julian had been a poor hunter, shiftless, and lackadaisical up to the time of the accident.

Our first awareness of the presence of Julian occurred at the time Ab shot the big bull moose in our first autumn at Cree Lake. When we returned to the site of the kill next day to pack out the meat, we discovered, on arriving at the spot in deep bush, that half the rib cage had been cut away with a sharp instrument, probably a belt axe. On a nearby jack pine the bark had been neatly blazed off and a legend in the Indian script was pencilled upon the white wood. Being unable to read the message, I made a copy on paper. Not until I showed it to Indians at Cree Lake Outpost in the following winter did I learn who the author had been and his message. It stated, in effect, that Julian had been on the trail of the same moose, but Ab had come upon the fresher trail and had killed the moose before Julian could do so. Finding himself a long way from his hunting party and being almost without food, he had taken away a piece of meat. It occurred to us that Julian may have been two or three days on the trail because he was a long way south of his usual hunting grounds. Somewhere to the south he had heard the shot and even though no snow was on the ground had, by some uncanny instinct, found the kill.

One summer Ab and I joined Henry Weitzel's brigade of riverboats at Meadow Lake for the return trip to Cree Lake. In this brigade were eight large wooden boats, powered with outboard motors with which we ripped the river and lake silences in a deafening staccato of exhausts—the mufflers had all been removed to get maximum power. At Patuanak, we were joined by several Chipewyan families, on their way to the northern caribou grounds and their winter traplines which were scattered all the way to Lake Athabasca. Henry was well aware of the abilities of these men in white water. The racing waters of the Drum and Leaf rapids were a menace to the heavy boats and their cargoes of trade goods and winter food. When we reached the Drum the boats were run through, one at a time, the "Chips" shouting and laughing as they were drenched by the spray on the way down. All boats were run through without damage. The process was repeated at Leaf Rapid.

Proceeding up the Deer River day after day, I had the opportunity to observe these people as never before. Their canoes were tied to the boats and were towed along. There was much laughter about their camps in the evenings and one felt that these people lived one day at a time and worried not at all about tomorrow. They did not have adequate food supplies of their own for this trip, but augmented the store grub that Henry doled out to them with fish and such game as they might obtain. One day

I observed one of the women clubbing to death a big fat porcupine. In short order the animal was prepared for the pot. Surprisingly, the meat was little more than brought to a boil, when it was cut up, still red, and fed to the children. Above Grand Rapids on the Deer River as we set out early one morning, with our boat in the lead, Ab shot a moose where it stood on the river-bank. The kill was divided among each Indian family and the white men of the party. This helped a great deal to sustain the Indians for the balance of the trip.

The children were cute though somewhat dirty, according to the standards of the white men of the party. Little Francois was the cutest of them all. About five years old, he was everywhere on the portages and often underfoot. However, in skidding the heavy boats when dragging them over the ground, all the children assisted as did Francois by stoutly pushing at the flat stern of the boat since he was not tall enough to grab hold of the gunwhale. One quiet evening as we camped on a small lake in the upper Snag River region, I heard a splashing noise in the river, such as a dog makes when he wades out into the water and laps up a drink. When I stepped over to investigate, I saw Francois' mother pull him from the water. He had fallen in and thus received an accidental bath.

In one family there was a girl of sixteen or seventeen. She was well-favoured, tall, and healthy looking. She smiled easily, and flashed even white teeth. Henry said she was to marry George, a young Chipewyan, tall, thin, and suffering from active tuberculosis of the lungs. Henry had known these people for many years.

One of the married women was called The Queen by the white men. She sat, when they camped, in front of her tent, and smoked one hand-rolled cigarette after another from a foot-long wooden holder. Rumour had it that she had once been married to a white man. While travelling, she sat well in the front section of her Chipewyan husband's canoe, with the inevitable long cigarette holder very much in evidence. I never observed her to touch a paddle at any time. Nor did I see her chop wood and carry water in camp as did the other women. She was an adept seamstress. When I called on her to sew up a rip in the canvass of our tent, I found the inside of her tent unexpectedly very clean and well ordered.

In the party was a partially paralyzed old man. One of the younger married couples assumed responsibility for his welfare and gave him meals in one corner of their tent. All his movements took about four times as long as it takes a normal person. Thus, in quiet water, on a windless day, he was sent out to tend the fishnet with the canoe. Paddling with deliberate, terribly slow strokes, he reached the net finally and did the work there. The children, of course, thought him great fun and pushed at him from behind to hurry his steps, thus making him run, yet I did not see him fall. With great difficulty, he fed himself, pushing the food into his mouth with his fingers so that much of it dribbled onto his chin and into his lap. Henry said that the man had been in this condition for about twenty years, since he had a near-fatal attack of influenza just after World War I.

We were much impressed by the respect shown by the Chipewyans for their dead. Ornate wooden crosses carved by hand and neatly painted were to be found along some of the lonely beaches of Cree Lake. The graves were fenced with carved and painted wooden fences, and kept painted and in good repair. One of these tiny cemeteries stood well into Long Bay in our hunting and trapping grounds. Located on a level spot above a cut bank the dead were placed so that the grave faced out onto the lake. Ab, while examining the location, allowed that this was as good a spot as any for a man to be buried. We found two such graves on the Highland Portage about halfway across. I asked Ab, "Do you think that the dead were buried here because this is approximately the highest point in the area?"

"My guess is that they grew tired of packing the corpses and decided to bury them instead of taking them all the way across," he said.

"Bum" Edward was a trading-post Indian. He admitted quite readily to me that he was a failure as a trapper and hunter or at any work where he must think for himself, yet he was quite capable when working under the direction of others. So he forsook the wilds and worked for the outpost manager at Cree Lake for a time as guide and general handyman. He set a good deal of store by the healing qualities and medicinal value of tea. The new manager, John Lawrie, told us that one day when he and Edward were on a long winter trip, one of the sleigh dogs became acutely lamed with a frostbitten foot, whereupon Edward administered to the stricken beast a drink of strong tea. The foot eventually healed by the process of allowing the animal to ride in the toboggan and then to rest at home for some weeks while natural healing did the job.

Throughout the North the people of mixed Indian and white ancestry are called breeds by white men. They generally congregated in groups near the trading posts all summer long, and "pitched off" in small parties in the autumn to their remote trapping grounds. Occasionally, you saw some of them travelling with Chipewyans, and with white men on another occasion. Not entirely accepted by Indians or whites, theirs was the curse of belonging to no one. They were, therefore, destined to a lonely life by circumstances and not always by choice.

Celestine was half Cree and half French. When others of mixed Indian and European ancestry dallied about the trading posts in summer, Celestine moved his family to faraway places where he lived off the country, lived the good life, faring well where there was no competition for the fish and game that he was expert at taking. His relatives did not at this season elect to follow him and eat the meat that he shot. We found him to be frank and straightforward and quite reliable.

Joe was said to be a man with "long fingers." I met him one day on my trapline early in the trapping season where he was setting his traps alongside mine. Then I noticed his snare hanging in a game trail. I did not like it at all, but under the existing game laws, Joe could set traps any place that pleased him. I made no issue with him and eventually he lifted all his traps and moved to another location. He was not so particular with his snares. He left several which I found in the following autumn, one of which contained a summer-caught cross fox.

Abraham was versatile. A big man physically, he had from time to time been employed by the Hudson's Bay Company. He was outpost manager at Cree Lake when Ab and I left the country. Abraham could trap, hunt, fish, run white water, and get along as well in the bush as anyone. He could administer the affairs of the outpost. He was vocal and persuasive and a good salesman. By no means the least of his accomplishments was that of being a linguist, for he conversed fluently in English, French, Cree, and Chipewyan.

Solomon was half Jew, half Chipewyan, and the only breed I ever saw who had a full black beard. I have seen these people with red hair and dark skin. Over Lac la Ronge way there were breeds with the blonde hair of their Scandinavian ancestors and they all chewed snoose, or snuff.

The debris lying about a long-time winter camping area of Indians is something that must be seen to be believed. The whole place is littered with wood chips, heaps of deer and moose hair, paunches of animals, gnawed bones, antlers, legs, and scraps of hide. As the weather warms, all this garbage that has been worked over by the dogs, is scattered through with dog feces and the whole mass begins to stink. Blowflies are everywhere. The Indians solved the sanitation problem by moving to a new site on the lake.

These people must have been the inventors of the idea of disposable diapers. Since dried sphagnum moss has great moisture-absorbing qualities, moss bags for the babies were much in evidence in their camps. The washing of diapers was therefore not necessary.

They lived, for the most part, a hard life. They endured the intense cold and often near starvation in far off and lonely places. At Christmas time most of the men made the over-four-hundred-mile round trip to Ile-à-la-Crosse, a feat not attempted by the white men in the dead of winter. Some of the Indians from our region ventured as far as the Arctic tundra to the northeast in winter. In summer they endured the heat, flies, and mosquitoes that one cannot escape in the North. They suffered terribly from the white man's diseases such as syphilis, gonorrhea, tuberculosis, and glaucoma. The hospital at Ile-à-la-Crosse served the entire area. The ordinary childhood diseases such as measles and whooping cough killed off the children. On our way Outside one spring, we were hailed by Bernard, a breed from Patuanak. We pulled in to the riverbank and visited with him. He told us that over forty children had died in the past winter, along with several adults. He concluded with the remark, "No one white man die!"

The Indians and breeds were forever and always in debt to the Hudson's Bay Company. Their furs, for the most part, were applied against the debt so that they were always at least a year behind the white trappers. Most of us paid cash for our grubstakes. The government "handout" had not yet caught on.

At the trading posts in summer, the young men wore blue serge trousers, white cotton shirts, and red bandana kerchiefs knotted around the neck. They took great pride in keeping the trousers pressed so that the creases stood out "like a knife," they said. The young women wore long dresses of vividly coloured cotton cloth and bright shawls on their heads.

All the trading posts stocked canned extract of malt. At first I thought this was used as a food supplement but I was enlightened when first introduced to Indian homemade beer, a cloudy yellow liquid whose aftereffects include the sensation of dry sand being dribbled on the top of the head.

In those days certain white men established commercial fishing camps on the most productive lakes in the Churchill River chain. Permanent camps were built for winter operation and supplies were freighted in, usually just before freeze-up, on large wooden scows built and loaded at Big River. The white men coming out with their canoes and outboard motors sometimes brought with them one or more Indians to assist in freighting the supplies through the river rapids. George, a Chipewyan from Buffalo Lake, was one of these.

George had never before been Outside. He spoke no English. I saw him standing on a small rise near where a steam locomotive was shunting boxcars to the Waite Fisheries warehouse. All at once I realized that this Indian was looking at his very first steam locomotive. He stood quite rigid and very still. His mouth hung partly open and his eyes never left the engine and he stood there until the engine pulled out. There was no telling what was in his mind. Perhaps he thought the same as did a Chipewyan with whom I once talked.

"The devil helps the white man!" he stated.

16

THE WILDERNESS BEARS

From early April until denning-up time in November we were often aware of the presence of bears but rarely did we see them.

These bears are not to be confused with the garbage-eating and begging bears that frequent our national parks. The wilderness bears were truly wild. In the areas of the Cree Lake wilderness that were off the main travel routes, it was likely that if you came upon a bear in the woods, that bear was making its first contact with a human. The bears, as a rule, faded silently into the bush, like evening shadows, as soon as they became aware of us. They were about at all times in summer as evidenced by their tracks, strongly resembling human footprints, the tracks that showed up in minute detail on the sand beaches where each toe was imprinted, the ball of the foot, and on the hind foot, the heel imprint. There were clawed tree boles in the woods. Big dung heaps were quite common in the bush and there were unmistakable ursine doggy smells along certain game tracks when these cut through dank swampy terrain where we walked on a warm autumn day and where mosquitoes and sandflies gave us torment.

Upstream, above the Cree Lake cabin, the Indians had built numerous deadfalls for the taking of bears. The remains of these log deathtraps were so old that the logs were all but decayed away to yellow dust. The Indians had probably made these sets to secure bears for meat, but possibly there had been a market for bearskins at that time. When we were trapping there was no demand for bearskins at all.

A bear just before hibernation carries a great deal of fat. I have seen, in winter, Indians eating back fat of bears. From their

food bags they drew out long strips of back fat, with the black hide and hair still upon the strip and the fat of which was three or four inches thick. Jim Buchan showed me a big pail of snowy white bear fat which had been given to him by an Indian. Since we had constantly craved fats in our winter diet, we decided to make a special effort to gather in a fat bear just before the following winter was to set in.

That summer we purchased a bear trap. Harry MacDonald, Hudson's Bay Company factor at Ile-à-la-Crosse, led us out to the company warehouse where, amid the bundles of used traps that the Indians had turned in to pay for summer purchases, he lifted out the great steel trap and sold it to us for five dollars. This was an instrument of torture that must have had its original design in Inquisition times. Two powerful steel springs clamped together the jaws on the inside of which steel teeth were offset. The jaws, when opened, had a spread of twelve inches. The trap was swivelled and attached to a short length of logging chain. The free end of the chain was linked to a steel ring six inches in diameter. The trap could not be set by hand so that a clamp was made of two poles tied together at one end and with which each spring was depressed, tied down, the trap set, and the tying cord cut away.

It happened that Ab took the bear trap to Albert's House, his outcamp on lake one, on an October afternoon, just before the lakes were to freeze over. On a previous trip to the secluded cabin he had sat on a hilltop on a fine warm evening and watched two black bears feeding in lush blueberry grounds on a neighbouring hillside, as the sun set in the western wilderness. He watched for some time as they fed heavily, pausing occasionally to bat away the troublesome sandflies that bother bears constantly and bite them particularly about the ears, eyes, and nose. Ab figured that this was to be the locale for his attempt at trapping a bear for our larder, come denning-up time.

On the visit during which the bear trap was brought in, Ab decided to put a wooden floor in the small cabin because the sand floor had proved somewhat annoying and unsanitary the previous winter. Behind the camp was a fine stand of straight jack pines. He cut down enough of these to make a floor. He squared off three sides of each log and cut them to fit so that when they were placed side by side and partly buried in the sand of the original floor he had a new white wooden floor surface, the fresh-cut logs giving off a pleasing pine fragrance. Then as evening approached, he launched his hunting canoe and paddled around a nearby point where big pike could be caught so that he could fry a fish steak for his evening meal. He had no trouble at all landing one of the largest pike that he had ever caught in these waters.

When he paddled around the point as he travelled cabinward, he thought that from a distance he saw a fleeting dark shape near the cabin. On paddling closer he saw that the door stood ajar. He was positive that he had closed the door and set the wooden latch before he had gone away. On arrival he saw that the door had been opened by forcing it inward and breaking the latch off.

A bear, having crossed to the cabin from the other side of the river, had approached wet and dripping. It had walked over an area where we had burned all the branches of the pines when we built the cabin and now a good deal of charcoal lay there. Thus soaked and dirty it had smashed the door inward and entered.

The new floor was as black as the top of a wood stove. Inside the cabin there was a sour, doggy smell. The tin stove had been knocked off its sandbox base, cuffed about, and the ashes scattered. The tin smoke pipes had been clawed down and flattened, the grub box overturned and the contents devoured, the bedroll torn from the bunk and befouled, and the hand towel ripped from its nail hook and dirtied.

Ab was understandably vindictive. He set to work cleaning up the cabin. It was already dusk when he took the bear trap a short distance back of the cabin. Using the head and entrails of the big pike for bait, he constructed a crude pen of dead logs and in it hung the bait from a pine branch so that it dangled about six feet above the ground. He topped a lesser pine and stripped the trap ring over it, spiking it down to ground level with three spikes that were in the cabin. The trap was laboriously set, placed in a hollow scooped in the sand just below the bait, and all evidence skillfully camouflaged with reindeer moss. He returned to the cabin in semidarkness, satisfied that he was now in a position to retaliate should the bear return.

When he had finished cleaning the soiled cabin, he retired to his bunk, for darkness had descended upon lake one. He fell asleep at once. Sometime later he was jolted awake by a great roar. The ground actually shook. The bear was caught, was fighting mad, roaring with pain, and periodically moaning, scratching, and ripping at the thing which tortured and made it captive. At intervals it lifted the trap as high as the chain allowed, then crashed it to earth so that the ground shook.

The night was cloudy, moonless, and black as only such a night can be in the woods. Ab had to respect the bear. To go out there, even with his rifle would have been sheer foolishness. It could be suicide. The bear might break loose, and it was possible that, in its condition, it would attack him. Out of compassion for a dumb animal and out of rage for its misdoings Ab would very much have wished to dispatch it with a .30-.30 slug between the eyes. He did not have a flashlight to attempt this task in the dark. Thus he endured the noise, falling asleep when the bear lay quietly for short periods and then he was reawakened by the roars, scratching, snarling, and rattling of the chain.

As soon as the dawn light came Ab arose quietly, readied himself, checked his rifle, and stepped outside, approaching carefully the site of the bear trap. There was fog rising from the river at dawn. The area where the trap had been set was partly shrouded in mist as he stepped closer. He saw the bear lying down and he heard it moan. Then the bear became aware of the careful footsteps and whirled to its feet, looking at the man with its little piggish eyes. It was a mature black male, well caught at a front paw as high as the wrist. It began to struggle with renewed vigour, so agile that one moment it tore at the base of a tree and a split second later the claws of its hind feet ripped the bark from a tree at a height of seven feet from the ground! A more savage, wrathful, and soul-shaking exhibition Ab had never seen. The brutality of the trap struck him forcefully. Deliberately, he rested his rifle barrel over a convenient limb. As the dawn light grew a bit brighter, he looked through the rifle sights. The crack of his rifle ripped the morning silence far downstream where some resting mallards rose almost vertically and flew swiftly in a big arc toward the far end of lake one.

Frank Fisher shot a prime bull moose as he paddled his canoe along the shore of an unnamed lake near the headwaters of the American River. It was late September and Frank had ascended the river from his home cabin just to assess the signs of fur animals in preparation for the coming trapping season. After he had skinned out the meat he hung it all carefully from the trees that it might drain and cool out properly. As night was coming on, he returned to his outcamp near at hand, and planned to pick up the meat early next morning and freight it down to the home cabin.

Frank was a man of neat and methodical habits. Imagine, then, his chagrin when he returned for the meat next morning to find it all ripped to the ground, and rolled in the sand, the tallow chewed off, the meat dirtied and ruined for human use. Even the hide had been dragged away. What had been order and promise was now a filthy mess.

Frank did not own a bear trap. He possessed, however, a .38 revolver which he often wore in a holster when on his lonely travels, rather than pack a cumbersome rifle. After his original shock his thoughts began to collect. The moose meat was ruined but there was a chance to kill the responsible bear. He constructed a log platform on which he piled the dirty meat. He blocked off three sides of the platform with logs and brush so that the bear must approach from the open side. Here a key log was set so that when the bear stepped on it an attached cord would pull the trigger of the revolver that was attached to a jack pine limb just overhead.

Frank went away for a day, returning the next morning. Only

the whisky jacks were about the meat. The set had failed. The bear had returned in due course, but as it stepped onto the platform its weight was so great on the key log that the revolver had been pulled askew, discharging it at an angle that missed the bear completely. Left on the ground were the bear's tracks where the moss had been raked off the ground as the starter pistol had barked the signal for a great leap on its way to more quiet parts where no trapper was operating.

It was the first week of December. Ab and I were ranging far south of the main cabin, hunting moose. We opened our eyes wide in surprise as we came upon the trail of a bear in the snow. The track was large, indicating a full-grown bear, and it was also quite fresh. What surprised us most was the fact that the bear was still abroad even though winter was well established. We had assumed all bears to be in their dens at this late date. The weather was very cold, the lesser lakes had been ice covered for some weeks. Even the ice on Long Bay was so thick that we had crossed on it some days before to set traps on the far side.

We reckoned that the bear was travelling to its den for it moved generally straight southward, it seemed, like a homing pigeon. We figured it to be rolling fat so that we would track it down and shoot it to obtain a supply of bear fat.

The bear did not stop to investigate anything or to do anything that bears normally do on their travels. Straight through the bush the trail continued. After several miles the trail led through big jack pines where the land was fairly level.

In a section of a smaller, thick stand of jack pines the tracks abruptly vanished. There simply were no more. It seemed that the bear had taken wing. We looked at one another, puzzled for a moment. Then Ab's keen eye studied the last few tracks and discovered that their pattern was somewhat altered—the bear had backtracked itself! Carefully, we followed the trail back and found where the bear had leaped to one side of the trail, over a low bush, and continued on its way. Twice more it made this maneuver before reaching the shore of a lake. Without breaking stride the bear had stepped on the lake ice and legged it to the far side in a beeline for its den. We picked up the trail on the far shore and followed it into a heavy black spruce stand that bordered on an open swamp.

It proved that our bear was a late-retiring individual indeed. We approached the thicket carefully, yet it heard our approach and we found only its bed in a shallow depression under a partly fallen black spruce. We did not consider this to be its winter den for it was too exposed. The bear was apparently not ready to den up. Certainly we had been outsmarted for the bear was gone. That day it snowed heavily so that the trail was lost.

We had two separate encounters with bears on the same day. I had set out for Caribou Lake on foot across country in October to do some work at my outcamp. I had moved to a new location where the two small creeks entered the lake's western end. I deviated somewhat from my usual trail and veered off to the westward into unfamiliar country toward a high hill that I intended to climb in the hope of sighting a moose. I reached the hill and started up its steep side. I found that the hill was surrounded by small lakes, divided by narrow sand beaches, all lying clear and blue among the green pines. Near the crest of the hill I crossed a bed of lichen-covered rocks that were made slippery from a sharp rain shower in the night. On a rock shaped like a loaf of bread my foot slipped and I fell heavily on my right knee so that the sharp edge of a rock struck me just below the kneecap and in the knee joint.

I felt the knee. It throbbed dreadfully but there did not appear to be broken bones. I could not bend the knee and there was an ugly blue welt forming where the rock edge had made contact. By walking stiffly on the leg, I could make some progress. I would have to get home somehow though the way would be long and painful. I set out at once coming down the hill in a straight line toward my trapline trail where the ground was more level and the walking easier for a man with a game leg.

I judged my speed to be about half my normal walking pace. Every step was so painful that I stopped to rest at the base of a small hill. As I resumed my journey I climbed the hill slowly—and came upon a big brown bear. When I saw the bear it was standing on its front feet with the hindquarters still in a lying position. The head was cocked to one side for it had heard something as it lay digesting a blueberry feed. A brisk wind was carrying off my scent so that it could not know what was approaching. Then it saw me and bolted. I shot twice at its vanishing backside from which blueberry residues streaked at every leap. I missed the target each time and blamed my poor shooting to the fact that I was in considerable pain and not able to maneuver properly for accurate shooting. At sundown, I limped into the home cabin.

Ab, meanwhile, that same day was returning to the home cabin from Albert's House. He had staged his canoe above a rapid, and since his pack was light, he decided to walk the last six miles to camp in the hope of running onto a fresh moose trail on the way.

As he neared the falls he saw a dark object amid the pines. The thing was at a considerable distance and he stopped and peered at it. He was about to take it for the base of an uprooted tree when it began to move. It gained speed and was coming toward him. He suddenly saw that it was a she-bear with two cubs that scampered off in another direction. Meanwhile, the bear charged on toward him.

Ab had sometimes wondered just what he would do in such a situation. He found himself kneeling on one knee and drawing a bead on a target that loomed larger and larger. When he saw the white marking on her chest, he squeezed the trigger. As the slug ripped into her she veered off to one side, crossed the river, and died in the black spruce stand on the far side.

Somewhat shaken, Ab arrived at the home cabin earlier than I. When I limped in we had a conversation that lasted well into the night.

The bears of the Cree Lake country survived through periods of such scarcity that they were all but starving; and then fed through times of such plenty when they gorged themselves to such a degree of gluttony, that I am certain they suffered a good deal of physical pain. At the time when the blueberries were ripe it was an easy life for the bears. I have come upon the beds of bears where they have slept off the effects of gargantuan feedings of lush blueberries. The bed is easily discernible for here the reindeer moss has been flattened down so that it is as smooth as a floor where a bear's fat heavy body has rolled from one side to the other to relieve his great bellyache. Ringed round the bed at a few paces are heaps of what are apparently blueberry residues for the piles are dark indigo in colour. Here the animal has lain for some hours until the digestive process and the emptying of the bowels has relieved the pain of the pressure of its bloated stomach. It is then ready to take on another feed.

In the season before the blueberries ripen life is more serious for bears so that they range far and wide, eating the ants, beetles, and grubs that they find by cocking an ear to the wood. When the insects are heard working inside, a bear will demolish a rotten stump with one cuff of a forepaw. Not a small item of its food are mushrooms that grow on the forest floor. The one food that it favours above all else is to be found on the rotting carcass of some animal which it mauls about to lick up the maggots that drip from it.

In the beginning of one trapping season, Ab caught a silver fox. It had been recently trapped and was not at all crippled. He decided that the pelt was not yet fully furred, so he built a small pen of logs and threw the fox a couple of fish each time he passed the pen on his trapline rounds. After a couple of weeks the fox was seen to improve in the length of its fur. Ab would pelt it on his next trip. In the meantime a ranging bear, attracted by the smell of fish found the pen. It scattered the logs of the pen left and right and the fox escaped. These happenings were shrugged off as bad luck.

Bears caused us considerable annoyance at the beginning of each trapping season. When it was not yet quite cold enough for them to den up, they were attracted to our fox baits, set off the traps, and ate the food. One of them caught the large toe of the hind foot in one of my number four traps. It gave one lunge and

17

KINOOSAO

The Cree word for fish is *kinoosao*.

Any time that you visit with a long-time northern dweller the talk includes, without fail, a discourse about fish.

Henry Weitzel, Ab, and I sat on the front steps of Leon Sargent's store on a fine July evening in the town of Meadow Lake. We had chosen, that summer, to outfit there instead of at Big River. Henry was there also to gather his supplies, as he did each year to stock his little trading post at Cree River which he operated with his two partners, Otto Okerberg and Pete Charlebois. Henry had had a varied career that ranged from camel driver in the land near the delta of the Danube where he was born, to blocking hats in a Winnipeg factory, plus many years of knocking about in the North.

Henry was, above all else, an accomplished teller of stories. He held forth in the long evening twilight at some length on the peculiarities of camels, their miserable dispositions, and filthy habits. Then he talked of his years in Winnipeg. Then he began to speak of the North. I recognized in him a veritable walking encyclopedia of facts and figures about northern Saskatchewan. He was as wise as an old owl in the ways of the wilderness and there was no doubt that he was an authority on the Chipewyan Indians with whom he traded.

Then said Henry, "Where the Cree River runs out of Cree Lake, there are swarms of graylin's."

Then followed in detail many facts about the appearance, habits, and peculiarities of the grayling and that he will rise to a fly. At this time I had already been in the country for a few years, yet had never heard of graylings. We had never caught any and as far as we knew they did not frequent the waters in our trapping area. We therefore knew nothing of the species. At any rate, we assumed that there were none of these game fish in the area where we fished. The outside world was apparently as generally ignorant as I of the existence of graylings in northern Saskatchewan. It was at least a decade later before the presence of grayling was "discovered" in northern Canada by the American sports fisherman. Stories about them were published in such magazines as *Sports Afield* and the *Saturday Evening Post*. As a result, the fly-in fishing camps were established. To these a steady stream of American sports fishermen has been flown in each summer ever since, to fish in northern waters for grayling, pike, pickerel, lake trout, and Arctic char in a sprawling green and blue panorama that extends from the last roads all the way to the Arctic islands.

Incongruously, the average Saskatchewan resident could not care less about flying into the wilderness to fish. Of course, there are exceptions. The Indian eats fish only when there is no meat. Much of the time there is no meat. Indians hate the constant fishing for dog food. The latter-day Indian is interested in guiding sports fishermen at the fly-in camps and will feign a delight for panfried fish to impress his affluent customers.

No one will argue the fact that there are lots of fish in the North. Elsewhere in this book I have mentioned the numbers of jackfish and pickerel that swarmed up Rat Creek to spawn—numbers that staggered the imagination. If this phenomenon took place simultaneously throughout the land, the numbers of fish in the country could only add up to a figure of astronomical proportions.

Places like Big River boosted their economy as a result of the fish industry. The hauling industry, using horse team and sleighs, transported the frozen winter catch to town from widely scattered winter fish camps hundreds of miles away from such places as Buffalo Lake, Snake Lake (later named Pinehouse for the benefit of tourists) and Lac la Ronge. Old-timers in the North

today will tell you anecdotes that describe hundreds of teams strung out over the lake ice when the fish haul was in full swing and the tremendous catch was being moved south.

On our first trip to Cree Lake when we entered Crooked River we saw hundreds of suckers which darted away from our boats as we passed over shoals and rocks. On entering the Beaver River, we found the water to be so murky that fish were not seen. We had known for some time that Ile-à-la-Crosse Lake was loaded with fish: the Indians congregated there in summer and are present only at good fishing grounds. On this trip we were not aware of great numbers of fish until we reached the quiet waters below Drum Rapid. Here the air had the unmistakable odour of fresh fish and we assumed that swarms of pickerel and pike were there but we did not take time to fish, for we had to travel. The same odour existed below Leaf Rapid, but here also we did not bother to wet a line.

On another canoe trip when we had our dogs with us, we camped overnight on the lower Deer River, at one of the many sharp bends of the river where the current eddied back upstream while the main water movement was a millrace towards the wide Churchill River. We had a piece of a fishnet about fifty feet long which we set at night to obtain dog food. I set it where the water moved in small circles and boiled up from the riverbed so that the net was not strung against the current but hung more or less stationary in the uncertain eddies and crosscurrents just out from shore. From the canoe I hammered a spruce pole firmly into the riverbed and from it strung out my net, anchoring the other end to a stout willow that grew at the water's edge.

At dawn I looked out at the mist-covered river surface. All the net floats were under water, indicating that fish had been caught. Then we hauled in the net loaded with fifty-four jumbo whitefish. We had not thought it possible to catch so many large fish in our small net.

In the upper Deer River, Frank Fisher cast his lure into an eddy. A ten-pound pike struck on the first cast and was landed without difficulty. As it was time for our noon meal he proceeded at once to fillet the fish while standing on a great rock that tilted into the river. All went well until Frank's feet began to slip on the slime-covered rock so that he slowly slid into ten feet of fast water. He exhibited some fancy swimming, the big fish in one hand, his hunting knife in the other, finally slinging one after the other on shore where I retrieved them. Outside of an affront to Frank's dignity, no damage had been done and much merriment was made out of the incident.

On our arrival at our cabin site at Cree Lake we began at once to fish so that our diet could be supplemented for we had no meat. We found big pike along the edges of the water-lily beds that grew in the little lake below the cabin. The water was so clear that on windless days we could look into the water and see pike so large that they looked like a section of log. On closer examination they were seen to be fish that looked up at us with eyes as large as our own. Then we stopped the boat and cast our lure toward the individual fish and saw it strike and become hooked. Sometimes the fish would just lie there and after several casts take the lure. These pike, we estimated, ran as high as twenty-five pounds. We did not think it essential to own a scale.

Where the river poured into Cree Lake, we saw a big pike stationed at a spot in an eddy near the north bank in deep water. I tossed the lure toward it and the fish struck on the first cast. We dragged it over the gunwhale and into the boat. After a few days another big fellow was seen lying there and was also caught. Always another took its place after a few days so that if we wanted a pike it was a reliable spot at which to fish.

A big pike when hooked puts up a lively fight but tires soon enough. It was brought alongside the boat and as soon as the big head broke water, it was struck with a short, heavy club just where the head joins the body, and the tension on the line was simultaneously released so that the hook would not tear out. This rendered the creature docile enough to be boated easily. Then the fish was picked up by the eyes—as you pick up a bowling ball—taking care not to get the fingers near the mouth and the thousands of sharp teeth that slant inward.

Cree Lake proper is a haven for lake trout. After we had acquired sleigh dogs, I spent many an hour each summer day fishing from the boat to obtain food for the dogs. Generally, I met with much success, yet some days they were not anxious to take my lure. There were certain locations on the lake where the fishing was much better. Long-Haired Cree told us that from where he had sat on a rock slab that hung over deep water, somewhere on the south shore, he had in a single day landed more than three hundred trout. I had no reason to doubt his story. He had lived on the lake all his life and had learned from his father the best fishing locations on the lake.

The Chipewyans from Cree River were camped one autumn near the northeast extremity of the lake for a time. On returning to Cree River they told Henry Weitzel about a giant lake trout that they had caught in a net. Henry asked some questions about its length, depth, girth, and general appearance. The Chips said it took them a week to eat it all. Henry sifted the information and decided that the fish had weighed 100 pounds. I did not take the story seriously at the time, but in the years that have flown since I heard the story, commercial fishermen on Lake Athabasca netted a lake trout that weighed 102 pounds. This specimen was mounted and hangs today in Saskatchewan's Museum of Natural History in Regina.

Our handline equipment was primitive but effective. Starting with a sturgeon hook, we fastened it to a heavy wire leader and swivel and above the hook attached a bent piece of a baking powder tin with the red label paint on one side. We used a heavy green line or even the side line used in making nets. The lure was cast by twirling it around and around the head like a cowboy twirls a lasso before he throws it. We became so adept that we could cast in any spot we chose to place the lure even while standing up in the boat. This equipment was built to land a fish that might weigh as much as a fair-sized dog or occasionally a large dog. The largest lake trout I ever hooked we estimated at forty pounds. Once in a while we hooked a whopper from the depths. The ensuing tussle was always quite a thrill and the fish actually was seen to tow the canoe on occasion. We were sometimes a little awed when such a big fish broke water. There were, of course, many smaller fish caught for each big one.

Neither Ab nor I liked to eat fish. Although there were times when fresh fish was eaten with relish for a meal or two, after a while the taste of fish became unappetizing. After many months of eating meat I recall the pleasure of eating tasty trout fillets roasted with butter. When we had to eat fish in summer because there was no meat, the thought of eating fish became repulsive. We considered the prolonged eating of fish to be the diet of a poor hunter, and strove to obtain fresh meat at such times.

Cree Lake fish were infested with parasites. We used big pike for food because there were no yellow pockets of infection in the meat, although tapeworms were seen to be present in the alimentary canal. Trout and whitefish were full of parasitic infection so that we must cut out all infected pockets in the meat before cooking. We could not get too enthused about fish as food for this reason. We used fish primarily for bait and for dog food.

We learned quite early that it is much easier to take fish with a gill net than with a handline. We made two nets each of which stretched for one hundred yards when set in the lake. These were fashioned by hand from linen thread and net accessories purchased Outside. We used a wooden gauge and a wooden needle and spool combination tool to weave and tie the mesh. Once we had learned the knack of net making the nets were made in surprisingly short time. These we set out from shore and thereafter we removed the fish daily when the winds would permit. Our take was lake trout, whitefish, and pike.

We had some trouble in locating the best spot for the nets. We first tried to set where the sloping sand of the lake bed faded to the green of deep water. From the anchor pole we laid out the net, drifting with an offshore wind. When we tied a rock weight to the free end, we found the net to be hanging almost straight down from end to end! We realized then the tremendous depths that were to be found in the lake. The net was reset in shallower water where the bottom sloped gently and the deep end of the net was in thirty feet of water.

We caught no pickerel at all where we set the nets. Apparently, they did not frequent the waters where we fished, just as the grayling did not. I was much disappointed in this for pickerel is my choice of Saskatchewan fish for eating. We were assured that pickerel did exist in other parts of the lake by Indians who talked of good pickerel fishing in certain areas of the lake.

We walked on a game trail that generally followed the shoreline of lake one, the first lake upstream from our main cabin, on a warm sunny afternoon in early autumn. We were trying to find a caribou whose fresh tracks we saw on a sandy beach. In a sheltered small bay just out from shore, we saw the white turned-up belly of a big pike. The fish was apparently dead, for it looked very bloated and blowflies crawled on the pike's belly and buzzed about it. We looked closer and saw that the tail of a trout, about a foot long, hung from the pike's jaws. Then we noticed that the pike was still alive for its gills moved slightly. Suddenly Ab recalled having read somewhere that a big pike will on occasion swallow a fish so large that all of it cannot be ingested into the gullet, whereupon it becomes torpid, rolls over onto its back so that the belly breaks water, and the warm sun assists in the digestion process. He grabbed the .22 rifle and shot the pike through the head. At once the water was churned to a frothy pink as the fish struggled in its death throes. We dragged it ashore. I pulled the partly digested trout from its mouth. The piece weighed three or four pounds.

Back among the hills the many lakes ranged in size from tiny potholes to some that were several miles in length. Many of these had no visible outlet but drained away by the filtration process through the sand into the next lake and so on until a small creek was formed to carry away the overflow. Apparently, all these lakes contained fish for dead specimens were seen on shore even on the landlocked lakes. I pondered how the fish happened to get into these lakes in the first place. The only solution I could reach was that fish eggs are probably carried from one lake to another by ducks. Ducks feed upon fish eggs and it is possible that these are carried, accidently stuck to the duck's feathers or his bill, or possibly regurgitated on arrival at another lake.

I heard tales of trappers who had set fishnets in some of these remote lakes and taken fish whose size and quality they had never seen taken from the large lakes. As I have stated before, Ab and I were not interested in fishing and never made a cast for fish in the many lesser lakes that we crossed in winter or skirted on our travels in autumn.

Among the wild creatures that fished for food none can match the otter, which seems to be as well adapted to water as the fish itself. They can wreak real havoc if entangled in a fishnet. Henry Weitzel told me of a mink he sat and watched. This mink had seized a big pike by the neck and after a stout battle almost succeeded in dragging the fish onto a rock ledge that sloped into the lake. The pike then gave a mighty flip which landed both mink and fish back into deep water. This process was repeated many times until, successful at last, the mink fell to the feast.

The bald eagle is a formidable fisherman. I read the story of his fishing prowess upon a lonely beach of a secluded bay on Cree Lake. The bird had dived from considerable height and taloned his prize—a ten-pound trout, according to the size of the fish head that lay upon the sand. It had to carry this fish some distance, for big trout normally do not come so near shallow water. From the size of the bird's tracks and the way that the fish had been dragged about, I was left with the impression that this bird is capable of great feats of strength.

The dead fish that were washed ashore were quickly disposed of by crows, foxes, coyotes, bears, and other carrion-eaters. The rotting flesh had the odour and consistency of Limburger cheese.

We found that when heavily fished, the small lake below the cabin became fished out and some time elapsed before it was restocked from Cree Lake. We took this as a warning that even the big lakes could be fished out by overnetting. It indicated something of the unproductiveness and infertility of this land where the soil grows only moss and jack pines, where there is no topsoil at all, and whatever grows, by some miracle grows from almost pure sand.

18

THE TREES AND THE FIRES

MY TRAPLINE TRAIL from Rat Creek to the Crooked River country led me through stands of almost every kind of native tree to be found in northern Saskatchewan.

Beginning at the Rat Creek cabin the trail led through a lush stand of mature white poplar, the most common species of wood in the area. We cut them down for stove fuel, for the wood was clean and burned evenly and quietly. When frozen, the wood split like glass under the axe. When we packed in a supply of stovewood for the night, the distinctive aromatic poplar odour filled the cabin. The wood is off-white in colour, with a brown heart line. The woodsmoke of poplar can be used for smoking meat. Seen from a distance poplar smoke indicates human habitation, warmth, and the means whereby a meal can be cooked.

Passing through the poplar stand, I cut across Rat Creek on the ice. It was here that it first became solid enough to bear my weight. Upstream from this point the ice was always uncertain because warm currents from the lake were constantly wearing it thin. Immense stands of grey willow lined both sides of the creek where coyotes and foxes stalked the many varying hares that frequented the willows. These were the trees from which the Indians had made stretching hoops for beaver pelts in the times when beaver were present in the land. Dead grey willow, we found, burns with little smoke. This is the wood frequently used by canoe travellers who make their campfires of willow. This was the haunt of ptarmigan which migrate from the High North in winter. Below the next bend I could see a stand of red willow where moose often browsed.

Where my trail entered the big woods on the east creek bank stood an immense black poplar whose broad leaves shaded the whole swampy spot in summer and seemed to smother the smaller spruce that would surely grow taller than the poplar one day, barring the possibility of a forest fire that might wipe them all out.

Having left the creek behind, I skirted a small open muskeg where there were no trees at all, but along the borders of which grew great tamaracks. The lower branches were hung with moss, the trees appeared venerable and nearly dead for the tamarack sheds its needles in autumn. Back at the cabin we had once cut some dead tamarack for stovewood. We soon gave up on it for the wood burned with such intense heat that the top of the stove became slightly warped. I was later warned by Bill Mahoney that tamarack wood will burn out an iron stove in short order.

Beyond the open muskeg I entered an area of giant white

spruce. These were over-age trees that were nearly all dead. Many had fallen, so that it was difficult to walk across the giant deadfalls, and the thick, heavy branches had to be cut away to make a passable trail. Some of these rotting hulks were more than three feet in diameter at the butt. Here foxes ranged in winter, hunting for ruffed grouse and spruce hens. Occasionally, I saw fox tracks in the snow on top of a deadfall where the fox had travelled along the dead log from end to end. Some of the spruce still stood, some were still alive, and here we found the largest living tree that we ever saw in the North—a white spruce, thick, towering and as straight as a die. It was a much better and larger tree than the one from which our dugout canoe had been fashioned for it contained no knots for a long way up. It rose from the ground at least four feet in diameter, branched out in a high symmetrical cone to its pointed top that I guessed was one hundred feet from the ground. It was a tree to notice, for it was without blemish and its immense size was unusual. It stood far above any surrounding trees.

A little way beyond there stood a strip of jack pines, straight and very tall. This had once been a suitable prime tie-cutting area, but there had never been any logging done here and now the wood was ripe, overage, and showed signs of rot. Here Ed Benoit was to set up his railroad-tie-cutting operation in our last winter in the country.

Coming out of this ancient forest I entered an area of second-growth poplar, as thick around as my forearm and shooting skyward at a rate of three or four feet a year, for they grew in fertile soil and were well on the way to forest recovery after a bush fire that had blackened this section some time back when I had been a little boy.

The poplar growth gave way to black spruce as I approached a great open muskeg over toward Voisin Lake. Here black spruce grew so thickly that one must follow the game track to get through the trees, the terrain so hummocky that the footing became uncertain when blanketed by deep snow. The black spruce diminished in size until I reached the edge of the open muskeg, where the trees were only a few inches high. Sombre islands of tall black spruce could be seen far out in the great swamp, ideal habitat for the ever moving woodland caribou.

From out in the centre of the open muskeg I could see, back in the lush timber stands, the tops of great white spruce that raised their crests against the skyline in saw-toothed profile, far above the lesser growths of poplar. In winter their snowy crowns rose starkly white against a sapphire sky just after a heavy snow and before the winds had swept them bare.

Here, in the country far off the beaten paths of men, the logger's axe had not yet swung nor had the whine of his Swede saw been heard. The chain saw had not been introduced in those days. Hand-sawing and hand-chopping was the order of the logger's day.

At the north end of the muskeg I came upon a stand of mixed poplar, spruce, and birch. The birch was one of our most useful trees; from its wood we made snowshoe frames, axe handles, cabin furniture, paddles, and in later years the dog toboggans that held our trail hardware, bedding, and food. The wood was tough, resilient, and durable. The bark had long been used by Indians as an outer covering for canoes. The bark is obtained from mature trees at the spring season when the sap rises, and the tree is debarked in great sheets. I have lit many a campfire with birchbark which burns furiously. I noticed dead birch that had all but rotted away, yet the bark was intact and seemed almost impervious to weathering. I talked with a man who had spent some time timber-cruising back in the Big River forest reserve and who stated that he had come upon a stand of white birch that were as big around as gasoline drums. I have thrilled to the vivid yellow of birch leaves in autumn.

The teamsters around Big River had their horse-drawn sled runners made of steel-shod birch, mill-sawed from the butt of the tree, for the grain sometimes curves at the base of the birch.

The trail led through alder bottoms. The wood is so delicate in texture that I could cut down a three-inch tree with one hard chop of my belt axe. When the blade cut clean through, the inner wood was pale yellow but it turned a deep orange after a few days.

Occasionally I passed stands of balsam, our favourite tree. When camping out overnight, we were often favoured by the presence of a balsam grove from which we cut the flat branches on which to sleep. The aromatic qualities of the balsam tree are strong and heady. It was said that the balsam gum, found inside the lump that forms just under the outer bark, is used for medicinal purposes by the Indians. The white man uses it in medicinal pastilles and patent cough cures.

The trapline route through the woods ended where Rat Creek joins Crooked River. The return journey was on the creek ice, a narrow open road between the grey willows and the timber towering on each side.

We missed very much the lush and flourishing timber stands when we moved to Cree Lake. Here the bush was smaller, thinner, and monotonously the same—jack pine and black spruce. Singularly lacking was the topsoil that is essential to poplar growth. Only in the farthest recess of Long Bay did I see poplar growing in this country: three trees only, about three inches in diameter and ten feet tall.

Jack pine grew here in different stages from very old trees to new seedlings that sprang from the ground in places of recent burnings. In some places new growth grew several feet tall and so thickly that a man had much difficulty walking through them. Here the bull moose, when alarmed, laid his great antlers back and charged through like a juggernaut scattering branches in a wide wake.

Some stunted birch was on Cree Lake's shore and on the islands. In certain favoured places, I cut birch for snowshoe frames and we found them of sufficient size to make toboggans, but the trees had to be found, sometimes after much searching and far travel.

Merchantable timber for sawlogs did not exist here. The country was covered with much younger growth and in mature jack pine stands I saw few trees that would yield more than three or four railroad ties. Some areas had such thin stands of trees because the soil was too poor even for jack pines. These trees grow very slowly for I have counted sixty-five annular rings in the end of a jack pine log that was only nine inches in diameter.

Down in the southward curve of lake one in an obscure bay there is a remote and small creek. The mouth of this stream was difficult to see from the lake and we came upon it by accident. It meandered between the hills and linked some small lakes to the main body.

At the upper end of this mile-long stream stood a dead jack pine. It had been dead so long that all the bark had long ago fallen off and decayed. Only two main branches remained near the top and reached gauntly to the sky. The wood had weathered to a silvery grey. Thus, dry and bald, the wood had checked along its grain that spiraled like a stripe on a barber pole, all the way from its butt to its top. It stood now a dead and dry stick about forty feet high. It was what we called a dry snag.

By the thickness of the tree just above its buttresses I judged that this tree had been a seedling some 250 years previous. Cut off at the base I could undoubtedly count more than 200 annular rings. How long it had been dead could also be determined, for the new green growth of jack pines around it had trees that were probably fifty years old. This would put the beginning of the dead tree somewhere in the year 1700.

So the jack pine had emerged from the sand as an insignificant, green, feathery shoot, one inch long in its first year. Then it had grown and flourished, adding to its stature and girth as the years passed. Here it had grown for a couple of centuries, but the poor soil, harsh winds, and the tremendous cold of winter had caused it to form a twisted grain and to taper sharply so that it never acquired the tall and straight sawlog shape that is seen in more favoured latitudes.

The tree had grown through 800 changes of season. Two hundred springs when crows flew overhead and sometimes lit on its top branches. Then sudden spring thaws swelled the little creek that ran a few feet away and the water swirled down to lake one. The summers were lonely and quiet. Occasionally, a pair of crossbills twittered in its branches. When it grew tall, the tree was frequented as a lookout for bald eagles. The silence was sometimes shattered by the crash-dive of beavers. Loons passed over each summer on their travels from lake to lake. Then the little valley was hot and humid, the blackflies and mosquitoes were present in great numbers. A beaver had once cut a small notch above one of the buttresses and the scar was still visible. It had been diverted somehow from continuing its work. Sometimes in an autumn a bull moose came rampaging along the creek, to disappear and return no more. Otters were now travelling upstream to a winter haven in the unknown lakes far to the west. In the quiet of evening, the splash of leaping fish could be heard. In winter the temperatures tumbled so that the little creek froze solid to its bottom, the only stream I had seen do so. At this time, the red fox, resplendent in its winter robe seemed to float silently by on its hunt for snowshoe rabbits. Wolves were ever present and passed through the valley each winter. When the caribou overran the country in the early years, they were everywhere so that the creek became a pathway where the snow was packed down by countless hooves. In the spring that followed, the melting snow water ran off on top of the creek ice, eventually melting it down to the frozen bed.

A game trail followed the south bank of the creek and passed by the base of the tree. In places the trail had been cut down a foot deep in the sphagnum moss over the years by travelling bear, moose, caribou, and the lesser animals. Except for the time the caribou were in the country there were few animals in the area, for it was somehow a harsh, unproductive part of the land.

The tree had been killed by fire. The tree bole had been filled with resin that had burned out at the time of the forest fire, and charcoal could still be seen in a crevice. Other large dead logs lay on the hill slopes, all in various stages of decay. Jack pines decay very slowly in this country, but eventually the roots rot and the tree falls. From the outside the bole softens and turns to dust, the resinous knots disintegrate only years after the tree has crumbled into yellow dirt that leeches into the sand with the summer rains and does not contribute notably to the fertility of the soil.

We saw no axe marks of previous visitors to this site, although we looked all about. It is certain that Indian hunters had explored the little creek throughout the years, yet for all the time the tree had been standing it was possible that we were the first white men to stand at that spot.

Occasionally, we found big jack pines that carried one or more burls—large wooden lumps that form on the side of a tree trunk and may be larger than a man's head. Along one of our bush trails, on one tree, there was a great lump the size of a watermelon five or six feet from the ground. Ab worked on it with his belt axe and roughly carved out the shape of a man's head, complete with facial features. In time it became something of a landmark and, as we approached it from certain angles, bore a striking resemblance to a human head. As the years passed, the healing resin dripped over the scars, solidified and sealed the bared wood so that it preserved the face from weathering. Jack pine burls were many years later sought out in our national parks, and sections of such trees were cut, peeled of bark, and varnished to be made into strikingly ornate signposts within the park boundaries.

In growths of old black spruce we found certain frost-riven trees where the spruce gum had formed in rows of lumps as big as the end of a man's thumb to seal over the split in the bark. These lumps, we found, could be chewed and, after the first disagreeable bitter taste was worked out, became an acceptable, if flavourless, chewing gum with a delicate pink colour.

In the Cree Lake region there were many high steep-sided hills whose crests overlooked vast expanses of wooded country. Any of these hills would have made a base for a fire-lookout tower yet in those days I had never seen a fire tower in the country

north of Churchill River. Bush fires were not fought in this area but burned themselves out when the whims of the wind and weather so dictated. As soon as the snow melted, and until the snow returned in the fall, we were ever mindful of bush fires. Reminders came in the form of the smell of woodsmoke from distant fires or smoke palls when the summer sun was a red ball in the sky. Sometimes we watched smoke rise from afar and saw it streak the sky in the distance. A fire in the Stony Narrows area smouldered and burned most of one summer. Luckily there were few days of high winds and eventually a three-day drizzle put it out. A much larger conflagration far to the west of Cree Lake brought smoke clouds to our area one fall and continued to do so until the first snow fell.

Among the creeping smoky flames of a bush fire, I saw red squirrels dead upon the ground in areas that were close to the flames, but they were unburned—apparently they had been suffocated by smoke.

We were struck by the number of old burnings in the land. Jack pines in various stages of growth could be found in all locations indicating that fires had burned and reburned the bush from time immemorial.

Very few people have heard of the fire at Sandy Lake. This

lake is marked Gwillim Lake on the Saskatchewan map and it lies on the canoe route from the Churchill River to Cree Lake, and in the heart of Saskatchewan's northern wilderness.

The person who first referred to the North as "God's Country" must have been inspired by a sight like that of Sandy Lake in summer. I saw it first in 1935 when it was a place of rare natural beauty, a lake about five miles long and shaped somewhat like the continent of South America. Its clear blue water was ringed with fine, long, clean, sandy beaches. The land rose above the lake where mature dark-green evergreen forests covered the hills in a thick stand. There are a great many lakes in northern Saskatchewan, but often, by reason of recent fires, they look bleak, desolate, and forbidding. Sandy Lake had about it the look of idyllic beauty and profound peace.

The Hudson's Bay Company had once operated a trading post on Sandy Lake's west side. The post had been closed for a few years, but the several buildings were still there and painted white. They stood out against a green backdrop of forest-clad hills, serving the canoe traveller as a landmark. It can be said to the credit of the company that no damage had been done to detract from the lake's beauty and charm. Sandy Lake lay then, in solitude and in peace, a delight to the eye of the occasional traveller as he moved through its length.

Ab and I had travelled the route several times as we moved each year in and out of our trapping grounds west of Cree Lake. We always arranged to stop at Sandy Lake to rest up after tracking in the rapids and labouring over the portages. Here we regained our energies for the road ahead. Sandy Lake always appeared the same: secluded, peaceful, and wonderfully clean and beautiful.

Sandy Lake lies within that area where reindeer moss has superseded grass for a ground covering. The moss is spongy when wet, but in a prolonged dry spell of summer the moss becomes hard and brittle, crunches underfoot, will burn readily and creates a touchy fire hazard. Here the moss was old and thick and formed ideal feeding grounds for the barren ground caribou.

The region was at the approximate southern limits of the caribou migration.

In July of 1937 Ab and I returned to Cree Lake by our freighter canoe and outboard motor. Travelling through the Deer River country, we neared the place where the Sandy River forks into the Deer.

We had made considerable progress through green-timbered country up the Sandy River when, coming around a long bend, we noticed brown and yellow stains on the hillsides. We knew well that this condition is caused by ground fires where the fire creeps through the moss and scorches the pine needles enough to turn their colour. Since the fire was out we decided that there had been a small fire here recently. As we progressed upstream, however, the truth slowly dawned upon us as bend after bend in the river told the same story. Then we came upon immense stands of burnt pine and spruce, for the fire had climbed to the treetops and raced with strong winds. Finally, when we pounded on into Sandy Lake that evening the whole appalling truth struck home.

The rolling hills as far as we could see in all directions were black and dead. The fire that had raced through the timber, pushed on by high winds, had whisked away all the needles and lesser branches leaving the naked boles as black and shiny as if they had all been sprayed with tar. Because the moss had all been burned from the ground great patches of bare sand could be seen on the hillsides.

The site of the Hudson's Bay Company buildings was empty. We beached our canoe here and found the perimeter of each building to be marked only by rows of nails, hinges, and fused glass for the rains had washed away the ashes.

We climbed a hill behind the old trading-post site. As far as we could see to the north, it was the same blackness, silence, and death. We could now realize something of the magnitude of the conflagration. At its height the blaze had roared northward, flaming branches thrown out of the main fire to kindle new blazes ahead. Since we had seen no smoke pall in the south, the wind had probably drifted it as far as the tundras of Keewatin where it would be recognized by Eskimos as woodsmoke in a land where there are no trees.

The red squirrels that had chattered and scolded at us on former visits were silent now for they lay cindered on the ground. No birds sang. Out on the lake there were no waterfowl at all. There could be no foxes, bears, moose, or any land animals in the whole black region for there was no food for those that escaped, should they return. There would be, in winter, no caribou here for decades except if they passed through seeking their former lush feeding grounds. A grim lifeless desolation existed here.

We walked back to the canoe with curious feelings of despondency as when you lose a trusted friend. Each time a black branch touched our clothing it left a dirty streak on trousers, shirt, or cap. Sandy Lake was now a place to be shunned.

We did not tarry there that evening but proceeded upstream for seven or eight miles. The river ran through ravaged woods all the way. On our arrival at Little Sandy Lake which is aptly named Solitude Lake on the map, we found that this miniature of Sandy Lake had fared little better from the fire although on one point a few trees stood intact, somehow miraculously spared.

Near the Highland Portage the fire had suddenly stopped its advance. A miracle had saved our trapping grounds on Cree Lake's west side. Snag River was in flood. A heavy, sudden, summer downpour had vanquished the red, roaring, ripping monster.

On a hot, sultry summer night, we tried to sleep in our tent set up in an open grassy spot in front of the Hudson's Bay Company's store at Ile-à-la-Crosse. A summer electric storm grumbled and fussed over on the east side of the lake. Lightning flashed and peals of thunder were heard in the distance. The storm passed over and only a few drops of rain spattered on the tent canvass. Next morning when I awoke and looked out over the lake, I saw three smoke columns rising from the bush on the lake's east side.

19

NORTHLAND NOTES

We experienced, on occasion, such fantastic happenings that the experience could be shared only between us. If we had related these anecdotes to our friends they would have heard us out and smiled tolerantly, and silently catalogued us as prime candidates for membership in the Liar's Club. It is public knowledge that the Northland is the source of uncounted lies and often the unusual occurrence is not recorded, for the hunter knows that no one will believe it.

Early November is the desirable time for the taking of furs. The pelts of foxes, minks, and coyotes are prime. The colour is deep, pristine, unbleached, and the pelt at full hair length. The lakes, rivers, and creeks are frozen over except in the vicinity of springs and where river currents thaw away the ice to form the natural habitat of otters. The travelling is easy now for the snow is only a few inches deep on land while the lake and river ice is either bare of snow or has just enough snow cover so that it is startlingly white and your moose-hide moccasins grip on the snow to make for unhampered walking. It is a time of lowering skies, soft winds, and moderate temperatures. There have been extremely cold nights to freeze up the lakes, but winter is taking a breather before another more intense arctic front, already poised to the north, begins to move down to the Cree Lake country.

The furbearers then become seized by a frenzy of curiosity and wanderlust. Fox and coyote tracks are everywhere on the ice just out from shore. Every snag, rock, or other projection above the ice must be investigated. They are particularly attracted to the animal smells at muskrat push-ups and houses and beaver lodges and dams. So strong is the urge to travel that once in a while they swim across rivers where the ice has thawed away. At this time the woods' furry denizens take a brief vacation from the grim business of hunting their food and are apt to act a mite foolishly. The whole land has for them become a vast playground and out on the ice they are exploring a whole new range previously denied them. They revel so greatly in this changed environment that much of their usual shyness and caution vanishes for just a few days. This is the time that the greatest fur harvest takes place for many fall victim to the trappers' snares, traps, poison baits, and rifles.

Ab, out on the Rat Lake ice, was following the outer edge of a big stand of reeds and rushes frozen solidly in the ice and towering six or seven feet high. He could see through the reeds to the strip of ice on the other side; he saw four coyotes approaching on that side. His shot through the reeds missed, probably because the .22 lead slug was deflected by a reed. The coyotes milled about while he reached for his hunting knife to work out the empty cartridge that did not eject due to failure of the rifle's ejector mechanism. The tawny, tantalizingly close coyotes continued to move leisurely on their way so that they were beyond range when the rifle was once more loaded.

At Cree Lake during such a season of the year, I had ascended a small creek on the ice and set a string of traps upstream along the watercourse that drained many small lakes into Caribou Lake. On my return downstream, I saw a red fox streak down the slope of a hill, nose to the ground, and come out on the creek ice, by which time I had dropped prone, my .22 repeating rifle cocked and ready. The fox kept its nose to the ice until it came upon my tracks. It faced me as it stopped, raised its head, and saw me at once. The shot, at long range, missed. I continued on to Caribou Lake.

Then I stepped from a thick stand of black spruce onto Caribou Lake. There I surprised a large coyote nosing about for mice in the long dead grass along the shore in a little bay. We saw each other simultaneously. My shot whistled over its speeding back as he legged it down the lake ice and out of sight to the north. I cut across the lake in disgust towards my outcamp on the other shore one and one-half miles distant. I walked at a brisk pace for the sun was down, the sky ominous and hung heavy with cloud. Darkness would come early that night.

As I walked I glanced over my shoulder to the spot on the ice where I had last seen the coyote. Keen young eyes picked him out there, a tiny speck that faded and reappeared like a gnat against the snow. I continued to look at it as I walked and saw that it moved with me, parallel to my course. "Aha," I thought, "he is curious. He has probably never seen a human being in all his life and thinks I am a big game animal. Well, I will try a little experiment, play on his curiosity, and attempt to bring him back within range of my rifle."

We paced each other steadily in this growing dusk, yet the lighting was such that the speck was visible from time to time all the way as we crossed the lake. Finally, as I watched him and he watched me, we neared the far shore. I had completed the planning of my strategy. Now I would attempt to outsmart him.

I reached a place about two hundred yards from shore. As the coyote had appeared large and mature, chances were that it had seen caribou upon the ice in previous seasons. Now, I affected the slow awkward pacing that is characteristic of the caribou run when not thoroughly alarmed. I bent over from the waist and swung my legs in the long strides of the pacing caribou. I ran faster and faster, then straightened up and charged into the bush, circled toward the coyote into a thick stand of small spruce as fast as I could and flopped down on my belly, rifle ready and pointed out at the lake. Now I lay completely hidden, with a good view of the lake at a spot about fifty feet from where I had entered the bush. I hoped that the coyote would make for the spot where I had entered and thus cross my line of fire.

I looked out on the lake. Sure enough, there he was looming larger and larger coming as effortlessly as a breeze. Straight as a surveyor's sighting, it seemed, he was drawn closer. I experienced a new and unique hunting thrill as he advanced without hesitation and no change of pace. Suddenly, I had him in my sights, then led the target and squeezed a shot. I did not lead him enough for he was hit through the hips. He pivoted then, biting at the red hot thing that burned through his hindquarters. A standing target now, the second shot, laid him dead twenty paces from where I lay in hiding.

I stepped on the ice and picked him up. The largest and heaviest male coyote I had ever seen, I dragged him up the hill and rolled him into the cabin. That night, as I skinned him out, and before chucking the carcass outside, I made an incision through the stomach wall to see why the belly was abnormally distended. I found it so full of blueberries gleaned from the snow-free hilltops, that I felt that this coyote was hardly capable of eating more and had not followed me because he had been hungry. He had only been fatally curious.

On a very cold February afternoon, Ab hunted through some dense growth of young jack pine on the trail of a moose. He flushed a whisky jack from a low bough and spotted its nest. Built at eye level, he peeped into the nest, pushed the down lining to one side and discovered three tiny eggs which were warm against his fingertip. He recovered the eggs and moved on along the trail.

"A strange bird," he said to me, "that will incubate its eggs at thirty below zero!"

On certain sunny winter days when the temperature had moderated, as we snowshoed through the woods we sometimes saw in old tracks of wild animals in the snow that the depressions contained tiny black specks, usually concentrated on the inner surface of the track that faced the sun. On close examination the specks were found to be tiny insect life, shiny black in colour, that moved on the snow as we watched. Many years later I learned that these minute creatures are called snow fleas.

The Cree Lake country abounded in red squirrels. These active little fellows were everywhere. Great piles of pinecone remains were common in the bush where squirrels had fed for many generations. Although there was a market for their skins in those days, they were valued at only a few cents each, and their pelts were not easy to handle so we left them alone. We found that squirrels fed on mushrooms in summer. I once found a pine sapling decorated with mushrooms where a squirrel had fastened his gatherings in the tree so that they would cure for storage. I had to shake the tree most vigourously to dislodge a single mushroom.

We were often entertained by the antics of red squirrels, for they gave many acrobatic displays while leaping from one tree branch to another on a neighbouring tree.

While hunting moose, many a time we were spotted by a red squirrel which, from some high treetop, would chatter and bark at us as long as we were within earshot. I am certain there were times when our quarry was thereby alerted and moved out so that we did not see it at all.

The red squirrel for all its agility and mobility in the trees was outmanouvered by the pine marten. In prime squirrel country we found the marten's tracks in the snow one day. We saw where the tracks ended at the base of one tree to reappear in the snow below another tree to prove that it moved from tree to tree as did a squirrel. A slim, beady-eyed, serpentine animal, it preyed on red squirrels. There should have been more marten in this country, but this animal is one of the easiest to trap since it will go for any kind of bait and seems to have no suspicion at all of a steel trap.

The otter possessed unsuspected strength. I caught one on a little creek above my outcamp on Caribou Lake. This fellow ripped apart the pen that I had constructed to hold the fish used for bait. It had dislodged all the poles of the pen, including the heavy drag to which the trap was anchored. It made off then under the ice of a small lake and became lost to us together with the trap and connecting chain.

Ab, with his usual ingenuity made a periscope using two pocket mirrors and a packing-case board. It worked well, too, so that we could peer for some distance under the ice. Although we spent most of one day in the search, we were unsuccessful. We gave up too soon—I found the trap containing the foot bones of an otter on the far shore of the lake the next autumn. Still attached to the heavy drag this otter had accomplished an incredible feat by pulling such a weight for such a long way.

The ptarmigan while in flight often hurls itself into deep snow and tunnels under the snow crust in order to become sheltered from the cold and to hide from its enemies. Along its path there are small holes in the snow at intervals where it has poked up its head from the tunnel to see what is going on. Apparently ptarmigan spend a good deal of time in these tunnels, for if you break them open with your foot, you discover many of their droppings along the way. The ptarmigan, difficult to see at best in winter, is practically invisible when its head protrudes from below the snow, so that you may nearly step on him before he thunders into the air and explodes powdery snow in your face. On a day when I craved a roast bird as a change from caribou meat, I shot one. On taking off the skin, I found a piece of spruce branch that was driven into the breast at least one inch. The bird had impaled itself on hurtling into the snow.

It seems that every living wild thing must, at least part of the time, be infested with parasites—fleas, ticks, lice—and such internal curses as tapeworms. In the Rat Creek country the moose were sometimes found to be so loaded with wood ticks that, as we split the skin along the belly when field dressing the animal, wood ticks were seen on the skin in such numbers that it made one a little sick at the stomach to see them, heads attached to the skin, their bodies blood-loaded. I believe that there are cases where moose are so weakened by wood ticks that they are a factor in the demise of the big animals.

Bears are tormented by flies, fleas, and the like and they are always scratching themselves or rubbing on trees. A bearskin rug on the floor of my outcamp was discovered to be alive with fleas, causing me to throw it outside for good. Squirrels and weasels are hosts to fleas and must stop to scratch frequently. When these animals are caught in a trap and freeze solid the fleas crawl out to the hair ends where they are rendered immovable. Strangely, these fleas will again become animated when the carcasses are brought into the cabin to thaw out.

Wild ducks harbour big ugly flat ticks that will run up your arm as you pluck off the duck's feathers. These insects lie so flat against your skin that they are as difficult to lift off as a bit of adhesive tape.

The barren ground caribou seems to be the most susceptible of all the big game animals to parasitic insects, for in addition to being host in winter to many larvae of the warble fly they may also carry a legion of nose botfly larvae and tapeworms. The cruel attacks on caribou by blackflies and mosquitoes in season must be seen to be believed; all the warm-blooded creatures suffer when the hair is thin and short in summer.

Foxes sometimes escape the steel jaws of traps by a combination of chewing and tearing off the foot. Often they die after such an ordeal. Occasionally, they survive. Ab caught a fine dark silky female cross fox who had one front foot off at the wrist. The remainder of the foot had been in use, for a small pad had grown on the severed end. We guessed that this fox though disabled had made its way for some years on the stump of a front foot.

A yearling bull moose blundered into one of my snares in a game trail. It had stepped into the loop by accident and stood caught around a front foot as I came up the trail. I shot it at once but found it to be only bones, skin, and hair and thus fit only for dog food. The moose had a broken front leg that it had suffered some months ago, for I found it to be knit together. This injury had so hampered the young moose that it could not move about to forage enough food. By the miracle of its tenacious hold on life, it had survived an unusually cold winter. Since it was early March when I caught it, I would have bet that it would somehow have survived the winter but for my snare.

We were packing a big load of moose meat from far back in the hills down to the river where we could load it into the canoe and drift with the current all the way down to the home cabin. At one of our rest stops in the bush, we sat in a thick stand of jack pine at a spot where we had never sat before. It was the kind of place that possibly had never had a human visitor for it was far from any definite trail and far from any lake or river. While we were sitting side by side on a fallen pine log, Ab reached over and picked up a round object from the caribou moss. It was the rusty bell from a dog harness, the kind used by Indians.

"They put bells on their dog harnesses because they are afraid," Jim Buchan had said. "They believe that the sound will keep away the devil when they are far out on the trail."

Ab, familiar with placer-mining methods for gold from experience in British Columbia, made some experimental washings from time to time in the creeks that ran through rock country. He dug gravel from the base of rocks that were in the creek, taking material from the downstream side. He showed me black sand residues which he said were similar to those he had seen on the Fraser River, yet never a flake of free gold did we find.

We took many rock samples in the outcroppings south of Cree Lake but found nothing of interest. We became aware, however, that if there is gold in that country it is bound up in solid rock, and mining development must be by big operators with financial backing of great magnitude.

At the time I first entered the Northland, I discovered the parka, for this garment was not then in use for winter outerwear in the south. The northern parka, properly constructed, is without doubt the most superior outer garment that is available. North country dwellers, I found, wore parkas that were loose fitting and hung nearly to the knees, with a deep fur-trimmed hood that could be pulled over the face to keep the nose and chin from freezing in severe winter weather. These coats were not lined but were sewn from tough, light, windproof material. Usually, a leather belt was worn around the waist, outside the parka, in which to tuck the belt axe and to hold the sheath for the hunting knife we carried over the right hip. In cold weather the hoarfrost collected at the shoulders from body moisture, but underneath we wore one or more woolen sweaters, a heavy bush shirt and a woolen undershirt of good quality.

We found that heavy cumbersome clothing was not suited to us for we must be active and walk much of the time. We wore blue denim pants which were cheap, windproof, and tough. Under them one or two pairs of woolen drawers kept out the cold. Two pairs of moccasins and three pairs of socks completed our clothing except for moose hide-covered woolen mitts and a light windproof cap with ear flaps. In this clothing we were comfortable and I never suffered a frozen finger or toe or frostbite to the face.

We were continuously plagued by mice. Our fur storage was checked regularly to see that mice were not using our furs for nest-building material. A pine marten pelt hanging on the cabin wall became ragged in one night. I discovered that a mouse had been stripping off the fur while we slept. Well known to us was their damage to dead and frozen foxes out on our traplines when they cut off expensive fur to line their nests. We always kept mousetraps as part of our equipment in order to eliminate them when they entered the cabins. Chris Timson told me how he had once stored a ten-pound sack of sugar at one of his outcamps. He suspended the sack from the ridgepole inside the cabin on a string so that mice could not get at it. When he returned next autumn only the empty sack remained. Mice had approached along the ridge pole, climbed down the string and cut a hole in the bottom corner of the sack so that the sugar poured to the floor like sand in an hourglass.

In summer mice were ever on the move on the forest floor. I

have seen them swimming across creeks, riding high on air-filled fur. Asleep in my tent one summer night, I was awakened when a mouse ran over my face. I felt its tiny claws as they gripped my skin for a foothold. One mouse that entered the home cabin through the moss chinking of the cabin wall set off my trap without being caught. It became trap-shy and would not go near it again. It rustled about at night and kept me awake. Finally I drowned it using a pail half filled with water on which a light packing-case board was balanced, one end resting on the stove sandbox and the other on the pail rim. This literally proved its road to ruin: it spilled the board, bait, and itself into the pail as it approached the bait along the board from the sandbox.

We had a bone to pick with the manufacturers of our rifle cartridges. Far out on my trapline I experienced a hangfire. I shot at a ruffed grouse high in a tree with my .22. As the firing pin struck home there was no explosion. I lowered the rifle, was about to eject the faulty cartridge when it discharged. Ab out on the lake in forty-below weather shot at a coyote only two hundred yards away. The .30 calibre cartridge cracked strangely weak, and the projectile fell to the snow fifty yards away.

One spring as we travelled Outside up the Beaver River, we found that the Crooked River water was so low that it was hardly navigable for our canoes. Frank, Martin, Ab, and I decided to continue upstream to the junction of the Green and Beaver rivers and thence to Green Lake, there to hire an Indian and his team and wagon to transport us overland to Crooked Lake. As we passed up the quiet Green River we encountered homestead lands. One homesteader was seen unloading manure into the river. Around the bend a bloated dead cow floated with the current.

I heard Frank curse softly.

On long journeys over the frozen wilderness, we often experienced great thirst. Our dogs suffered thirst also for they frequently gulped snow. Far out on the big lakes we did on occasion chop a hole in the ice, lie face down and drink.

20

DEVIL'S VISIT

WHEN THE FULL FORCE of winter's heavy snows and extreme cold falls upon this land, there comes a feeling of uncertainty and depression to those who dwell there all alone. A search of the records reveals that dark deeds are committed in such a season. Shocking misfortune stalks and sometimes strikes at the isolated souls in this remote wilderness. Such was the mood of the 1938-39 midwinter.

Matt and Johnny arrived in the Cree Lake country in the summer of 1938. No strangers to us, we had met them in Big River over the years. They were both young, had spent some time trapping in various locations in the northland. In spite of their youth, they were already veterans of the bush. Just arrived to trap in the territory to the south of our area they would operate from Black Henry's former home cabin, recently vacated by him.

We had learned via moccasin telegraph that the partners had ascended in the late summer the watercourse known to us as Muskeg River into the back country where Black Henry's cabin stood deserted, empty, and silent. When winter came we heard nothing further. We saw none of their sign for our trails did not cross. These men were known to us to be able, experienced, and resourceful; it did not occur to us that they could be in difficulty.

It turned out that the trappers had been doing rather well. They had established their lines and, working hard, had gathered some sixty fox pelts, some mink, otter, and lynx, assuring themselves a grubstake for the following year.

One day in mid-February Matt arrived at the home cabin after a three-day trapline patrol. Johnny, from a window in the cabin, watched the dogs hauling the bush toboggan, heavily loaded with caribou meat. He felt elated, for the caribou had come only in scanty numbers to Muskeg River that winter. They were extremely wary and difficult to hunt successfully in the deep snow.

Matt was a born hunter. He was also a dead rifle shot, the kind of fellow that is given the assignment of sniper in battle, or who can get a job demonstrating the wares of the cartridge manufacturers. Never once in the eight years that the partners had worked together did Matt fail to supply meat when it was necessary. Now Matt was twenty-eight years old and wise in the ways of the bush. Congenial, big, agile, and iron-muscled he possessed a rugged endurance that made him a difficult man to pace when on the trail. His was a genuine love for the life he led. I had once heard him state that trapping, his chosen vocation, he preferred to anything on the Outside.

Johnny was tall but slighter of build than Matt. He had a gritty quality, an inquisitive and adventurous spirit, along with a pretty fair sense of humour that did much to cut down on the monotony of long months of isolation. The fact that his shooting eye had a minor astigmatism caused him to shoot less deadly than did Matt. Johnny had for some years proved his ability as a trapper so that he contributed his share to the fur catch. At twenty-five years of age he had already spent a third of his life in the wilderness.

The partners visited together all the next day. Matt presented a detailed account of his trapping trip which had taken him into a country of unknown lakes, creeks, rock outcroppings, and frozen swamps. He talked of wolves, foxes, and minks, of beaver and otter, for he had seen much fur sign. The highlight of the trip had been the caribou hunt. He had run onto the fresh tracks of a small herd somewhere in the headwater country of the Muskeg River. He had trailed them and then stalked them, drawing on all his knowledge and experience to get within reasonable shooting range. He had shot three adult animals where lesser marksmen would have failed completely.

The partners had only one dog team so that they worked their traplines alternately. The big yellow husky bitch of the team had recently given birth to four fat, round, woolly pups and she was not being worked while she suckled her offspring. This left three mature huskies, the present working team.

Next morning it was Johnny's turn to travel. He had breakfast ready long before daylight. They ate together, then Johnny loaded the toboggan and harnessed the dogs. He looked in and said good-bye to Matt who was eating slowly because it was his time to relax and rest. As he left, Johnny closed the cabin door firmly against the cold. By the light of his flashlight the thermometer outside read forty degrees below zero Fahrenheit.

Johnny's first day out was uneventful and unproductive. In the bush there were no tracks of game or fur and it felt unusually cold. It was a bitter season of the year, for at the time when the sun is moving back to the Tropic of Cancer the temperatures in this land can fall very low. He felt chilled, frustrated, and depressed as he made it to his small line camp that evening. The cabin inside felt like an ice-box. It seemed that the jack pine shavings caught fire reluctantly from his match and the cabin warmed less quickly than was usual.

That night aurora borealis flashed with a weird blood-red light.

Johnny had settled down for the night. Somehow he felt uneasy but could not explain why. He thought that perhaps he had already been at this business too long and should quit in the coming spring. By the light of a paraffin candle he tried to read from an old magazine he had brought over from the home cabin. Finally he made plans for tomorrow when he would head the dogs up an unexplored creek. He liked going into new country. He fell into a sleep from which he woke from time to time throughout the night.

In the morning it was colder than before. It was so cold that the dogs whined a little as he put them in harness. They looked rather low-spirited and sad of eye. Abruptly Johnny cancelled his plans to explore the creek and headed the dogs for the home cabin. To gain time he followed his trail of the previous day instead of circling back by a string of small lakes, an alternate route; nor did he stop for a boil-up at noonday.

By early afternoon the dog team emerged from the jack pines onto a high rock ridge that overlooked the river valley and the tiny clearing that circled the home cabin. Johnny observed at once that no smoke rose from the tin smoke pipe. Puzzled, he stopped the dogs and looked intently down at the cabin. No heat waves shimmered above the pipe. The fire was out. He had an immediate premonition of disaster. He urged the dogs in a charge down the slope, so that he had to brake the toboggan with his feet as they descended. He drew up in front of the cabin in a flurry of powder snow, the dogs bunched at the door.

The door stood ajar. Moans could be heard coming from inside. Johnny stepped in. Matt lay on his bunk, buttoned into his sleeping bag.

"Johnny, thank God you are here. Johnny, I froze my feet!" said Matt.

Johnny peered at Matt's feet as he drew them from the sleeping bag. The toes were all swollen grotesquely and were discoloured. Great blisters covered his toes and the soles of his feet almost to the heels.

"Matt, how did it happen?" cried Johnny in horror.

When there was no reply he looked up questioningly into Matt's face. A strange glitter shone out of his eyes. There could be only one explanation and it came to Johnny at once.

As the horrible truth came to Johnny he felt a numbness creep into his soul. He and Matt had discussed this malady that comes to some who live too long alone, yet they had always considered it as a thing remote, like leprosy, that could happen only to others. Here it was, now, in this very cabin, stark, ruthless, and with a terrible reality. Matt was insane!

Johnny gazed numbly about the cabin. Equipment, clothing, and supplies were scattered in indescribable disarray. In one corner lay the shattered remnants of their radio receiving set.

Johnny turned back to Matt.

"Lie down, Matt, cover up, and I'll get you some food," he suggested. Matt obeyed silently.

Johnny lit the fire in the stove and made some sort of order about the table and stove, pushing the debris to one side. He found that most of their food supply was intact. When Johnny brought supper to the bunk, Matt wolfed down the food.

By candlelight he studied Matt's feet. The blisters looked shiny and were hard to the touch. He worried at the discolouration of the toes and the possibility of developing gangrene. Should he drain the blisters? He decided that Matt's chances of infection would be less if the blisters were drained; if he walked on them they would surely burst open. He found a darning needle, dipped the point in boiling water, punctured every blister and squeezed out the watery bloody liquid. Then he gave the feet a light coating of salve from their meager first-aid supplies. Matt lay ominously silent through it all.

It was night. Lying on his bunk, Johnny tried to sort out his thoughts. He had just experienced the shock of his young life and felt himself to be in a nightmare from which he could not waken soon enough. He did not dwell on why it had happened, rather he asked himself what could he do about it.

The nearest help was at Martin Brustad's cabin, almost twenty miles away by the river trail, the only route he had previously travelled to arrive there. There was a shorter straight trail through the bush but it would mean trail breaking and slow travelling. A day's travel to the north was the Karras brothers' cabin, the exact location of which he did not know, and another forty miles beyond that was the Cree River trading post. The Hudson's Bay Company had recently moved their outpost to somewhere on the north shore of Cree Lake. Westward lay an impossible desolation with no known human inhabitants as far as they had travelled this winter. Similar conditions existed all the way to the Churchill River, if you went south. There were no police or doctors until you got to Ile-à-la-Crosse, maybe two hundred miles south or at Stony Rapids, a similar distance northward.

Johnny had dozed off. He was alerted by the sound of Matt's bunk creaking. By the pale light that reflected into the cabin from the deep snows outside he saw Matt up and moving barefooted to the door. That explained how his feet had become frozen.

"Where are you going, Matt?"

Matt made no reply. He must pass Johnny's bunk to get to the door. As he attempted to rush past, Johnny made a flying tackle that brought them both crashing to the cabin floor. Never a match for Matt physically, Johnny somehow wrestled Matt back to his bunk. The rest of the night was spent there, Johnny talking to Matt and coaxing and restraining him to stay in bed.

While Matt had his quiet moments Johnny tried to form a plan of action that would ultimately lead to Matt's rescue. His goal, at least, was very clear: to get Matt back to civilization in the best possible physical condition. He had not ceased to worry about Matt's feet, appalled at the thought that he might have to amputate them. Matt must be kept off his feet. Johnny therefore could not strike out for Martin's cabin, nor could he freight Matt along in the toboggan. At daybreak next morning it was no longer forty degrees below zero. When Johnny went down to the river for water, a quick look at the thermometer gave a reading of sixty-five below. Matt, long ago had warned Johnny not to travel in such weather. Johnny decided to follow his good advice now; he would sit it out until the weather moderated. In the meantime he felt like an animal in a trap, pinned down by a force with which he could not cope.

Martin might call in a week, a month, or not at all. It was that indefinite. There was enough food to last out the winter, thanks to Matt himself who had freighted in the big load of caribou meat. Dog food could become a great problem. There was a good supply of cut and piled stovewood.

Matt sat up when Johnny brought him his breakfast. He ate in silence, then hurled the dishes violently to the floor. Then he was on his feet and advancing. His eyes glowed wickedly. Johnny, cut off from the cabin door, backed to a wall.

"Get back on the bunk, Matt."

Johnny tried to put authority into his voice. The effort was wasted. They grappled for a time but Matt literally had the strength of a madman. Down on the cabin floor now, Matt had Johnny's throat in a death grip until his head reeled. As quickly as the spell came, it left Matt, and Johnny was released.

"You had better keep off those feet," Johnny admonished. Matt lay down on his bunk. For some time thereafter Johnny was aware of soreness about his neck.

Johnny gathered up all the available rope and trussed Matt to his bunk. He coiled it round and round his body and the flat bunk bed. Matt lay relaxed and allowed his hands to be tied with a length of cotton lampwick which the partners used for snowshoe harness.

Now that Matt could not move Johnny snowshoed out to a nearby lake, just south of the cabin. He cut a number of small spruce trees and dragged them a long way out on the ice laying them out to form a large V, the official signal of distress to passing aircraft. The bush plane that flew between Prince Albert and Goldfields on Lake Athabasca's north shore, sometimes flew high over this country and occasionally stopped at Cree River post. When Johnny had completed this task he went back to the lakeshore where he turned and looked back out on the lake. In the cold afternoon sunshine it was empty, lifeless, and forsaken. For the first time he felt alien in this land. He turned back to the cabin.

He kept Matt tied down to his bunk over the next several days and nights, attending to his wants as if Matt had been a baby. Matt raved loudly and almost incessantly and fought his bonds, determined to free himself. Johnny watched him constantly lest he break loose. Matt's moods ranged the awful gamut of violent, cursing, struggling, roaring rage to genuine sympathy for his partner. One day he suddenly remarked:

"Johnny, you must be going through hell."

There was grim humour when he exclaimed after a long silence: "Well, well. So I'm the mad trapper at last!", alluding to Albert Johnson, the mad trapper of Rat River, who became internationally famous.

Johnny was awed by the turmoil in Matt's being and the malady that had reduced him, who had never been sick, to a state that was infinitely worse than helplessness. A horrible spectre had hunted him down just as surely as Matt had so recently stalked the caribou herd. This had been an apparition that had left no warning tracks in the snow. Johnny dug back in numbed memory for any unusual behaviour prior to Matt's breakdown. Always he came up with a negative answer. Obviously, a man who had just returned from a successful hunt must have had all his faculties. If there had been signs, they were missed completely. The realization of Matt's condition made Johnny feel depressed and angry that it had happened. Sometimes he cursed softly to himself.

How much can a man stand? On the sixth day Johnny asked himself this question. He recalled having no sleep in all that time and now he reeled drunkenly as he moved about, doing the endless camp chores. On two different occasions he thought that he heard voices outside, but on jerking open the door there was nothing but the sleigh dogs looking at him from where they were chained to their kennels.

He knew now that their only chance was a dash for Martin's cabin. At best he would be away for a whole day, and probably longer. The water in the bucket by the stove would be frozen solid before he returned. There had been no break in the extremely cold weather. Matt's feet would be refrozen. The idea was impossible. To sleep was also impossible. Johnny realized that it was quite possible that his own frayed thread of reason could snap and they would both be lost.

Towards evening Johnny made a decision. He had looked again at Matt's feet and saw that by some miracle the blistered skin had tightened to the flesh. Although the toes were still discoloured the swelling had subsided and he was sure the feet were healing. He felt that he just could not stand more of Matt's ravings; besides, Matt's arms were raw from the ropes.

"I will release him," thought Johnny, "and to hell with the consequences." He untied the ropes.

Matt arose quickly, evidently pleased to be free. He donned his moccasins, strode about the room, and gave no indication of pain. Johnny sank to his bunk. He could not remember ever being so tired.

"Oh, God, if I could only sleep. . . ."

He jerked to his feet when a rifle discharged in the cabin. Matt stood there holding his big game rifle, having just fired it into the opposite wall.

"Give me the rifle," demanded Johnny. Warily watching each other, Matt placed it quietly into Johnny's hands. Thereafter all the rifles were kept locked in the warehouse where the furs were stored. It was very strange but Johnny had not thought of this precaution beforehand.

A full week had passed. Johnny gave Matt the run of the place. Outside it was still bitterly cold and they both kept inside the cabin. Each day was another nightmare of noise and violence. The nights, it seemed, were worse. Many times the fate of the partners was in grave doubt. Some of these happenings Johnny vowed to tell no one, ever. There were occasions when it would have been difficult to determine which one was sane and which one crazy. Sometimes Johnny seethed inwardly at his own helplessness. He mustered all his patience during Matt's worst emotional storms. He dozed when Matt slept, which was not often. Then the dogs would howl and awaken him.

Matt's powers of concentration were gone. Underlying his entire activity was a mania of destruction. He wrecked, sabotaged, and burned his personal property, bit by bit, day after day. Johnny once had the disconcerting thought that since Matt was destroying those things that he valued, he might well attempt to destroy his partner, whom he valued a great deal.

The cute little pups became the first casualties. Since Johnny could not be away to hunt for caribou, their meat supplies must be conserved, if Johnny was to stretch out the dog food until spring. The pups would have to go. One day he took them from their warm kennel and killed them, one after another. He felt wooden as he did so, as though he were someone else. A few days later he heard the bitch whimpering at the door. Her dugs, greatly swollen and bared, had been frostbitten so that they presented a livid appearance and were extremely hard to the touch. Johnny shot her through the head.

Another day Matt in one of his flashes of violence smashed the windows from the cabin, then sat down on his bunk. As the very cold air rushed into the gaping holes Johnny sat at the table and put his head down upon his folded arms. There occurred about his eyes an almost forgotten drawing sensation. Suddenly he was sobbing. Johnny had not wept since he had been a little boy.

He thought back to his Christian training as a child. Certain Biblical quotations were recalled, which he repeated to himself:

"Though I walk through the valley of the shadow of death, I will fear no evil," and "I to the hills will lift up mine eyes, from whence doth come mine aid."

Johnny had not prayed for a long time either. His prayer now was simple and fervent:

"Help me, help me, Almighty God!"

He arose and repaired the windows. He tacked into the gaping spaces sheets of fine paper of certain maps which they owned. He nailed down the edges neatly with wooden strips and was rather pleased at the result for the openings were sealed and although they were no longer transparent, they were translucent so that there was plenty of light in the cabin by day.

Another week had passed with no improvement at all in Matt's condition or in Johnny's except that his hopes were dimming a little each day. Not once did he entertain the idea of dashing to Martin's to save himself.

One day the cold spell broke. In the morning warm winds blew from the south and by noon the air outside had a definite pine fragrance. The sky took on a delicate shade of blue and some of the great burdens of snow tumbled from the trees. Now was Johnny's chance. If he could succeed in roping Matt to the bunk again he would leg it as hard as possible for Martin's cabin at Stony Narrows, beginning at daylight. He began to make preparations for the trip.

Just after sundown he heard a shout. The dogs, full of life

after their long idleness set up a wild clamour as Johnny threw open the door. Incredibly a dog team appeared around the bend from upriver and the north. He saw two parka-ed figures, one walking in front and one behind the dog team. He stood there and watched them approach to the door, two young men. Johnny's first thought was how neat and clean looking were their outfit, dogs, and their persons compared to his own chaotic situation.

Over at our cabin very early that morning we had gotten under way on a chance visit to Matt and Johnny's place. Following the route generally that we had taken to Black Henry's in the previous winter, we spent a gruelling day in the unaccustomed mild weather breaking the trail through the hills. Once we almost turned back. This would be a chance visit just to break the monotony of winter and to see and do something different. Different, indeed!

When Johnny explained to us at the door we stood there a moment in disbelief. When Matt himself came out and babbled a welcome, we began to understand.

After a few days there and satisfied that there was no other way, Ab mushed down river to Martin's cabin. Fortunately, Martin was just in from his trapline the previous day. He volunteered to carry the word over fifty miles to Cree River since his long rangy dogs were ideal for a fast run. Ab continued on to our home cabin for supplies and dog food and he returned to Muskeg River on the third day.

During this time I had the opportunity to hear from Johnny his story in detail.

Four days later Martin Brustad arrived at the Muskeg River camp. He stated that no one at Cree River knew when the Goldfields plane would call—there was no schedule.

Moccasin telegraph, however, was spreading the word. In a few days Holgar Petersen and Henry Weitzel pulled in from Cree River. They were followed two days later by Chris Timson and Martin Engemann whose traplines were scattered northward of Cree River. Finally, Frank Fisher arrived. He had heard the news from Chipewyan hunters on Cree Lake's east side. Matt, they said, had "the bad sickness" as they referred to the malady in hushed, horrified tones. We now had representation from every known white habitation within a radius of sixty miles and some from beyond.

We stood in the little clearing at the cabin one day when Matt suddenly grabbed the big, razor-sharp axe used for splitting wood. With murderous eyes he strode towards Holgar. Holgàr met the oncoming Matt and laid a hand gently on his shoulder. This action could have been like placing a hand on a trapped bear.

"Put down the axe, Matt," said Holgar.

Matt set the axe down and hung his head.

At night we had the chance to enjoy Holgar's conversational ability. To pass away the time, he told us stories. There were tales from the seaports of the world, Christmas eve in a bar in Valparaiso, and humourous anecdotes from the ends of the earth. We had some good laughs, a tonic that we all needed.

One day Chris commented:

"Matt's case is not so bad, I have seen much worse ones in the war. I think Matt will get over it in time."

The days passed by. We were in our third week of hanging around the place and were getting fed up. Henry and Holgar returned to Cree River.

One day Chris spoke to Johnny privately:

"Martin Engemann and I will start for Ile-à-la-Crosse in the morning. We think that we can get a plane from there long before the Goldfields plane shows up here."

Ile-à-la-Crosse was 150 miles away by air and 200 miles by the winter trail, but it was linked to the outside by communication wires. Johnny started to protest. Chris stopped him by saying firmly, "We had intended to go down there anyway this winter."

It was a lie and Johnny knew it. A white lie.

Johnny gave each a token gift as they left. To Chris, short on dog power, he gave their finest dog. To Martin Engemann, his own strong snowshoes, made by himself. Martin's webs were badly worn.

In the morning we all walked down to the river ice to see them off. As they left they turned and waved a final farewell just before they vanished around a bend.

Two days later the Goldfields plane roared over the cabin and landed on the lake where Johnny had placed the distress signal. Long ago we had prepared for this moment. A Royal Canadian Mounted Police constable assumed the role of Matt's escort. Willing hands attended to all the other details.

At the plane Johnny shook hands with us and climbed aboard. Then the door closed and soon a small speck in the clear sky to the south was all that remained of them. Then the drone became silent and the speck vanished.

In retrospect, I see the little knot of men standing on the ice after the plane took off. I see two more on their long and unrequired trip to Ile-à-la-Crosse. All proven friends, allies, and brothers through adversity. It is just a bit different with Matt and Johnny. They are brothers by birth.

21

PIMIYAKUN

IN MY TRAPPER'S JOURNAL I noted each day a particular highlight that had happened on that date. As I look over the entries I find mentioned certain sightings and hearings of passing aircraft. They are recorded thus: "Heard a plane," or "Saw a plane."

One entry reads: "Heard a plane—in this weather!" It happened that it was snowing heavily at the time. In those days the bush planes carried no two-way radio, there were as yet no detailed maps available of the area over which the plane was flying and the pilot, in this case, was flying "by the seat of his pants" as the saying went.

With the coming of aircraft into the bush country a new word was introduced into the Cree language. *Pimiyakun* became the word for an airplane and when aircraft became common in the country it became a word that was heard often wherever Crees conversed together. They had all seen many aircraft and although many had never seen an automobile they accepted and took for granted the bush plane as part of their life. It meant that when pimiyakun came to the trading post, immediately there was a new supply of trade goods on the trading-post shelves.

Pimiyakun had been coming and going for so long that the feeding bull moose gave scant heed to its drone overhead, it merely turned an ear toward the sound and went on feeding. The plane must pass over at very low altitude before it caused the red squirrel to chatter and bark from its perch in the pinetop or the beaver to crash-dive where it cruised in the quiet waters of a flooded swamp.

In the early 1930s the Royal Canadian Air Force had a number of flying boats based at Ladder Lake near Big River. After most of these units had crashed into the bush at various times they were abandoned as unsuitable to northland flying. It was then that the cabin monoplane made its appearance; float-equipped in summer, it was readily converted to ski landing gear after freeze-up. Now certain commercial ventures began to freight fish out of the North, to bring in supplies, and to carry passengers. The firm of Mayson & Campbell began a freight and passenger service from Prince Albert. No schedule was established but the planes moved on a charter basis. Another of the original pilots was a short, stocky fellow who worked with a single plane of his own out of Big River. His name was Cecil N. ("Cece") MacNeal.

A few years later Canadian Airways Limited established something like a regular schedule between Prince Albert and Goldfields on Lake Athabasca's north shore.

At Ile-à-la-Crosse we saw the flying boxcar, a heavy Junkers aircraft that was used especially to freight heavy mining machinery into Goldfields. This plane, made in Germany, had a German mechanic who flew with the craft at all times.

Ab and I made it a point to be at our Cree Lake cabin one day in mid-January. In the previous summer in Big River we had arranged with MacNeal to deliver some freight to our cabin on this day. The bill of lading was to read:

300 lbs. flour, 100 lbs. sugar, one quart Hudson's Bay Co. rum.

As the day drew near we marked out for him a runway between two rows of spruce tree markers on the lake ice so that he would not encounter the river channel and trouble.

Sure enough, in the early afternoon of that day MacNeal circled the cabin and came down on the ice before we could harness the dogs.

Then we took the freight off the aircraft, loaded it into the toboggan and MacNeal came up to the cabin with us where we had a short visit over a drink of rum. A few hasty news items

were exchanged and he was away, just clearing the spruce ridge that separated his recent landing strip from the wide reaches of Cree Lake.

In the months of November and December bush pilots were bedevilled by fogs that were thick and persistent. Ice conditions caused planes to land on unfamiliar lakes where the ice build-up was assessed and, if possible, removed. Slush under the snow was a hazard and a worry to pilots landing on the ice. The great weight of a heavy snowfall caused the ice to crack and water seeped under the snow unseen so that airplane skis could become stuck in slush. In summer sudden violent storms buffeted the light planes about.

I talked with MacNeal nearly all one night at Cree Lake Outpost where he had brought in Alex Ahenakew, the Hudson's Bay Company factor from Patuanak who was an Indian and making an inspection of the outpost. MacNeal was a great talker, liked a funny anecdote, and gave me a general idea of the perils of bush-flying.

"I was flying Slavic John and his outfit into Black Lake last August," began MacNeal.

"When we were out somewhere beyond the north shore of Cree Lake a great black summer storm cloud appeared ahead. Rather than waste a lot of time and fuel in circling the storm I headed straight into it and disappeared like a mosquito into a cloud of smoke. Then the instruments went haywire, it became dark as night. When we came out of the cloud and into bright sunshine we were flying straight up! I levelled out and looked at John who sat relaxed and unconcerned—first trip for him and he thought everything was normal. Then we came in to Black Lake, and while unloading John's outfit I noticed that the door was bowed inward as was one side of the fuselage."

One summer at Ile-à-la-Crosse I heard MacNeal talking to another bush pilot. Said Ernie, his friend, "I'm flying this crate with a welded piston because we can't get the replacement part."

Later that day we took off for Meadow Lake with MacNeal. He had warned us beforehand that one of the floats was leaking and had taken on water making the aircraft list a little on that side.

"She'll drain out as soon as we're airborne," he assured us.

After an easy take-off over the waves of Ile-à-la-Crosse Lake we were soon over Big Island. My first flight. I was amazed at the thinness of the bush from above. Each tree, stump, and deadfall stood out as a single unit. There was no blending of trees as seen from the ground. Every path and game trail could be seen. An ant-sized horse grazing on the island lifted its head as we passed over. Then we were over the long and winding Beaver River where we had toiled with our wooden boats when we first entered the country. I could see rocks and water boiling over them where we were later to have trouble with one of Henry Weitzel's riverboats. I could see the swampy backwaters where we had been attacked by hordes of mosquitoes as we had camped on shore on a hot steamy summer night.

MacNeal put the plane down at Beauval. From here he had to make a side trip to Doré Lake while we hung around the Hudson's Bay Company store, now with bare shelves for it was springtime and most of the trade goods had been sold in the previous winter. In a short time our plane had returned to the river. Our first take-off run was blocked by the curving riverbank. MacNeal cut the motor with a few seconds to spare. The second run bore fruit for the riverbank slipped away below us at the last moment.

MacNeal got considerably more altitude for this leg of the trip to Meadow Lake. A vicious crosswind ripped at us from the east and the ride became bumpy.

A considerable conflagration was developing between Doré Lake and Lac la Ronge, and the high winds were now obscuring much northern scenery by scattering a smoke screen from extensive bush fires, for with the coming of spring and drying winds there is ever the danger of forest fires. I looked east towards Rat Lake but all was hidden by smoke. Suddenly MacNeal banked sharply and we came down on a small lake near the town of Meadow Lake.

In a Chinese restaurant over a cup of coffee I asked MacNeal if he had considered it rough going up there. He answered very seriously that the ride had been unusually rough.

Another summer at Ile-à-la-Crosse we watched a bush plane light on the lake and taxi to the dock. From where we sat we saw the pilot, a young, tall man, climb down on the dock and walk toward the Hudson's Bay Company store. Even from a distance he looked familiar. "He looks a lot like Ron Baker," I said to Ab. Ron had been one of Ab's classmates at school and we had heard that he had taken to bush-flying. We went up to the store then and had a long chat before he took off. Ron later rose to be one of Air Canada's top flight engineers.

On a summer day at Big River I watched an overloaded plane make a desperate take-off attempt down Crooked Lake. The pilot tried time after time, but failed even to get on "the step" which acts as a water ski. Finally he taxied back to the dock. There I helped him unload several large cases of beer. Then he took off and was lost to view in the haze to the north. We were not long to the realization that the purpose of most northern flying in those days was to freight in booze to slake the blast-furnace thirst of northern residents.

From deep in the northern wilderness when we observed passing aircraft it was certain that they flew generally on a south-to-north course when coming or north to south on the return trip. As the 1930s drew to a close we became aware one summer from our Cree Lake cabin that pimiyakun flew east to west and west to east at unusually high altitudes and on clear calm days. We thought this strange and discussed it at some length. The full realization of the purpose of these flights was not made known to us until the next summer.

We learned from Martin Brustad who had met a ground-survey party that an aerial photography project of the Government of Canada had photographed the Cree Lake country strip by strip and was presently mapping in detail, the scale four miles to one inch. The map that was later printed included the area of latitude 56° and longitude 106° and 107°, with Cree Lake the main geographical feature. Pimiyakun had made it possible, along with ground-survey personnel, to compile a map that showed for the first time in minute detail every bend in the rivers, all potholes, lakes, muskegs, the islands in the lakes, and the location of many cabins!

The Cree Lake map, which I did not see until after I had left the Northland, was pleasantly redolent with familiar names and memories. The map makers, probably not aware of the local names of rivers and lakes, had renamed many of the lesser lakes, bays, and rivers. Stony Narrows was designated as such, as was American River where Frank Fisher's trapping grounds were located. A large bay on Cree Lake's east side was named Lazy Edward Bay. There was Holgar Lake, Timson Creek, Weitzel Lake, and Engemann Lake. Caribou Lake, where I had done much travelling was now Abraham Bay. Brustad Lake and Brustad River had been Muskeg River and Muskeg Lake when Matt and Johnny had there spent a sojourn in hell.

Ab and I had been singularly honoured. The river upon which our home cabin had been located was named Karras River and far upstream on lake two of the ubiquitous shoreline was printed the name Karras Lake.

Pimiyakun was instrumental in the very best deal we ever made for our annual fur catch. We had mushed the dog team over to Cree Lake Outpost to visit with John Lawrie, the replacement for Jim Buchan who had been transferred to Fort Liard. Toward sundown a light ski-equipped plane lit on the lake ice below the outpost. MacNeal had brought in Alex Ahenakew on an inspection trip. That night Alex learned that we had made a good catch of foxes. Alex said that there had recently been a sharp rise in the fur market. He insisted that MacNeal take Ab and himself to our cabin. They took off at daylight.

Based on prices received in the previous year we had estimated our catch to be worth something like five hundred dollars. After two hours they returned. Everyone was smiling when Ab showed me a Hudson's Bay Company draft for just under one thousand dollars, more money by far than we had possessed at one time in all our lives.

Ab told me later that Alex wanted a couple of caribou to take back to his home larder. While MacNeal streaked the plane over the ice parallel to a fleeing reindeer herd, Alex opened the fusilage door and handed Ab his rifle. Ab, lying on the floor on his belly, opened fire. He continued to shoot until the herd attained the sanctuary of a wooded island. Ab was puzzled for a time that he had hit nothing at all, as were MacNeal and Alex. A bit of thought on the matter solved this puzzle. The plane had been travelling at a greater speed than the caribou so that Ab's aim should have trailed his target rather than leading it as he normally would have done. He had forgotten that he was not stationary while shooting.

Pimiyakun took us out of the North for good. A gradual build-up of certain events had forced the decision. We had been in the same location for four winters and the trails had become too familiar and monotonous. After seven years in the bush we decided that it was probably time to get reestablished. Besides, things were brightening Outside and we had been offered employment. The idea of a steady monthly paycheque seemed attractive, as did the possibility of finding a good wife. The episode at Muskeg River had made the whole business seem futile.

The final blow struck ominously in the spring of 1939. Our entire fur catch, an excellent one, brought three hundred dollars. We reeled under the blow and made a decision. We quit the country with a great deal of regret.

Arrangements were made for Frank Fisher to take over our traplines. On a journey to Cree River we had left word to be picked up at our home cabin, our destination Prince Albert.

Bill Windrum put his bush plane down on Cree Lake ice a mile below the cabin. When we joined him we found aboard several hard-rock miners from Goldfields, sporting fat wallets and on their way Outside for a holiday. The copilot was communicating with his base via two-way radio, the first such apparatus we had seen.

Airborne in a short run, we headed southeast in brilliant spring sunshine. I looked from the windows, noting in fleeting glimpses some familiar landmarks. I saw from the air the island where I had seen the many wolf tracks. Back over my right shoulder Long Bay stretched white and empty. Then we climbed rapidly over Stony Narrows with Martin Brustad's camp and trails visible. We climbed higher so that such details were no longer visible. We were slipping along at an airspeed of 185 miles according to an indicator mounted under the plane's wing.

Over to the west a snowstorm shone starkly white in the sun. The country, still in winter's grip though it was April, was a white and green panorama in all directions. I found that a tremendous amount of woodland had been burned over in recent times.

We travelled a straight course across Haultain River, Foster Lake, Churchill River. When we put down at Lac la Ronge we had been flying for an hour to cover some 170 miles from Cree Lake.

La Ronge was only a trading post at that time, having yet to be discovered as a sports-fishing attraction.

After we left it seemed no time at all until we were over rectangular-shaped patches in the bush, a sure sign that we were on the fringes of the settlements and the homesteader's domain.

Windrum put us down at Prince Albert on the ice of the North Saskatchewan River, near the heart of the city. Such was his mastery of the aircraft that I was not aware of the contact of the skis on the ice.

That same evening Ab and I sat drinking beer in the "licensed premises" in the Avenue Hotel.

Our trip Outside was something upon which to contemplate. What a contrast was this journey to others we had made to Prince Albert from remote Cree Lake! Other trips had involved several days of planning and preparation even to get under way. Out on the windswept Cree Lake ice we had to hold the canoe against the wind lest the whole outfit be rolled and the canoe smashed on the ice as the top-heavy sled was hauled by the dogs as far as Stony Narrows. We constantly had to watch that the dogs' feet did not become ice-cut and the trail become blood-streaked, as was the lot of the Indian's dogs. Then it was weeks of travel and portaging until eventually we arrived at the government dock in Big River from where we hired a car to run us into Prince Albert.

We called for another round of beer. Good-tasting draft, we had not had any since the previous July.

22

LAST NOTES

January, 1947.

A letter from Frank Fisher reads in part: "I have had several good years working your former traplines and have netted well over two thousand dollars a year on the average. . . .

". . . the country hereabouts has had many bush fires through the years. Last summer a big fire burned a stretch of the Karras River and Albert's House. . . ."

February, 1953.

Frank writes only once more, this time from Ile-à-la-Crosse:

"I have moved from Cree Lake to Ile-à-la-Crosse Lake where I am now mink-ranching. . . .

"Commercial fishing companies have built freezing plants on some of the big lakes including Cree Lake."

August, 1957.

By sheer luck I meet Johnny and his wife on the street in Banff Alta. We are all on holiday. Johnny has become a top car salesman. Matt, he says, made a complete recovery in a few months following shock therapy. He is married, has children, and is paying a lot of income tax. He is in the real estate business in a large western Canadian city.

July, 1961.

This is a dry summer and bush fires rage throughout northern Canada. I find a small map in a newspaper which marks in black the areas of all the major fires of Saskatchewan's Northland for

that summer. By far the largest is an immense black blob a long distance west of Cree Lake which signifies a tremendous holocaust that extends eastward to the headwaters of the Karras River. This burned-over area is so large that the whole area of Cree Lake will easily fit into it.

December, 1965.
The latest government survey on the barren ground caribou estimates that there are only 200,000 to 250,000 left in Canada. In small numbers they still trickle down as far as Cree Lake when the lakes are frozen over and their migrating urge brings them that far south. Their former massive feeding range has been cut tremendously by fires. The caribou moss takes many years to recover.

A road, originally planned to link Prince Albert with Uranium City via the east side of Cree Lake ends in the bush north of the Churchill River. The report is that road-building costs were out of all proportion to the original estimates. Although aircraft fly back and forth to Cree Lake it is relatively free from civilization. No road has reached Cree Lake.

April, 1966.
A sleek new jet airliner owned by Canadian Pacific Airlines approaches Tokyo International Airport. Coming in over the water

the craft is almost on the landing strip when it dips suddenly, bounces off a retaining wall, then crashes to the runway and burns. Among the dead is C.P.A.'s senior pilot, Captain Cecil N. MacNeal.

June, 1966.

I returned to Rat Creek. With a friend I was in the country to do some pickerel fishing. We motored up from the south on surfaced roads all the way to Meadow Lake. In the long twilight as we headed out of town I saw a roadway sign—"Cree Lake Fly-in Fishing Camp"—then we were past the sign and on the gravelled highway to Green Lake.

Green Lake village has not grown appreciably. There are a few stores, lodging places, and boats for hire for the sports fishermen. The highway forks here, northward you can motor to Beauval, Ile-à-la-Crosse, Buffalo Narrows and Portage la Loche. The route east and south leads to Big River and Prince Albert.

The Green River looked almost the same as it had thirty years before when Ab, Frank Fisher, Martin Brustad, and I had ascended it from the Beaver River and had our canoes hauled overland to Crooked Lake. The grey willows along the banks seemed no larger, the river ran as quietly, horses and cattle grazed along the banks as they did the first time we passed through.

All this I recalled as we rode downstream in the early morning in our rented motorboat as far as the junction of the Green and Beaver rivers, advertised now as excellent pickerel-fishing grounds.

We anchored just off the Beaver River shore. After an hour we had been joined by seven other boats.

On his third cast my friend hooked a pickerel. We had no trouble at all catching our legal limit that morning—eight fish apiece. They ran about two pounds each, the same size as those I had once caught on a still summer evening at the quiet bend below our cabin on Rat Creek.

We had been assigned to a red-painted cabin by our host in Green Lake village. Next door a cabin was occupied by a newly married couple from Elma, Iowa. Others in for the fishing were affluent, middle-aged Saskatchewan farmers, with their middle-aged wives, and sporting the latest in water transportation right down to spanking new blaze orange life jackets which they wore without fail when afloat in their fibreglass boats with overpowered motors. It struck me then that Ab and I had never owned a life jacket, much less worn one in all our travels in the Northland!

After another morning at the junction and with our limit again I took the fish to Virginia's filleting plant for processing and freezing. Virginia, of Indian ancestry, was so adept at filleting that she could do a fish in twenty-two seconds, I was told.

Then I suggested to my friend that we take a drive to Crooked Lake Dam, then take the Doré Lake road as far as Rat Creek.

Past open farmland and over surprisingly good roads, we drove through fine stands of white poplar. We soon covered the nineteen miles to the dam. The last few miles were through poplar saplings, for fire had ravaged the old timber that Ab and I once knew. This lay rotting on the ground.

A fine concrete dam holds back the waters of Crooked Lake. I noticed remnants of two previous earth and timber dams, one that existed in 1932 and a replacement built in 1937. Earth fills at each end still jutted into the lake.

The Saskatchewan Department of Natural Resources, called locally DNR, has constructed a fine tourist campsite at the dam. It is at an open spot, exactly where Bill Mahoney's several buildings had stood. Bill's old home cabin was there still, windows boarded over, the only building to remain.

No resident dam keeper lives there now.

As we looked over the site we saw that the young poplars grew straight and vigorously and the seedling spruce were already emerging on the forest floor.

I found many beer and coke bottles strewn about. I gathered some and threw them into the empty DNR garbage can.

We drove north then in a big arc on the Doré Lake road. We stopped at the wooden bridge that spans Rat Creek.

The creek, I was pleased to note, had not suffered the fire scourge since I had last seen it. The trees had become fat with more than thirty additional annual rings.

Downstream was a big beaver dam that spanned the creek from bank to bank. Beaver-felled timber was scattered all about the place. Even as we stood on the bridge, a mature beaver appeared on shore, quickly cut off a poplar sapling and swam off towing it downstream.

I walked up the creek for a short distance. The same kind of mosquitoes stung the back of my neck and behind my ears. About five miles away was the site of the old cabin. How I wished that I had time to hike up there and look it over! Was there any visible evidence of the cabin? Had the fires destroyed the fine timber?

I hoped to learn the answers on another day. Right now it was evening and we had a commitment in Meadow Lake next morning.

It was early morning when I picked up the pickerel fillets at Virginia's. Harry, her husband, asked me in to visit for a few minutes. His name, Harry Morin, rang a bell in my memory. I remembered him as trapping muskrats on Rat Creek one spring. I mentioned Rat Creek and our cabin of long ago. Then his face lit up.

"I remember you," he said with emphasis on the *you*.

He told me that old Red Iron had died some fifteen years previously and Harry Maurice whom, by the grace of God, I had not shot as a moose, had died a natural death.

Our leave-taking was filmed by the young couple from Iowa.

On our way out at a Green Lake service station I saw young Indian men and women sauntering about from house to house or just loitering on the highway bridge, much the same as they had done in 1936. In those days the girls wore gaily coloured shawls and vividly coloured long dresses, the boys in white shirts, red neckerchiefs, and blue serge pants. Now the girls wore tight slacks, jackets, and short hairdos. The boys had hippie hair and clothing. These people spent much of their time in the adjoining cafe at the coffee bar and playing the juke box and pinball machine.

September, 1967.
On a fishing trip to Doré Lake I talked with Harry Husak.

"I came to Big River in 1928," began Harry. "I spent many years at Beauval and finally bought this place." The "place" consisted of a dozen run-down buildings including a house, a store, warehouses, and tourist cabins. He had boats and motors and guides for hire, catering to sports fishermen and moose hunters in season. He told me that he did some mink-ranching and ran a trapline in winter.

His eyes sparkled happily as I named mutual acquaintances of the old days. He warmed up to a lively recollection of the past. Then he expressed some views on the future and on the present:

"If anyone had told me twenty years ago that a highway would be built to Doré Lake I would have told him to go have his head examined. Honestly, I miss the old days when a hundred horse teams in a string could be seen on the Doré Lake ice, hauling fish to market in Big River. Then the Indians hereabouts were a fine people. Right now I have five American fishermen waiting for my one available Indian guide to sober up. Yesterday he took them fishing and I paid him fifteen dollars. Today he is staying in his shack with a couple of jugs of wine. He slipped into Ile-à-la-Crosse last night over the bush road to the highway in his car. The opening of the roads has hit these Indians hard."

May, 1968.
With my son Jim, just home from university for the summer recess, I motored to Big River. At a service station there I studied the telephone directory for familiar names. I found just three, among them Alex, a member of the tie-camp crew of 1935. I had had no contact with him since, until I dialed his number.

"Alex, this is Art Karras."

Dead silence at the other end of the line, then: "Is it really you?"

We met and had a long talk. He said that access to the Rat Creek cabin was possible by car in dry weather, by turning off the Doré Lake road and onto the old road which he had helped cut out to haul ties over to Crooked Lake. He had driven in himself, about five years previously, he stated. The cabin still stood at that time. He judged that we would have to walk from there for the ground was currently very wet with the melting snows.

Over the flat, wide highway, where it had taken Ab and I a day and a half to walk to town in the old days, we covered the same distance by car in less than forty minutes.

I parked the car where the bush road led in the general direction of Rat Creek. This turned out to be a dead-end logging trail as did a couple of others that we tried. At last we struck out through overage poplar and spruce and came out on Rat Creek, two miles below the site of the cabin.

Moose were still in the country for we saw their droppings and we saw a yearling feeding among the red willows. A small white-tailed deer watched us approach, then dashed into covering brush.

The creek looked much as it had in the past, except that the water level was so low that it hardly ran at all. After a mile of walking we came upon two railroad ties, weathered to a silvery grey, but otherwise sound, and caught up in a clump of grey willows. These were Ed's ties without a doubt deposited here during high water long ago. The log bridge had vanished.

As we rounded a bend of the creek I saw a familiar landmark. Across the creek was the little hill where the big black bear had died after Ab shot it.

Just around the bend was the site of the cabin but we saw nothing of it from the creek. Then we climbed the slope and there it was—just a couple of tiers of logs remained about its perimeter. I was amazed at the condition of the logs for they were hard and white on the inside walls as they had been when we constructed the cabin in 1933. The log that had lain above the door was intact, even to the neatly cut section to allow the door to fit snugly, Ab's handiwork easily recognized.

The reason for the gradual disappearance of the cabin became apparent. To one side stood a small board shack. I looked inside. A few traps hung on the walls and a tin stove stood in one corner. Muskrat stretching-boards were scattered about. A pair of rubbers containing insoles made of grass had been discarded in a corner. The owner was absent. I noticed that he had been sawing off a piece of poplar log from the old cabin each time his stove required fuel.

The debris scattered about proved that the cabin had been occupied much of the time throughout the years. I found three burned-out stoves. I hunted for the remnants of our cast-iron stove but found no part of it. The place had the unmistakable disarray of an Indian camp and had been used as a base for hunting and trapping operations.

The view from the cabin site out towards Rat Lake had changed little. The same cattail beds and reed beds are there. The points of land that jut into the creek and were once covered with tall poplars are now dominated by taller spruce, with Rat Lake lying in the distance.

We sat on the old cabin logs and rested from our long walk, I pointed out to Jim the spot where Ab had felled the giant moose, only to lose him in the swamps. I pointed out the base of a slope where, as a youth, I had seen a bull caribou pass by while I looked from the cabin window.

We both fell silent. In my mind's eye I once again saw Ab swinging his axe among the big poplars and recalled his booming call—"Timber!"—as the treetop quivered just before it swayed and crashed to the ground.

I was brought back to reality by the sound of a jet aircraft ripping by above the heavy overcast.

I led Jim back downstream. A short walk and I pointed out to him the remnants of the moonshiner's cabin. Only the earth embankment about its perimeter remained. I recognized a few individual trees, now twice their former girth. A poplar stump, the tree of which Ab had felled when we feared it might one day fall upon the cabin roof, now protruded black through the tall grass. A thick clump of spruce only six feet tall stood where my bunk had been.

The remains of a rusted-out tobacco tin lay on the cabin site.

We found cruel man-made scars in the land. Logging roads had been bulldozed into the prime timber stands and the great spruce which mule deer had frequented had long since been hauled to the mill in Big River. Bulldozers have cut away the ancient moss beds right down to the yellow clay.

In front of the poplar cabin, brush and topsoil had been pushed into the creek to give trucks a roadbed to the other side.

A small break in this crude dam exuded a little trickle of water, all that flowed in the creek. Back in 1933, 1934, and 1935 the creek had run high in May. The water then had been quite clear and swarmed with fish. I peered into the coffee-coloured water above the dam and saw nothing.

That evening, in Big River, as we ate our steaks in the Chinese restaurant I watched a young man slide up to the coffee bar beside a couple of his cronies. From his conversation I gathered that he operated the road maintainer on the gravelled highway to Green Lake.

"Do you know how an Indian changes a tire?" he asked. "Well, since they never have a jack in the car they go back into the bush, cut a long pole, find a big stone and pry up the wheel. One fellow sits on one end of the pole while the other changes the wheel. Then they pull out!"

In Big River almost everyone drives some kind of motor vehicle today, but the cars are of older vintage by far than those seen in the rich farmland farther south. The big sawmill has been rebuilt, the tall sawdust burner once again belches smoke of spruce sawdust and mill tailings. I noticed that some of its lower steel plates had begun to buckle.

The railway station stood the same as I remembered it. I could find no trace of Morgan's Boarding House. Pete Godin's store looked the same from the outside. The hotel, and stores where we had traded were there, some deserted and in decay. There are two new service stations, a drugstore and chain food store. Near the mill stands a grain elevator. A few new houses are on the south, otherwise the village has not changed.

I walked down to the government dock. It was peaceful there and shorebirds waded at the water's edge.

I thought that a marker might have been erected at this spot to commemorate where began many a wilderness journey and where many others ended.

EPILOGUE

Attending a convention in Saskatoon in January, 1969, I heard one delegate say to another,

"The Saskatchewan River is so low that the city sewer outlets are bared. You can see sewage being discharged into the river. . . ."